Christine Faber

A mother's sacrifice

Or, who was guilty?

Christine Faber

A mother's sacrifice
Or, who was guilty?

ISBN/EAN: 9783741110702

Manufactured in Europe, USA, Canada, Australia, Japa

Cover: Foto ©Andreas Hilbeck / pixelio.de

Manufactured and distributed by brebook publishing software (www.brebook.com)

Christine Faber

A mother's sacrifice

A MOTHER'S SACRIFICE;

OR, WHO WAS GUILTY?

BY
CHRISTINE FABER,

P. J. KENEDY & SONS
44 BARCLAY STREET, NEW YORK

A MOTHER'S SACRIFICE;

Or, WHO WAS GUILTY?

CHAPTER I.

The rigid corpse lying on the marble table in the *morgue* was a ghastly sight—a loathsome sight, as the bright morning sun shone on its gory hair and made sickeningly visible the great gash that disfigured the countenance.

The eyes were only half closed, but the lips were firmly compressed, and despite the ugly cut that extended the whole length of the left cheek the face wore an expression of defiance as if even death had not terminated the passion which had raged in the last moment of life. The form was well and powerfully made, the limbs strong and graceful, and the constitution evidently had been one that, with regular living, might have promised to its possessor many years of vigorous health.

There were few stains on the black fashionably-made clothes—hardly sufficient to indicate that there could have been a struggle before the death-blow. In age the man might have been thirty, but it was difficult to judge; for at first sight his well-shaped head with its crisp black curls clustering thickly round his ample forehead seemed to mark him a very young man, but a longer look into the gashed face would make one decide that he must be in the very prime of life.

He had been found in the early morning of that day lying upon the sidewalk dead, evidently murdered.

There was no clew by which to trace the perpetrator of the deed; not even a trace of blood beyond the immediate spot where the corpse was found.

The object of the crime had not been plunder, for a handsome watch and a solitaire ring had been found on the body. Nor was his portmonnaie touched, but it contained nothing by which his identity might be discovered.

He had been borne to the *morgue* and placed on one of the tables between a dripping form taken from the river an hour before, and an unknown person who had died in the hospital, on the previous night, of *delirium tremens*. But there was something about the murdered man that attracted the most attention, and the people who visited the *morgue* during the day, whatever their motive, found their eyes, repulsive as was the sight, turning repeatedly to the ghastly, gashed face.

Relatives claimed the remains of the drowned man, and a friend was found for the wretched creature who had died in his drunken fit, but no one claimed the corpse of the murdered victim. All day long he lay with stray rays of the bright sun gleaming upon him, and no one came to identify him.

"It's a queer case," said one of the employés, in reply to the question of a visitor, "the doctors say it wasn't the cut as killed him, but a blow he got on the breast. I guess he's a stranger in these parts; no owner 'll be found for him 'till the description of him gets to other cities."

When it was nearly evening a woman, unaccompanied, sought admission to the *morgue*. She was very plainly dressed, and so heavily veiled that not a feature in her face could be discerned. She was slight and girlish in form, and her manner seemed to indicate shy youthfulness. Her voice was tremulous, but singularly sweet, with a peculiar intonation that once heard was seldom forgotten.

The officer who met her at the entrance accompanied her to the side of the murdered man.

She drew her ungloved hands from the folds of her shawl and clasped them together so tightly that the tops of her slender fingers under the nails became almost as ghastly as were those of the corpse.

"You know him?" said the officer in an undertone.

"I knew him once," was the reply in that singular voice, "but "—turning to her questioner with slight alarm in her manner—" there is no tie between us. I have not come to claim his body; only to see if he is the same whom I knew."

"But you may be able to throw some light on this strange affair?"

"None, none! I have not seen him for a long, long time," and with singular nerve for a timid-seeming creature like her, she bent to the loathsome gash as if to peer into its bloody depth, and she lifted the curls from the forehead as if searching for some other murderous mark.

"Is this all?" she asked, pointing to the cut when she had finished her survey.

"No, ma'am; there are bruises on the breast as if he was struck by some powerful body."

Her voice became animated.

"Which killed him the cut, or the blow?"

The man looked sharply at her before he replied.

"Why, the doctors says it was the blow as done it; but that looks ugly enough to do it," and he pointed to the gash.

The woman sighed and turned to depart.

Her questioner had all the smartness sometimes accredited to men in his position, and having strong inducement in the reward which he knew would be forthcoming for official expertness in this case, he contrived to intercept her. In a few moments she found herself confronted by other officials.

One of them, though suspicious of her agitation, could not help pitying her; she seemed so young and despite the plainness of her dress so much above those of her sex who usually visited the place. He said, kindly:

"This case is a very strange one and it requires rigid investigation. As yet not a single clew has been found to tell by whom, or for what reason the murder was committed, or even to reveal the identity of the murdered man. You say that you have known him. Then you will be able to tell us something about him—not now, child"—seeing her about to speak—" but at the proper time, before proper authorities," giving a sidelong glance at the man who had brought about the meeting.

"All we require at present," he continued, "is an assurance that we can find you whenever we may want you to tell what you know of this unfortunate man, and that assurance we must get by detailing some one to accompany you home in order to ascertain your correct name and residence. To-morrow perhaps some light may be thrown on this singular affair."

The girl was sobbing with all the wild abandon of passionate woe. The startled men glanced significantly at each other, but no one spoke, until the first wildness of the burst had spent itself.

As if in a moment of forgetfulness she threw up her veil, disclosing one of the loveliest and saddest countenances the world-hardened men had ever beheld; it was so delicately fair, with large eloquent eyes—now mournfully eloquent because of the tears with which they were filled—and every feature, from the intellectual forehead down to the small, sensitive mouth, regular and perfect; short dark curls had strayed beyond the confines of her bonnet, and lay in becoming rings upon her forehead.

"Calm yourself, my child," said the officer who had spoken so kindly to her before; "no one is going to harm you."

"Me!" she said in that peculiarly intonated voice. "Ah! if only I—"

She stopped suddenly, her very lips blanching, and her breath seeming to desert her for a moment.

"I must go home," she resumed when at length she recovered herself. At a sign from the gentleman who had last spoken, and who seemed to be highest in authority among the party, one of them prepared to accompany her.

He was not in official dress, but if he had been it would have made little difference to the trembling girl beside whom he walked; she thought only of what might happen from this unlucky visit to the *morgue*.

After a walk which occupied nearly three-quarters of an hour, she paused before a very handsome house. Her strange companion muttered some exclamation whose import she did not catch, and he looked with a puzzled expression from the plain garb of the girl to the magnificent appearance of the building—its situation in the very centre of a fashionable locality, and its style indicated great wealth. He mentally solved the difficulty, however, by supposing her to be an upper servant.

"Lady's maid, or some such," he said to himself; but she disabused his mind of that idea by saying, as they ascended the stoop:

"My aunt is an invalid, and of a very sensitive temperament. It would kill her to know of my visit to the *morgue*. If you have any inquiries to make, could you make them without letting her know?"

"I suppose so," he answered, too thoroughly puzzled to know quite what he ought to reply; "but I'd like to see some member of the family."

She looked at him with those thrilling eyes.

"There is no one for you to see save the servants.

My uncle is dead, my aunt is ill. You can ask the help to tell you all they know about *me*," uttering the last word a little defiantly, as if some sudden thought had dissipated her former fears.

The officer was in a quandary, and he stroked his chin, looking into her sweet face all the time. He could not resist the imploring glance of her mournful eyes.

"That will do, miss; I'll question anybody you like, and I won't say anything about why I'm doing it."

She put out her small, white hand, and caught his rough bronzed one, and to hear again the grateful "thank you," which fell from her lips, he felt he would be willing to go away without asking any questions at all.

A trim, tidy little maid opened the door.

"Oh, Miss Margaret!" she said, "your aunt has been asking for you."

The girl thus addressed looked significantly at her strange companion, but she made no remark until she had brought him with the maid, whom she had motioned to follow her, into one of the parlors opening from the tesselated hall. The heavy gilt chandelier was partially lighted, but the man had hardly time to observe fully the magnificence of the apartment, for she who had been addressed as Miss Margaret, leaning against the door which she had softly closed, said hurriedly:

"Tell this man, Annie, what my name is, and all that you know about me."

The maid was so astonished at the command that she only stared with wondering eyes and open mouth.

The officer stroked his chin a second time in perplexing thought.

"Answer," said Miss Margaret a little impatiently.

The maid stammered.

"Your name is Miss Margaret Calvert——but I don't know what else you want me to say about you."

"How long have you lived in this house?" questioned Miss Margaret.

"Two years."

"What have you learned about me during that time —in a word, who am I?"

But a wondering stare was the only reply.

"Let me question her, Miss," said the man, who at last had recalled his senses.

"Who is this young lady?" pointing to the form beside him.

"I told you her name once, what more do you want to know?" seeming to divine with the smartness which is usual to some of her class, that questions were being asked which it was not desirable for her to answer.

He assumed his most stern official tone.

"Is Miss Margaret Calvert a daughter of the lady of this house?"

"No, sir," awed a little by his stern voice; "she is a niece, so far as I know."

"Be quick, please," said the sweet voice at his side; "I fear my aunt is waiting for me."

He gave a puzzled look from her to the maid, stroked his chin a third time, and with a muttered:

"Hang it! I can't do it anyhow," turned to depart, saying:

"That will do for the present, Miss."

She accompanied him to the door, opened it for him, and waited on the stoop until he was half way up the block. Once he turned; her mournful eyes haunted him.

"Hang it," he muttered again; then remembering that he had not even ascertained the name of Miss Calvert's aunt, he cursed his stupidity, wished he had never been detailed for the duty, and finally compromising with his conscience by returning to one of the adjoining houses, he learned on inquiring from a servant, that Miss Calvert was the niece of a Madame Bernot, and that the latter had no family save a son who was traveling.

The maid had remained to close the door when the lady should return from the stoop.

The young lady strove to be calm; but the weakness and the terror of the past hour had returned to her, she clutched the oaken balustrade for support, and sank on the lower step of the stair.

The maid hurried to her with much concern in her manner.

"I do not need you," Miss Calvert hastened to say. "I am better now—leave me."

Prudence and compassion whispered to the servant silence upon what she had witnessed and heard, but her woman's curiosity, which she thought might be gratified if others assisted to discover the import of the strange affair, and her love of gossip that delighted to speak about it, even though so doing would be vain to unravel the apparent mystery, prompted her to tell about it in the servants' hall; but though each of the domestics commented, and offered various conjectures, not one of them thought of tracing the slightest connection between the strange murder of which the evening papers were full, and lovely Margaret Calvert.

Miss Calvert had grown calm at last and had returned to her room that she might put off her out-door garments before attending her aunt; but she had not quite finished bathing her face in order to remove the tear stains, when another summons came from the invalid's apartment.

It was a spacious, airy room, just above the parlors and luxuriously furnished; but the object which first and immediately attracted attention was a large, peculiarly-constructed chair. Even without seeing the form that reclined on its soft cushions, its use was at once apparent from the peculiar castors, the adjustable back ready to prop the occupant or to form a couch. Now, its back was turned almost upright, and the form that

reposed against it seemed to fill entirely its ample space
—so large a form that it was difficult to think it could
be a woman until the face was seen, and that, with its
regular, feminine features, though they were slightly
sharpened by severe physical suffering, told at once of a
noble and devoted nature. It was such a face as one
sometimes meets in rare old paintings, not beautiful because of perfection of feature, but because of the singular expression which the countenance wears, the indescribable something that lingers about it and that is remembered long after the color of the eyes and the hair
is forgotten.

Such was the face of this invalid. Few looking into
her eyes thought of their color, but few forgot their expression. For seven years she had occupied this chair,
leaving it neither by day nor night. It was so constructed
that she could rest on one side while her cushions were
being arranged on the other.

For seven long weary years she had not been moved
save as they wheeled her chair about, and lifted her in
strong arms while they changed her soft white robes;
but this last motion, gentle as they sought to make it,
caused her intense agony. The lifting of a finger or
the moving of a foot was accompanied with such pain,
that she preferred never to leave her invalid chair.

Her countenance, even apart from the lines which
suffering had worn in it, indicated her age to be fifty or
more; but her gray hair was abundant and glossy, and
free from cap or restraint of any kind, clustered round
her head in curls that many a youthful beauty might
have envied. She had never been known to repine at
this dire visitation of God—not even a hired attendant
had ever heard her murmur save when a throb of pain
unusually severe had wrung from her a half stifled cry.

It was this wonderful endurance and resignation
which gave to her character so noble a cast, that it was
reflected in her appearance, and invariably impressed
beholders with a sense of her exalted virtue.

"Is Margaret coming?" she asked of the attendant whom she had sent to summon her niece, in a voice that had nothing of the querulousness of sickness in it—clear, sweet-toned, and possibly as strong as it had been in her healthiest days.

Margaret entered and went at once to the invalid chair.

"You have been very long, child—your walk must have extended itself much further than usual."

"Perhaps it did, aunt," was the reply, accompanied by a kiss on the invalid's forehead; and then she proceeded to do the numerous nameless little things incidental to a sick room, moving about in so noiseless a manner that it was soothing to watch her.

But the poor invalid's eyes could not follow her very far, for the head was unable to turn without great pain.

"It was cruel of me to leave you so long when Hubert was not here to take my place," said Margaret, when, having finished her little services, she knelt beside the sick woman, gently rubbing the poor hands that could not help themselves. The soft pressure of another's fingers upon them seemed to allay the pain that at times started violently in every joint,

She slumbered at last; one of those infant-like dozes into which she sometimes fell, and which were the only sleep she knew even in the longest nights.

Margaret motioned to the attendant, a tall, stout, kindly-faced woman, to take her place, and rising softly she went from the room.

On the hall above whither she had gone, she was confronted by a white, startled face. It peered over the balustrade at her, and shrank from the hand she extended.

"There is nothing to fear," she whispered.

It came toward her then, to where the faint light from a lowered gas-jet beamed shadowingly upon it.

It belonged to a young man whose age could have

been little more than a score of years; but there was a manliness about the slight, straight form that might have belonged to thirty. A glance at his face told of the near relation he bore to the invalid below, but his features were not characterized by the peculiarly beautiful expression which marked hers.

Yet his eyes had the same look—the same look despite the wild, startled expression of his whole face now.

Margaret attempted to turn the jet that a brighter light might be shed through the hall.

"Don't!" he said in a tone tremulous from fear. "I can't bear the light."

She desisted, replying in as low but a firmer tone.

"You must nerve yourself; this fear will never do."

He drew her into a recess that even the faint light that shone, might not reach them.

"I *was* firm, Margaret, till I saw you from the window of my room coming home accompanied by a strange man; an unaccountable fear took possession of me then, and I am under its influence still. But, tell me quick, did you see *him?* Was *he* there?"

There was the sudden shutting of a door on the floor below. The young man started and shrank further into the recess, while Margaret looked over the baluster.

"It is only Annie who has gone into the parlor," she said, returning to him, and then she drew him into one of the rooms that opened from the hall, and for a few moments was busy in assuring herself that there was no person in either of the adjoining apartments. Then she returned to him, took both his trembling hands in her own, and said firmly:

"Hubert, you must be brave for your mother's sake. I saw him; it *is* he whom they found and carried to the *morgue*—I recognized him only too surely. But they say it was a blow on the breast that killed him."

He shook his head, while she continued:

"They found him in the street early this morning, but no one knows him, nor has a single clew been discovered to tell who did the deed. Be brave, Hubert.

"Yes," he said, turning away from her, "I shall be brave until the torture caused by remorse for this deed, and the secret fear of detection, goad me to desperation —until my life snaps under the strain. Tell me, Margaret," turning suddenly back to her, "would it not be better to give myself up at once—to face it all, the cell, the scaffold perhaps, the gaping multitude, my mother in her coffin from the blow, and our name a thing of scorn for all time? but "— with a sudden change of voice—"I cannot die—oh, God! I cannot die!"

He covered his face with his hands.

"No, Hubert, no;" she passionately answered, though in her secret soul she was struggling with her own scrupulous sense of duty, which told her that the course he suggested was the only right one. "The yielding of your life cannot restore the one you have taken—rather live and offer penitential acts and works of charity for his soul."

"Works of charity," he repeated, taking his hands from his face and smiling bitterly; then, as if impelled by some sudden and alarming thoughts, he asked quickly:

"Can *you* keep my secret? are you sure that *you* will never betray me?"

"Betray! oh, Hubert!"

There was such keen reproach in her tones that he could hardly bear it.

"I did not mean that you would denounce me, Margaret, but have you thought how heavily the burden of my confidence may press upon you—how in the future when you may become desperate from its weight, some unguarded word may fall unintentionally from your lips; have you thought of all this?"

"It is not necessary to think of it," she answered mournfully, "it is enough that you have trusted me—sooner would I die, than betray that trust by a look."

"Are you willing to take an oath to that effect—will you solemnly swear never to betray me?"

She replied, with her head bowed, and her voice more mournful:

"If you trust me so little as to require an oath—"

"It is not that I do not trust you," he answered passionately; "but my fears have made me cowardly and unreasonable—to know that you have sworn, will be an assurance to me, and it may be a safeguard to you. Will you take an oath, Margaret?"

She bowed her head, and repeated after him the the solemn words which bound her to inviolable secrecy; seeing her intense pallor, and noting the convulsed agitation of her form, he continued: "It is your own fault to be thus burdened—you sought my confidence, you implored me for it when I returned this morning. You must pay the penalty of your guilty knowledge—you must help me keep my wretched secret, even though it should burn into your soul, as it is now scorching, shriveling mine."

She did not answer.

"Poor child!" he went on, and his tone assumed a tenderness befitting the comforter of a penitent. It was as if *she* were the perpetrator of some dark guilt and *he* was showing her its horrible consequences; detailing the black remorse in his own soul as if it were a description of what was passing in hers, and his face came back to its own expression, and his attitude became more erect, for his guilty heart reveled in the knowlenge that another would suffer from the weight of his unhappy secret—he would have companionship in his hidden misery.

Still she made no reply, and he, as if to rouse her from her apparent lethargy, began tenderly to stroke her hair.

She started from him.

"You shrink from the murderer's touch," he said bitterly, "though you have consented to share the murderer's secret suffering."

She shook her head.

"Margaret," he resumed in a pleading tone, "a while ago you bade me be brave—you alone can assist me to be so—nerve yourself and I shall cast aside my fears—my plans are laid; safe ones, I think, since you have consented to bear part of my wretched burden, do not go back, nor falter now—help me, oh, help me, Margaret!"

The last words were a despairing cry that came up from the very depths of his sick heart. He extended his hands to her, and his face betrayed more than it had done yet, the insupportable anguish under which he labored. His cry, his look, raised all the compassion in her nature—flinging aside every thought save that it was in her power to aid him, to comfort him, she grasped his outstretched hands, and said tremulously:

"Fear not! I am strong again—use me as you will, I shall never falter more in your service."

He drew her unresistingly to a chair, and seating himself beside her, began to talk calmly of his future course.

"And, now, tell me about the stranger who accompanied you home this evening," he said.

She repeated without reserve what had taken place in the *morgue*.

His face darkened, and he shuddered.

"How near you came to giving them a clew."

"I know it," she answered, almost sobbing again, "but the sight of *him* unnerved me."

"And how do I know but that you will be unnerved again when they summon you to the witness-stand?"

"No! the worst has passed—I have gone through the most severe ordeal—you need not fear for me now."

She spoke calmly, and looked up at him with an

expression of firmness in her face which he had never seen before. He seemed satisfied, and rising, he said quietly:

"There is but one thing I wish to do before I leave —to see my mother. You must manage that for me, Margaret; arrange to have no one in the way."

"You had better not," she replied, "how will you account to her for your sudden return? and if you *should* be seen by any of the servants, it might cause sad consequences."

"It will be your business to provide for my *not* being seen," he answered somewhat imperiously, "and my mother asks so few questions, it will be sufficient to tell her I was delayed. But, Margaret, I *must* see her —I shall have more heart for the future knowing that I have looked into her face since—since the deed— than to think I must meet on my return her pure eyes for the first time since I have become the guilty wretch that I am."

She attempted no further remonstrance, but rose at once to obey him.

The invalid was awake when Margaret descended to her. She was wondering in her uncomplaining way at the absence of her niece.

The girl had taken the precaution to send the attendant from the room on some pretext which would detain her long, and then stooping to her aunt she said softly:

"Hubert's departure was delayed, and he desires to see you once more before he goes."

"Dear boy!" the invalid murmured, and so far from seeking to know the cause of his delay, she made no other remark, but turned her eyes to a picture which hung directly opposite.

Unable to bow her head, or to clasp her hands in the attitude of prayer, she had caused to be hung just before her a painting of the thorn-crowned head of Christ. It was only the head, but it was life size, and so vivid in coloring and expression, that the very blood drops on the forehead looked as if each moment they would tickle down on the cheeks, and the eyes as if they implored compassion from every beholder.

The invalid's eyes were wont to turn upon this picture with so absorbed a look as to convey the impression to those who had seen her thus, that her clear vision beheld something which was invisible to ordinary observers.

"Will Hubert see me now?" she asked when the mental prayer which accompanied her gaze was ended.

"Yes, I shall go and tell him that you are ready."

She hastened to the servants' hall to assure herself that each of the domestics was safely at his or her labor, and would not be likely to come up stairs for some time, and then hurrying to the room where Hubert impatiently awaited her, she preceded him to his mother's apartment.

The velvet-covered stairs returned no sound of their careful steps, but to Margaret's excited mind it seemed as if their descent was frightfully audible; often she paused to look above, or below, lest some prying eye might be fastened on them, but the spacious halls contained no person beside themselves, and the only sound was that of the laughter which floated indistinctly up from the servants' hall.

Both entered the sick room in the same stealthy manner, and Margaret softly turned the key in the lock, while Hubert went forward to his mother's chair, kneeling beside it, and resting his face on her hands lest she might read his guilt in his countenance.

Even then she did not inquire the cause of his return, only murmured as she had done before:

"Dear boy!"

It was not till Margaret knelt on the other side of the invalid chair that Hubert could summon sufficient courage to lift his face and look into his mother's eyes. He met there only the most tender expression, Evidently she read nothing of his crime, and he breathed freer.

"I thank you, my God," she said, "that I have again the privilege of blessing this, the only child Thou hast left me. Make him accomplish Thy will; put more suffering upon me if it so pleaseth Thee, but preserve *his* innocence."

Hubert's face sank suddenly in her lap again, while successive chills ran through his form; but his mother was indifferent to everything save the picture on which she was looking. Margaret Calvert grew white to the lips and lowered *her* face lest its pallor might betray her; but in a few moments the young man recovered himself, and rising, he said hurriedly:

"My time is limited, mother; I must go now."

She could not lift her face to respond to the passionate kisses he gave her, but he bent low so that her quivering mouth might touch his, and Margaret raised the poor helpless hands and placed them upon his drooped head. She turned her gaze to the picture while she said in a voice which brought the tears to the eyes of her niece.

"God bless you, my darling boy, and God protect you!"

He turned to leave the room, Margaret preceding him; she unlocked the door as noiselessly as she had locked it, and she looked cautiously into every room and hall ere she beckoned him to ascend to his own apartment.

Then she summoned his mother's attendant, and she returned herself to the invalid fearing lest any stray word might escape from her relative to her interview with her son. But her fear as she had felt it would be, was groundless; the sick woman had never during her illness referred to events after their occurrence; nor did she break her rule in this case—her son's name did not once pass her lips even to her niece.

When the evening was far advanced, Hubert Bernot

left his home; Margaret's adroit management had rendered his departure secure from observation, so that not even a stray neighbor seemed to be looking when he quickly descended the marble stoop and hurried up the street. The servants of the house supposed him to be hundreds of miles away, and little dreamed as they sat cosily chatting, of their broken-hearted young mistress above stairs. She wrung her hands, and walked the floor of her room, and tried to pray; but the words froze upon her lips, for in the giving of that oath to Hubert, she had gone against every dictate of her own sensitive and scrupulous conscience.

That conscience, tender and over-exacting as it had been from her childhood, would have urged her, nay, would have sternly insisted, that it was her duty to denounce the murderer, dear though he was to her; and because she could not do this cruel duty, because every impulse of her being rose in desperate resistance to such a mandate, she felt, that to approach the sacraments again would be a farce—that even to pray would be idle, for had she not chosen to serve a creature instead of her God?

CHAPTER II.

SENSATIONAL paragraphs headed the account of the strange murder in the numerous daily papers. Exciting descriptions of it filled many of the columns; a minute detail of the appearance of the dead man was given, and a large reward was offered for the discovery of the murderer.

But not a single clew was found.

Margaret Calvert was summoned (as they had said she would be), and, bracing herself for the ordeal, she appeared at the inquest with as firm a mien as though she were only entering her aunt's apartment.

The coroner requested the withdrawal of her veil, and she threw it instantly aside.

Her face was very pale but its pallor seemed to enhance her loveliness. She was unattended, and the world-hardened men wondered at her self-possessed manner, looking at each other with puzzled glances when she rose apparently quite unembarrassed, to tell what she knew of the murdered man. Her voice,— that peculiar voice, so remarkably sweet, that her hearers could have listened to it for hours, was slightly tremulous at first, but it grew firmer as she proceeded.

"I knew him long ago," she said, " under distressing circumstances of which even you, gentlemen," bowing to her listeners, "I think can hardly compel me to speak. I have not seen him since, till I saw him dead; but he has not been forgoten, for there is something in my home which keeps up constantly a bitter memory of him. In a second issue of one of the newspapers of that day—the day on the early morning of which he was found murdered—I saw the account. That account described his appearance—I knew that it was not unlikely he would meet some such end—and I visited the *morgue* and found it was he."

She was interrupted by a question:

"Why did you suppose him likely to meet such an end?"

"The girl paused for an instant as if to collect sufficient energy to make her voice sound with more force than she had hitherto put in it:

"Because he had neither pity, nor love, nor fear in his nature—because he was relentless and cruel—because he has darkened one home and broken one heart forever and ever."

She was trembling then;—so violently, that the hand which she raised to put back a stray curl shook visibly.

In one part of the room, there was sitting a man who seemed to be as interested as those who were immediately concerned in the proceedings. Permission to occupy that place had been granted him because he had gone to the authorities that morning, and having shown the credentials which proved his right to legal practice in the city, said he desired to work up the case, having been the murdered man's friend, although he had not seen him for some time owing to his own long absence from the city. He had also stated that the dead man had no relatives and that for years he had been the recipient of an income which came to him annually from a bank in Germany and which in default of heirs to claim it, would by will revert to a charitable institution in the same country.

Margaret Calvert, though aware of this silent presence in another part of the room, had not directed any close attention to his person, even though she saw him change his position once in order that he might better hear her evidence.

But while she stood trembling and hesitating

whether to speak further of the dead man, the strange gentleman arose. Every eye turned to him, he stood so erect, so firm, so still.

Margaret, in a vague way wondered if he always assumed such an attitude, if his head was always poised in that noble manner, and if his eyes flashed so piercingly on everybody as they were doing on her.

He could not have been more than twenty-eight—his beardless, youthful face was proof of that, but every feature evinced the strength and sternness of his nature.

He came forward, stood directly in front of the the wondering girl, and raising his right arm, pointed at her, saying in a voice so strangely distinct that the sound seemed to linger after the speaker had ceased:

"I charge you, Margaret Calvert, with a *knowledge* of Cecil Clare's murder.

Had a bomb-shell exploded amongst the gentlemen who composed the rigid, investigating committee, they could not have been more startled.

Margaret's manner while recounting her tale had somehow compelled them to believe in its truthfulness, and already they had begun to reject as absurd, the idea which one of their number entertained, that this young girl could in any way be connected with the murder; but the decided manner of him who made the charge, with the sudden faintness which overcame the girl on hearing it, was rapidly changing the prevalent opinion and leading them to think that the conjecture of their sage companion was correct.

She had lost all consciousness, and, but for the supporting arm of a gentleman near, she would have fallen.

They were obliged to bear her to an adjoining room, and summon to her aid some of the female employees.

When she recovered it was only to find herself an object of professed suspicion; to hear herself already convicted of complicity in the crime by some unguarded tongue,—as one coarse-looking official expressed it:

"Them sweet looks of hers ain't to be trusted."

The case, interesting before from the mystery that surrounded it, became intensely so now from its seemingly close connection with this beautiful girl, and preparations were made for a rigid investigation.

The young lawyer who had preferred the charge against Miss Calvert was determined to pursue it, till, as he had been heard to say, out of her own mouth should the murderer be convicted.

She was too important a person now to be suffered out of sight for a moment, and despite her passionate sobbing, her piteous entreaties, and the bribes she attempted to offer in the shape of her watch, and the costly rings she drew from her fingers, she was sent to the house of detention as a witness.

She was permitted to send home however, and in a short time the trim, tidy little maid whom she addressed as Annie, returned with the messenger.

"Oh, Miss Margaret!" she cried with blanched lips, "what have you done?"

"Nothing!" sobbed the half frantic girl; "They are detaining me as a witness for something; but oh, Annie, help me about my aunt—do something that she may not know I am out of the house—tell her that I am confined to my room, ill; anything that *she* may not know. Oh, I am so desolate, so frightened!"

Misery renders any companionship sweet. Dainty Margaret Calvert, who, while kind in her manner to the servants, yet always maintained a certain dignity before them, threw her arms about the maid's neck, and clung to her as if she were her sister.

The little domestic had a warm heart and quick sympathies. She was touched by this mark of affection and confidence from one so much above her in social station, and she hastened to assure the young lady that everything at home should be managed entirely to her satisfaction.

What a startling, exciting case it became; the astute

young lawyer who had undertaken to find the murderer through Margaret Calvert, proceeded with his work in such a peculiarly systematic way of his own, proving so much and so clearly from little, odd, incidents collected by his unflagging energy, that many a time beneath the mask of calmness which by great effort the girl had assumed, she felt her courage utterly fail.

"I cannot save him," she thought, and, on leaving the witness stand she invariably burst into hysterical tears.

The case reached its critical point; the sharp young lawyer had carefully wrought it up; and on a certain bright morning in the crowded court-room, with the eager glances of bright eyes, and the swaying of charming attire about him, he drew himself up in his firm impressive way, turned a triumphant look on the fair witness then under examination, and said in his startlingly distinct tones.

"There is a member of the family in which you reside—a young man—a son—he knew the murdered man, Cecil Clare. Where is this young man now?"

The girl knew that her face was like monumental marble; but that in a second it would be as red as a young belle's crimson fan flaunting near, and while the vivid tide swept suddenly over her cheeks, and brow, and neck, she looked steadily at him, and answered firmly:

"Traveling."

The sharp lawyer with his penetrating look, questioned again.

"When you, having seen an account of the murder in an evening edition of that day's paper, visited the *morgue* where at that time was this young man?"

Her face was pale again, and she drew herself up, and answered as firmly as before:

"Traveling."

She felt herself growing strangely bold; a feeling for which she could not account unless it was produced out of the very thought of the imminent danger which threatened her cousin. She flinched no more from the sharp questions; she did not vary in the least from the statement she had first made; and the skilful lawyer found in Margaret Calvert a sharper witness than from her previous examination he had thought she would eventually prove to be.

The case was adjourned till subpœnas should be served on the domestics in the household of Margaret Calvert's aunt.

From the daily papers the help all knew the particulars of the strange case, and the connection of their young mistress with it.

At first it created consternation and horror. The coachman, on the morning after the detention of Miss Calvert as a witness, had read aloud in the kitchen, as he was accustomed to do on most days, accounts of the strange and wicked doings in the city, and the cook, suspending her work for a moment requested him to see if there was anything more about the man who had been found murdered and taken to the *morgue*.

How had he skipped it?

There it was on the first page, with the startling heading with which the sensational press prefaces its accounts of exciting events.

"SOME LIGHT THROWN ON THE STRANGE MURDER!

"ACCIDENTAL DISCOVERY OF AN IMPORTANT WITNESS!

"VOLUNTARY ASSUMING OF THE CASE BY MR. CHARLES PLOWDEN, A STRANGE YOUNG LAWYER!"

Then followed an account of all that had happened on the inquest; the singular charge which Mr. Plowden had preferred against the lady-witness, with her name and her complete description.

The cook let the plate, which she held, fall, so great was her amazement and horror, while John the coachman stared blankly about him, and the other servants held up their hands and uttered sundry exclamations.

All had learned from little Annie on the previous evening that Miss Calvert was detained as a witness for something, and though they marveled much at that, and sought to assist each other to a discovery by their various conjectures, no one dreamed that her detention had anything to do with this affair.

When the cook recovered her voice, she laid her hand on the coachman's arm, and said with her good-natured face all aglow from indignant feeling.

"Do you, John, think that young creature had anything to do with the like of that?"

"No!" said John emphatically, an opinion in which the help without exception heartily concurred; and each one of the kindly-feeling domestics assisted the little maid's efforts to keep from Madame Bernot all news of what was transpiring in the outside world—an easy task, for no newspaper ever found its way into that sick-room, no reading but that which pertained to the spiritual life, and the few—very few—who were ever admitted into that apartment, by tacit understanding, refrained from mentioning anything which bore the slightest relation to crime.

Indeed, her mind seemed to have voluntarily severed all connection with the outside world. Her son, his prospects, that which she desired him to become, were merged in the thought that all was in God's hands, and while she prayed for him with all the fervor of ardent affection, she never suffered herself to think of the worldly circumstances, or perils, or joys, with which he might be surrounded. She kept no account of dates—the very days of the week with her were merged into morning, noon and night. When Sunday came, her niece, or the attendant, acquainted her. She did not or would not remark the passage of time; and when, as on rare occasions it happened, she was asked how long she was thus afflicted, she always referred the questioner to her niece, or the attendant, as she could not tell the exact time. So that which required most stratagem on the part of the servants was to account for Miss Calvert's prolonged absence from the sick-room.

Annie reported her ill, and Madame Bernot, though anxious, for a time appeared to be satisfied. But she worried at last in her gentle way, lest the child, as she called Margaret, was seriously ill, and did not have proper attendance; lest she should die, and turning her eyes to the picture she said sadly:

"O, my God! why am I so helpless?"

It was the first murmur which, since her affliction, had escaped her lips, and in a moment, as if to atone for the sudden repining, she murmured, her eyes still fixed on the picture:

"Thy will, my God, not mine, be done!"

She asked if a physician attended her niece, and on being answered in the affirmative, Annie feared she would request to see him; but before she did so, subpœnas were served on the servants, causing more consternation and horror among them, and calling forth more indignant exclamations from the ruddy-faced, warm-hearted cook.

Margaret Calvert's examination was at last concluded, and the sharp-witted lawyer, though he cross-examined her with an adroitness which excited the envy of much older members of the bar, and questioned her about facts in her life, of which she was startled to find he had a knowledge, he had not succeeded in causing her to implicate any one.

As she stepped, tremblingly, from the stand, she glanced, while in the act of lowering her veil, toward Annie, the maid, the witness who was to succeed her, and when she reached her seat she lowered her face in her hands under cover of the friendly veil, and she bitterly thought:

"I have not committed him, but *they* will.

Annie Corbin took the stand, and deposed that she was two years in the household of Madame Bernot. Miss Calvert had engaged her, and engaged all the servants about the same time, as Madame Bernot and her niece had only then arrived from the South. The son, Mr. Hubert Bernot, was at college then; he rarely came home. On the night on which it was supposed the murder was committed, Miss Calvert had been in steady attendance upon her aunt from early evening; she, Annie Corbin, had been asked by Miss Calvert, at six o'clock on the next morning, to bring some tea to Madame Bernot's room; Miss Calvert's attire was precisely what it had been on the previous evening. She looked pale and tired from watching; Madame Bernot had desired her, Miss Calvert, to go to her room, as she must be weary after the long night.

Mr. Charles Plowden began his adroit examination; the company who were supposed to visit Miss Calvert, the acquaintances she had formed; but he only elicited that the young lady led a life more befitting the cloister; company of any description had never been received during Annie's term of residence in the house, and the young lady rarely went out save, when she, Annie Corbin, had attended her, and then it had been to make purchases. On such occasions, she rode in the carriage.

"This son, Mr. Hubert Bernot," said the lawyer, "does *he* never bring young friends, or college mates home with him?"

"Never since *I* have been in the house," was the reply.

"When was Mr. Hubert Bernot home last?" and just for a second there shone in Mr. Plowden's bright eyes a triumphant glance. He had asked that question of Margaret Calvert, and she, confident that the servants had not seen her cousin since the day that his trunk was despatched, and he a few hours later had followed in the carriage, had given the date of that day. But he *might* have been seen, and she almost suspended her breath while awaiting Annie Corbin's answer.

The maid could not remember the precise date, but

on reflection, she said it was so many weeks and days ago, which brought it exactly to the time Margaret had designated. And on being examined further, she deposed that he was then about to start on a traveling tour,—his trunk had gone by express in the morning, and he had followed in the carriage as she had already stated.

John McNamee, the coachman, was next called. He deposed to the same facts so far as they had come under his observation. He was about the same time in the house as Annie Corbin; he had been engaged by Miss Calvert; though he drove the young lady out, she was attended by the maid,—sometimes twice a week, when purchases were generally made. On such a date, he remembered it distinctly—the same date given by Miss Calvert—he drove Mr. Hubert Bernot to the depot, waited while he alighted and went into the ticket-office, then drove home.

The evidence of the other servants was of the same nature; all deposed alike to the main facts of the case, and all were agreed on the date at which Mr. Hubert Bernot had left home.

Margaret Calvert breathed freer; the rapidly changing color in her cheeks had given place to a steady glow, and her eyes had a hopeful look. She felt almost bold enough to draw aside her veil, but prudence forbade, lest her emotion should again betray itself in her face.

The last witness called was Hannah Moore, the cook. She was a large formed woman whose round, ruddy face, indicated the good-nature, and good-humor so characteristic of her country people. Her manner showed that she had never been in a court-room before, and that even now she was in some trepidation lest her appearance there should be derogatory to her character. Her ruddy complexion grew ruddier, and her embarrassment prevented her looking directly at anybody for some minutes.

Sharp Mr. Plowden, only made more determined
and eager by his failure to extort from the previous
witnesses sufficient to cause the issue of a warrant for
arrest, on suspicion, of Hubert Bernot, changed the
manner in which he had conducted all his other examinations, and came directly to that which he wished
to elicit when he questioned Hannah Moore.

She had gained a little more courage, and had given
her evidence, the same in effect as that of those who
had preceded her, becoming bolder as she continued,
and raising her voice with its rich-toned brogue, until
it was distinctly heard throughout the crowded place.

While she was speaking there came a strange expression into the lawyer's face. It seemed to change
its whole contour, to banish the hard, cold, firm look
which struck even casual beholders, and to put into his
eyes a wistful tenderness, a passionate longing. But
its coming was so sudden, and its stay so brief, that no
one observed it, and when Hannah Moore had ceased,
and people looked expectantly at him, waiting his
questions, he was the same cold, exact, professional
gentleman he had previously been.

"When did you last see Mr. Hubert Bernot?"
he asked, and for the first time the ruddy-faced Irish-
woman's eyes rested fully upon his countenance.

She appeared disconcerted for a moment, as if that
full gaze into his face had paralyzed her. But the judge,
and other important officers and even only curious
beholders, attributed her hesitation and apparent
embarrassment to another cause—that of not being able
to give the same answer that her fellow-servants had
done.

Sharp Mr. Plowden saw at once his chance for an
advantage. He appeared to give that interpretation to
her strange manner which he knew others were giving,
and he repeated his question in a tone the triumph of
which caused Margaret to lift her veil and look at him.

But Hannah Moore had recovered herself: whatever

had been the cause of her agitation had passed entirely away, and she answered loudly and firmly that she wasn't good at remembering dates, but the gentleman could count back if he liked; it was as Annie Corbin had said, so many weeks and days ago. Mr. Bernot had come down in the kitchen that morning looking for the coachman, just in the same off-hand, pleasant way that he always had when he happened to be at home; that he wasn't above speaking kind to the servants, and saving them trouble. And here Miss Moore's voice became slightly indignant.

Mr. Plowden bent another of his penetrating looks upon her, and said:

"You affirm upon oath then, that the morning of—" mentioning the date—" was the last time upon which you saw Mr. Hubert Bernot?"

"I do."

"And you affirm also upon oath, that at no time afterward either within your sight or hearing, there occurred anything to make you think Miss Calvert's actions strange, or to make you suspect that Mr. Hubert Bernot had possibly not left home at all?"

There was a sudden buzz in the court, as if sundry examinations had burst forth together; but it was instantly checked.

Margaret impulsively threw up her veil, and while the convulsive feeling in her heart was betraying itself in her face, looked anxiously at the witness.

Hannah caught the look, a peculiarly earnest one, and she seemed to derive from it that of which no suspicion had previously entered her mind. She pretended to be seized with a fit of coughing that she might gain time to frame her answer; and all the while Mr. Charles Plowden's sharp eyes were fastened upon her face, and Mr. Charles Plowden's own countenance wore a look of triumph.

The witness replied at last, boldly and firmly as before, but in a very indignant tone:

"Nothing happened to make me think anything strange; and you'll make nothing of trying to pull out of me what I would not tell if it was there to tell, which it aint; for I could speak of strange things about other people that might stop their questions."

She paused to take breath, and was about to proceed in her queer strain, but Mr. Plowden stopped her as not being pertinent to the question.

The judge leaned forward and said:

"On your oath do you know anything about anyone here present, which would help to clear the mystery of this murder?"

"I do not."

It was remarked that after that, Mr. Plowden hurried the examination to a close, asking but few more questions, and apparently careless of the replies.

Margaret Calvert once more breathed freer, clasped her nervous hands together, and tried to murmur a prayer of thanksgiving that the dreadful ordeal was so nearly over; but there was to be another test.

The last witness was dismissed from the stand; then Mr. Plowden made an eloquent resume of the case, dwelling on the careful examination just concluded, and recapitulating the elicited facts, harrowing his listeners' souls by his impressive account of the horror of the crime committed, and drawing tears and sobs from fair ones by the picture he drew of the murdered man's sad and lonely death. Then he ended with a firmly-avowed conviction, which he doubted not was shared by every one who heard him, that no witness who had been examined knew anything of the perpetrator of the terrible crime.

He sat down with a half suppressed sigh of relief, wiping his perspiring brow, and pressing his fingers on his temples as if to still their throbbing.

Another of the legal gentlemen arose—one who had been listening for something by which he might show that Mr. Plowden had not collected all the evidence. He rose slowly and glanced triumphantly about him before he spoke.

An undefined fear of what was coming sent the pain into Margaret Calvert's heart again, and made her weak and trembling.

He said in a distinct and sonorous voice, that the eloquent and searching gentleman who had preceded him had forgotten one very important witness—Mr. Hubert Bernot's mother. Though she was an invalid her evidence could, and ought to be obtained—it was certainly of moment to know when *she* had last seen her son. He hoped the court would feel the importance of his suggestion.

"She may not be able to say; she takes no account of time," Margaret murmured to herself, pressing her hand over her veil, lest even through that the ghastly pallor of her cheeks and lips could be seen.

Mr. Plowden's face wore something like a scowl as he rose to answer this implied neglect on his part. His tall, erect form seemed to assume a more commanding height, and his voice had a cutting sarcasm in its startlingly distinct tones.

He described Madame Bernot's pitiable condition; drawing so accurate a picture of her sufferings that Margaret started, wondering how he knew. He told of the little knowledge which the invalid had of the outer world, and ended by suggesting that if her evidence must be obtained, it might be taken in a guarded way so as to keep from her all knowledge of the purpose for which it was required.

His suggestion was adopted, and the case was adjourned till Madame Bernot's evidence could be obtained.

Margaret at last was permitted to return home. She was hysterical, and she would have the servants to accompany her in the carriage which the coachman hastily brought.

Hannah Moore and Annie Corbin were both unaffectedly weeping because of the distress of their young mistress.

CHAPTER III.

MADAME BERNOT'S evidence *was* taken—taken in her own room while Margaret stood beside her, pale and nervous enough to have been considered another invalid.

The young girl never forgot that morning.

From the time that her own examination had been concluded she had watched for this promised official visit to her aunt, and she had recognized at first sight the face which looked out from the carriage that stopped before the door—it belonged to the gentleman who had suggested that this evidence should be obtained.

She flew to the sick-room, dismissed the attendant with an injunction to rest, as *she* was now prepared to wait on her aunt, and when she was summoned to meet the strangers she rang for Annie Corbin to attend Madame Bernot.

Three gentlemen met Margaret on her entrance to the parlor. The professional man whose suggestion was the cause of this visit, said blandly:

" You shall see, Miss Calvert, that we have arranged every detail of this call in such a manner that the slightest alarm cannot be given to your aunt. This gentleman," pointing to a florid-faced man on his right, "is a physician; he will ask all the questions so that Madame Bernot shall be led to think that she is simply answering a doctor's necessary inquiries. You can prepare her, if you choose, by telling her that he is skilled in such cases and you have engaged his services for her.

"And this gentleman," pointing to a sharp-visaged

man on his left, " is a reporter who will accurately note down everything that occurs."

Margaret only bowed, but she fancied that the fluttering of her heart could be seen through her dress as she left the room.

She knelt beside Madame Bernot while Annie Corbin retired to a window, and said with as much firmness as she could assume :

" Aunt Bernot, an eminent physician is in the parlor, I heard of his skill in the cases of others and so have engaged him to visit you. For my—for Hubert's sake, allow him to see you."

" Dear child ! " was the reply ; " it takes long to convince you that my disease is beyond all earthly remedy —my sufferings are entirely in God's hands."

" But see him," pleaded Margaret, " for just this once ; I wish it so much."

" Be it so then," the invalid answered, and she fixed her eyes on their usual resting-place, the picture of Christ's bleeding head.

The three professional gentlemen evidently were not prepared for the sight of this patient, suffering woman. Only one, he who was to make the inquiries, came in her sight; the other two, in obedience to a request from Margaret, remained near the door, so that Madame Bernot supposed she was in the presence of only one stranger. They looked embarrassed for the first few moments, and the physician hesitated as if fearful how to begin.

At length he commenced by inquiries about the amount of pain she suffered, all of which Madame Bernot patiently answered. Then he asked the length of time she had thus suffered.

" My niece will have to tell you," was the reply. " I remember no dates and know nothing of the passing of time. I am simply here waiting the Master's call."

It was impossible to discredit her. Her angelic face, her clear eyes, with their peculiarly touching expression, told too convincingly the truthfulness of her statement.

The physician again hesitated while he pretended to rub softly the helpless hands lying in her lap, and when he spoke his voice slightly trembled. He asked a few unimportant questions, and then he casually inquired about her immediate attendance, saying that hers was such a peculiar case she should seldom be left entirely to the charge of hired nurses.

Margaret tremulously answered:

"I attend her most of the time."

The gentleman assumed a more confident air. He was slowly but surely approaching his point and he felt sanguine of success. Raising his eyes to Miss Calvert's face, he said:

"But this care does not devolve entirely upon *you* —there are other relatives I presume——"

"My son!" interrupted Madame Bernot with true maternal tenderness in her voice,

"So there is an equal division of the duty I suppose," he said, smilingly. "You have reason to be proud, my dear madame, of such dutiful kindred: but I shall have some directions to give that the care which your case requires may be rendered in accordance with my mode of treatment, and, if possible, I should like to see your son."

"He is not at home," said Madame Bernot; "he is traveling."

"Ah, then!" looking again at Miss Calvert, "the affectionate duty does devolve entirely upon *you*."

He bent his head to Madame Bernot's hands and appeared to study intently their delicate veins.

Margaret bowed her head and tried to quiet the wild beating of her heart. She knew he was but seeking a pretence on which he might ask one question of the invalid; and what if the latter should correctly answer! The girl's heart beat wilder at the thought, and a choking sensation came into her throat.

The physician lifted his head and looked sharply into the sick woman's eyes.

"At some time in your life," he said, slowly, "**you have** received a very severe shock, of which your present condition is the consequence. Your mental state now is far from being quiet, and you have experienced recently some new agitation—perhaps due to the departure of your son—which has left baneful effects. When did you last see your son?"

Margaret's heart gave a thump which, to her excited imagination, seemed as if it must be as audible to every one in the room as it was to herself; and the choking sensation in her throat increased, till it seemed to her that she must be experiencing all the sensations of a drowning person.

Madame Bernot's eyes had not once turned from the vivid picture opposite.

She was not startled by the physician's words, for every practitioner who had treated her, had told her that her illness was the result of a severe shock to the mental system; neither was she surprised by the rather abrupt and unnecessary question with which he had concluded. She answered, quietly:

"I have said before that I keep no account of time. My son *was* here, but he has gone. The time of his departure I am unable to tell you. He bade me goodbye, and left me; my niece will tell you when."

The strange sensation went suddenly out of Margaret's throat, and her voice was quite firm when she answered—the same answer that she had given in the court-room.

The physician looked discomfited, and stole a hasty glance over Madame Bernot's shoulder at the two silent figures near the door—one so busily writing—as if imploring help in his emergency. The lawyer answered with a glance that seemed to say:

"On no account must you give up yet."

And the medical man swept his hand across his forehead, and said in a slightly nervous tone:

"I should like to know precisely, my dear madame,

for the reason that it is necessary for me to have such particulars in order to determine with greater accuracy upon your case——have the goodness to make an attempt to remember—was it in the day time or in the evening that your son took his leave of you ? Perhaps in that way we shall arive at the exact time."

Poor Margaret! the lump was returning to her throat. But Madame Bernot answered as quietly as before :

"Neither am I able to answer that question. Since it has been the Divine will to afflict me, I have allowed little incidents to drift in and out of my life without thinking, or ever after remembering the *time* of their happening. All I know is, that my son *was* here ; he kissed me while I sat as I am sitting now, and left me. My niece will give you any further particulars you may wish ; and, pardon me, but I seldom give so much time to strangers."

The expression of her eyes still fixed on the picture, and the motion of her lips, conveyed to her immediate listeners the fact that she was praying.

The physician glanced again for his cue, and receiving a nod from the lawyer signifying that sufficient questions had been asked, said he would leave his directions with Madame's neice, and he departed gently from the room followed by his companions and Miss Calvert.

All repaired to the parlor, Margaret going slowly that she might gain time to calm herself.

The gentlemen grouped themselves near the door, and Margaret, on entering, leaned slightly against a marble pillar which supported a large arabesque vase, and asked in a low tone :

"Are you satisfied, gentlemen?"

The lawyer had been talking eagerly to his companions, and he answered Miss Calvert in the same eager tones :

"By no means satisfied ; the case remains precisely where it was before. We have gained nothing ; we have learned nothing. Sufficient evidence has not been elicited to warrant the arrest of Mr. Hubert Bernot; and this murdered man will not be avenged just yet. It is probable that the case will be dropped now, for others do not entertain my views of this affair; but murder will out in this as in other instances, and when it does, you and I shall meet again. That you may not forget me, here is my card."

He placed in her listless hand a little square of enameled pasteboard, on which she read, in a mechanical way, the single and singular word:

"ROQUELARE."

Even in her strange state of feeling the singularity of the inscription struck her, and she found herself wondering if that was the name of the gentleman; and then she looked at his heavy face again, and seemed to be making a special examination of each one of his features. They were not easily forgotten—square cut, and prominent, and yet with a heavy, fathomless expression about them which, on first sight, frequently conveyed the idea of lack of intelligence.

He seemed to desire her close inspection for a few minutes, then, as the mental examination still continued, he turned to his companions and signified his wish to depart. Margaret accompanied them to the door in a half abstracted way.

The lawyer was the last to descend the stop, and while his companions entered the carriage, he paused to say to Miss Calvert in a significant tone:

"You may calm your fears; nothing more will be done for a while; but remember, that truth is sometimes strangely revealed."

He followed his companions into the carriage, while Margaret turned from the door and repaired to her aunt's room.

"Did this eminent physician leave a prescription

dear?" Madame Bernot asked, as her niece having mentioned Annie to withdraw, took her accustomed place beside the invalid's chair, and there was a slight smile on the patient face.

"No, ma'am," was the reply. "I think your case puzzled him.

"I think it did," said the invalid, "and I think also he asked rather strange questions, but I suppose the eminence of his profession made it necessary for him to do so."

Her eyes returned to the picture and it was evident that she wished all thought of the late visit dismissed.

Annie Corbin's face on her descent to the kitchen wore a half frightened expression, which at once attracted the attention of the cook, who hastened to her with a sympathizing look in her own countenance, and asked:

"Have they gone? And how does that young creature up stairs feel?"

Cook's sharp wits had discovered the object of that unusual visit as quickly and correctly as Miss Calvert herself had done.

Annie told hurriedly all that her memory retained of the conversation between Madame Bernot and one of the strangers, at which the cook sagely shook her head, and made other signs that there was an assured connection between Annie's statement and her own previous thoughts of the affair.

"What does it all mean?" Annie concluded, "surely, Miss Calvert had never anything to do with that murder?"

"Is it that baby?" said the cook in strong indignation. "That pretty chit of a girl who would'nt harm a fly? Don't be taking leave of your senses, Annie!"

"I don't mean that," answered the little maid. "Of course I know Miss Calvert herself wouldn't do such a thing, but don't you think—mightn't it be that she might know that Mr. Hubert Bernot——?"

"Tut, tut, tut!" interrupted the cook, with an uncalled-for energy in her tones. "Never let such a thought as that into your head. Both Mr. Hubert and Miss Calvert are two innocent babies that have been unaccountably mixed up in some other body's sin. Here, as you're down here, mix up this batter for me."

And ruddy-face, warm-hearted Hannah Moore bustled most unnecessarily about her culinary duties; but when Annie Corbin had mixed the batter and gone up stairs, and she was alone in the kitchen, she ceased her work very suddenly, and standing quite still, placed her arms akimbo, and said, audibly:

"*He* wasn't one of them that came to-day. Well, perhaps he won't have anything more to say; if he does, then I'll have *my* speech and maybe the tables will be turned."

So the mysterious murder case was dropped; neither the public investigation nor the private inquiries of the man whose card bore that singular inscription, having discovered anything further about the matter. And after many days had passed, during which nothing occurred to cause a return of Miss Calvert's fears, she began to be almost her own placid self.

The servants ceased to talk of the murder, and at length even to think of it; all, save Hannah Moore.

But Hannah gave expression to her thoughts only to herself, and not even Miss Calvert suspected that the cook knew that which, had she told it, could have been worked up into damning evidence against Mr. Hubert Bernot.

The murdered man had long since been consigned to an obscure grave.

Just before his burial, the keeper of a private boarding house in the lower part of the city, had identified him as a boarder, who had mysteriously disappeared from his house. He had been an inmate of the house but a few days, and had given his name as Cecil Carter.

The authorities immediately proceeded to the room which Carter, or Clare, had occupied, but, beyond a trunk filled with handsome clothes a few letters bearing the signature of the banking house in Germany of which Mr. Plowden had spoken, and a check for a large amount of money, payable at one of the city banks, they found nothing to show what friends he had possessed.

A letter asking for particular information of him had been despatched immediately to Germany, and the reply tallied exactly with what Mr. Plowden had told of the dead man's affairs. The check had also been forwarded to Europe, but his watch, and ring and clothes disappeared through some of the meshes of the law.

So, at last, the public regarded the affair as one of those mysteries which would only be cleared at the Divine Judgment Seat.

Hubert Bernot's letters came regularly, and Margaret always hastily scanned the contents before she read them to her aunt, lest there might be a sentence referring to the fearful event of the past weeks, or a stray word to betray the unhappy state of the writer's feelings; but each missive was calmly, even happily written—detailing only the pleasant events of his journey, or describing in his graphic way, the novel sights he witnessed.

Margaret in her replies was equally careful not to touch on the murder; but she thought sorrowfully how his crime seemed to weigh less upon him than the knowledge of it did upon her. *She* carried about with her a worm, the gnawing of which never ceased. Her face never for a moment now lost its sad expression, and her manner, contrary to its old wont, was frequently languid and abstracted.

Months went by, and at length a letter from Hubert announced his speedy return.

"God is very good," said Madame Bernot, "to have spared me to see my son again." And she smiled, but made no remark when Margaret said to her one bright morning:

"This is the day Hubert has fixed for his return to us."

Miss Calvert herself was nervous and wretched. An undefinable dread had seized her—a terror which she felt would not desert her even in his presence; so she went forth slowly when the carriage, which had gone to meet him, returned, and she heard him alight, and a moment after his quick springing step on the stoop.

He did not wait for the door to be fully opened, before he bounded within, and bestowed on Margaret a passionate greeting.

He was too eager, too excited to notice that she hardly returned his affectionate salute, and he proceeded to inquire hurriedly for his mother.

"Her health is the same," said Margaret. And she led the way to her aunt's room.

He wore such a bold, confident air; he looked so handsome and well, even his mother delightedly commented on his appearance.

While a special repast was being prepared for him he entertained his two auditors with a lively descriptions of his tour; and when he rose to visit the servants, as had always been his wont after a lengthy absence, Margaret thought with a sick heart:

"It is only on me the burden is pressing; *he* has cast it off."

With what a hearty greeting he met each one of the domestics!

Annie Corbin said when he had left them:

"Just his being home makes the house like another place!"

And Hannah Moore, when she was alone that night, soliloquized:

"An' its on him, the kind-hearted *gossoon*, he wanted to put the crime! Thank God, I said nothing!"

Hubert partook of the tempting dishes prepared for him in his mother's room, where her eyes could fix their loving glances upon him. As if to apologize for her desire to have it so, she said, smilingly:

"I wish to feast my eyes this once; we have been parted so long."

But when he had partaken of the repast she insisted that he should retire for rest after his journey, and he playfully obeyed. Margaret as usual busied herself about the invalid; but there was a choking sob in her throat and a squeezing pressure about her heart which made her gladly resign her charge to the attendant, and seek her own room.

As she was about to ascend the stair, she heard her name called from the hall below and looking over the baluster she saw Hubert standing there. He beckoned her to him, and when she reached his side he drew her into the library.

"I *must* see you, Margaret," he said, "I could not go to my room without speaking to you, and I waited for you, feeling that you must soon come forth."

He closed the door, and, leaning against it, extended his hands with just such a cry as that with which he had extended them to her on the night after his crime.

Ah! the mask had fallen completely from his countenance and his manner, and Margaret shuddered at the suffering face which met her.

"Help me, Margaret, help me!"

The cry found an echo in her own sad soul, and the pressure about her heart and the sob in her throat dissolved in a passion of tears. The sight of her grief seemed to have a soothing effect upon him, for he took her hand between his own and said tenderly:

"My poor, brave darling! that I could take this cup

from you; that I could pour back into my own heart the bitterness that has come into your life—but bear it for me awhile, and one day perhaps you shall be free; but not yet, not yet!"

He released her suddenly, and resuming his former position against the door, continued, his voice sinking to a hoarse, ominous sounding whisper.

"You are the only one to whom I can wear my own face. To every one else I show the mask you saw me wear below. I have worn that mask during all the time of my absence, and I fancy that I have schooled myself to wear it even in my sleep. I jested and laughed with the very paper in my hands in which I saw the account of your examination, and the rigid means they were adopting to discover the murderer. I laughed the loudest when my fears of arrest were greatest. Unexpected grips made me start, and strange voices suddenly speaking made me shudder, but mighty effort kept start and shudder from being perceived.

"I shouted with mirth when there were gaunt devils whispering all sorts of evil things to my black heart. I thought time would inure me to my wretched secret, but it has failed to do so most miserably. If the phantom which pursues me grows a little dim while I am talking to others, and light and mirth are around me, it is only to come out more startlingly distinct when I am alone—to pursue me relentlessly then, to hold me, and compel me to look at the bloody thing as it was— as it was—"

He stopped suddenly and put his hands before his eyes, as if he saw that which he was describing.

His words were harrowing Margaret's soul. She, too, covered her face, not to shut out the imaginary scene he pictured, but that she might not look upon his suffering.

In her pity for him she had almost ceased to pity herself.

Minutes elapsed before either looked up, and then

It was Hubert who withdrew his hands first and said in that same dread whisper:

"I have disclosed to you now a part of the agony which I continually suffer. I have been so long alone with it that the mere telling of it to you has afforded me intense relief. It has given me courage to assume my mask again and to wear it perhaps even in *your* presence,—I shall plunge into the work I have planned for myself, letting the worm that is here," placing his hand on his heart "gnaw, till it has eaten the very cords which bind me to life."

He turned away, moving with a firm step toward the centre of the room. Margaret followed: her own sad heart was full of tenderness, now that she knew he had not cast aside his wretched burden.

She had words of hope and comfort upon her lips, speaking them sweetly, while her face had such an expression as an angel might wear. He listened calmly, and even something like hope lit up his own countenance, until she said:

"And after a little, Hubert, God, in pity for your suffering, and in love for your repentance will give you grace to kneel at His tribunal and confess."

He became furious:

"If you would drive me to commit suicide name confession again. I tell you I shall *never* confess to mortal man, and, did they arrest me, this hand," raising his right arm, "should end my existence before Hubert Bernot would stand in a felon's dock."

Her passionate sobs calmed him.

"Never again, Margaret, speak of confession to me. Remember your oath, and remember also that you are the only one in this wide, wide world who can afford one ray of comfort to my desolate soul."

He stooped and kissed her forehead.

She flung her arms about his neck and clung to him as a frightened child might do to its parent. Alas! she felt the need of companionship in her misery, and she tried to imagine that the love and tenderness of a creature could compensate for the God she had resigned.

When both had grown outwardly calm, she sought to tell him of his mother's official examination, and of the card bearing the strange inscription, but he interrupted.

"No, Margaret! let the dead past bury its dead as much as we may do. I read the papers carefully and wish to know no more than they contained; if anything else has happened do not tell me, it might but add to my fears."

She made no more attempts to tell him, but bade him good night.

He accompanied her to the door, clasping her hand for a moment before opening it, and whispering:

"We two, bound by a bloody bond."

She shuddered at his words, but even while she shuddered, a thrill—an undefinable thrill—ran through her form. Now, too surely she knew that a creature usurped her Creator's place in her heart. God help her! Murderer as he was, she loved Hubert Bernot.

CHAPTER IV.

HUBERT BERNOT began the study of the law, and as he had said to Margaret, he applied himself to it with a vigor of heart and mind which alarmed his mother for the effect of so many hours of close study upon his health; but he laughed at her fears, said Margaret had exaggerated her account of his diligence, and kissing her, returned to his room to drown in study his ceaseless remorse.

It had been Margaret's custom to use the carriage in going to church on Sundays, but on the Sunday succeeding her cousin's return he requested her to walk, saying:

"I shall tell you why when we reach the church."

Great was the surprise of John the coachman, when the usual Sunday morning order for the carriage was countermanded, and he scratched his head in a perplexed way and said to the cook:

"Faith, its a queer way the world has; them that has carriages not wanting to use them, and them that can't have them not content because they have to use their feet at all!"

But a half hour after, when he caught sight of Hubert—tall, lithe, handsome fellow that he was—and pale, lovely Margaret arrayed in her plain, dark, but charmingly becoming costume, he declared to Annie Corbin that it would be a pity to shut such a pretty sight in a carriage.

When near the church to which streams of people were hurrying, Hubert bent and whispered :—

"The reason why I would not have the carriage is,

I shall not enter with you—I feel as if I were banned by God for my crime, and I dare not enter His temple. But do you go in, Margaret, and pray for us both. I shall wait for you somewhere here."

She stopped short, looking at him in horrified affright.

He drew her arm through his own, and forced her on. "You will attract notice," he whispered.

When she recovered herself she besought him to alter his determination; but he was as flint to her passionate appeals. Mournfully and with many a sad, lingering look after his retreating form, she at last ascended the steps of the church.

Poor Margaret! She drew little comfort from the mass. Pray! she could not. What had she to do with prayer who held a murderer's secret, and who refused to denounce the murderer?

Oh, that unhappy secret!—if she could only lay its miserable burden somewhere! But her love for Hubert Bernot bound her to its weight with a strength that her will could not conquer, and she could only bury her face in her open prayer-book, and let her scalding tears wet the leaves through and through.

Hubert was waiting for her, after mass, at the door of the church.

The homeward walk was silent and dreary.

Every Sunday the same course was pursued, even on stormy ones; Hubert giving out that it was but proper, something should be endured in the service of the Lord; at which the coachman and the cook held up their hands and praised God there was so much goodness in the rich.

"Why go at all?" Margaret said to him once, a little impatiently; for her own remorse of conscience was so sharp. He answered:

"To avert the suspicion of the servants—they are very sharp sometimes." And she silently acquiesced.

The patient, long suffering invalid, whose eyes had

turned so often and gazed so long on the sacred picture near her, that they had acquired something of the expression which the painter had depicted, worried in her gentle way about the monotonous existence led by her son and niece.

"I am afraid I have been very selfish," she said to Margaret one day when her niece was tenderly bathing the helpless hands. "I have kept you so long attending to an old woman's whims. I thought that when Hubert came home to remain, he would be your passport to society; but he is almost as great a recluse as I am, and I have fancied, Margaret, that you were suffering——"

The girl bent low over the vessel she held, that her sudden start might not be noticed.

The invalid continued:

"That you are not well, and fear to tell me lest it may make me anxious. You look pale and sad my poor child; you have looked so for a long time. Is there anything the matter?"

Margaret forced herself to look up and to meet those calm, passionate eyes. Oh! how she yearned to be able to tell that there *was* something which was eating her very life away—to lean her head against that tender breast and sob out the grief with which her heart was breaking. As it was, it required a mighty effort to keep the tears from bursting forth. She looked sadly into the face before her.

"I am not ill," she said, "but I do not feel quite as well as I used to feel—I am unaccountably depressed in spirits."

"Ah! I see how it is. You have associated so long with suffering, my poor child, that you have grown to suffer yourself. But I must remedy this in some way. Tell Hubert to come to me, and you return with him. No; call Kreble to remove that"—as Margaret was about to remove the vessel she had been using.

Margaret put her mouth to a speaking-tube which

led from her aunt's apartment to the attendant's room, and in a few moments a large-formed, coarse-featured, but kindly-mannered German woman appeared to take her place by the invalid.

The breakfast bell had not yet rung, and the busy happy clatter of the servants below came faintly up to Margaret as she stood for an instant in the great hall to steady her trembling limbs. A pang of envy shot through her heart, and as she leaned her burning brow on the baluster, she thought bitterly how cheerfully she would exchange with the lowest menial in the house if so doing would break the heavy chain that bound her—would free her from the weight of the murderer's secret.

There was no immediate response to her timid knock at Hubert's door, but she heard a hurried movement inside as if he had been startled from some occupation; after a little, he asked hoarsely, "Who is there?"

"Only I—Margaret! your mother wishes to see you."

He opened the door and stood before her, his face frightfully pale and drawn up into an appalling expression of suffering.

"It's a relief to look at you," he said; "to find some one who reflects the agony that is in my own soul."

She did not answer him; her eyes were looking past him to the lighted astral on the table; he followed her look and attempted to laugh, but he only produced a hoarse, discordant gurgle:

"Ah! Margaret! noticing the evidence of my vigil, I see; it was a ghastly one, as they all are—"

He stopped abruptly and gasped as if a sudden pain prevented his utterance.

"You are ill, Hubert;" she said, wildly; and she was about to rush to the bell to summon aid, but he intercepted her.

"Do not call any one," he whispered, "and go down to the library. I will join you there."

He turned back to his room, and Margaret, faint and suffering herself, descended to wait for him.

She heard his heavy, uncertain step descending the stair, and she could not help contrasting it with the buoyant spring of his old-time gait. He did not take the precaution to close the door when he entered, only sank into the nearest chair, as if his weakness left him no alternative.

Margaret softly shut the door and stood before him.

"I frighten you," he said, looking up at her; "but the torture of this secret crime is getting to be more than I can bear. Oh, Margaret! rather than endure it, rather than face the phantom which so frequently rises before me I would gladly, nay, exultingly, fling my guilty secret far—proclaim it from the housetop and then die—die anywhere, die anyhow, so that I had flung my burden off; but I cannot while my mother lives—I cannot destroy *her* with such a fell blow as that would be,—she who has suffered so long, I cannot bring such dishonor upon our name. So there is nothing left for *me* but to bear life as I may. I have forsworn every tie. No wife shall ever clasp my red hand, and if a thousand years of such torture as I am enduring now, could restore the life I have taken, or could cleanse my soul of its bloody stain, I should unflinchingly bear it all. Pity me, Margaret, and pray for me!—

"And yet, what do I ask?" he continued, moodily; "you to pray for *me*, when *I* am not willing to make the atonement which alone will satisfy my conscience! This it is which keeps me from the sacraments, from church, from prayer—of what avail would all be when I cannot, when I will not, give myself up to justice. Oh! that one crime should so blight soul and body— would that I were never born!"

She could not answer him—for, was not her soul

also blighted by that one crime, and unwilling, nay, positively refusing, to do what she deemed to be her duty, how could she exhort, or comfort him—and of what should her exhortation consist, but a plea to give himself up, and that would be to lose him, and crush his poor invalid mother.

She could not do it, and she was silent. He resumed:

"Prove your regard for me, Margaret, by bearing with me, and by guarding faithfully all the wretched things you know about me. Now, tell my mother that you found me a little unwell, but that I shall be with her soon."

But Margaret could not go immediately to deliver his message to Madame Bernot; she felt that she must relieve her own wild, maddened feelings first; so she went in a bewildered way to her room, and walked the floor, and wrung her hands, and sitting down at last before her dressing-table rested her head upon it, and burst into violent weeping; but they were tears that brought no relief, and she dashed them aside at length in a desperate, defiant way, and sat looking sullenly before her.

A little fancy-basket was on the table, and a white embossed card shone through the meshes of its silken lining.

She took it idly out and read again the peculiar inscription, "ROQUELARE."

This time the letters seemed to assume fantastic shapes, and the word itself to conjure up frightful images of her cousin brought to justice by some mysterious means.

"I believe that I am going mad," she said, and she dropped the card back to its place with a shudder. Then, rising, she hurriedly bathed her face and descended slowly to her aunt's room. The patient invalid had evinced neither surprise, nor impatience at the tardiness of her son and niece in obeying her request. She thought they had waited to fulfil some duty, and when

Margaret told her that Hubert was slightly unwell she desired that he should not come to her until he had breakfasted.

The breakfast bell had rung a second time and the cook was slightly indignant, and the waiter impatient, because no one had appeared in the breakfast room; but Hubert and Margaret came down at last. Both were so absorbed in painful thought, and both made so poor a pretence of eating, that even to the waiter their mental suffering was visible. He attributed it to physical illness, and spoke of it as such to his fellow-servants who thought it probable from their knowledge of Hubert's studious habits, and Margaret's unremitting care in the sick room.

But when Hannah Moore was alone she shook her head, and muttered:

"I know me own know. Its no bodily sickness that ails them. God help them!"

When the silent, scarcely-tasted meal was ended, they went together to Madame Bernot's room, and Hubert was obliged to kneel and lift his face to his mother that she might discover in his features the extent of his illness. He met her gaze calmly enough, only, when her hands rested on his shoulders, placed there at her own request by Margaret, he winced like one in pain; but he lowered his face at that particular moment, and his mother little dreamed that she had been pressing on raw wounds which were being constantly opened afresh before they were permitted to heal.

Margaret, by whom no motion was unobserved, suspected his suffering and its cause, and she averted her face lest its expression might betray something to her aunt. The mother was saying:

"Dear boy! I have a request, which is very near my heart, to ask of you to-day."

"Speak, mother; whatever it is, it shall be granted."

"It is that you will go more into society; that you

will bring gay, young companions to the house for Margaret's sake. We owe it to her for her long and devoted care of me. I have made her too much of a recluse."

A strange look came into Hubert's face—a sudden brightening of every feature for a second, but it was immediately succeeded by the appalling expression with which he had met Margaret on her entrance to his room that morning, and he bowed his head that his mother might not see. When he raised it he wore his usual look and he answered calmly,

"You are right; *we* owe her much," (with an emphasis on the word we which Margaret alone understood), "and I shall begin this week to do as you desire. I shall renew the acquaintance of my college mates."

He rose, standing erect, and poising his head with the manner of one into whom some new hope has been suddenly infused. A sudden hope had also filled Margaret's heart—a hope that society would wean him from his dreadful ideas of self-torture, and eventually would bring quiet, if not happiness, to his troubled spirit. But no such thought had entered Hubert's mind. He had hailed his mother's proposition because it seemed to afford a prospect of lightening for Margaret the burden which he had imposed on her—the hope that eventually her happiness might be secured in the love of some good man. Yet at that thought his own heart throbbed with exquisite torture, for wound about every fibre of his being was a passionate love for Margaret Calvert.

The gentle invalid, unsuspicious of what was passing in the minds of the young people, smilingly responded:

"Thank you, my dear boy, and God bless you both."

Her eyes returned to their wonted place, and Hubert, kissing her, went softly out, while Margaret began her usual daily duties in the sick-room.

Hubert kept his promise. He went abroad that very day, and returned with a couple of jovial fellows the ring of whose mirth could be heard through the house. He had taken them to his own room first, and had despatched a message to Margaret to meet them in the parlor. She was in her aunt's apartment when the request was brought, and Madame Bernot, smiling, said:

"And I insist that you will change your dress, and make yourself as pretty as possible. Come, I want obedience *now*."

Margaret went slowly to her room, donned as plain but a less sombre costume than the one she wore, and gave a careless brush to the curls which clustered so thickly round her head and neck. She cared very little for the impression she might make. Her one thought, her sole care, was for the miserable creature whose image was shrined in her heart. It made little difference to her that this was an unusual way of being introduced to fashionable society—that Madame Bernot in her life of suffering and retirement, and Hubert, in his little knowledge of the conventionalities of fashionable life, had *waived* the usual mode of introduction. She only knew that the one object of her life was Hubert's welfare, Hubert's happiness.

The grand state-parlor which had never been used for the reception of company since it had been in the possession of the Bernots, looked grim, and in a slight measure awful to Margaret when she entered it—she had so rarely visited it, and the two last occasions on which she had done so were intimately connected with the gaunt secret that she carried.

She paused a moment to remember more distinctly the features of the man who had given her the card with the strange inscription, and then with a shudder she tried to dismiss the painful thoughts which the memory caused.

An indistinct sound of the merriment in Hubert's room was wafted to her ears, and once she fancied that his voice was raised in mirthful tones. She bent forward, clasping her hands in her eagerness, and murmured:

"Already they are doing him good."

She was not mistaken for his door just then opened and his voice sounded in loud and mirthful protest against some proposition urged by one of his companions, as the three began to descend.

A sudden color dyed her cheeks, and never, perhaps did she look lovelier than at the moment that her cousin entered with his friends; but the color flitted as suddenly as it had appeared, and she stood as motionless as the marble image just in her rear, for she had recognized in one of the strangers Mr. Charles Plowden, the young lawyer who had held so prominent a position in the recent murder case.

He too, seemed embarrassed, and looked appealingly at Hubert; but Hubert said, gayly:

"My cousin is slightly startled, gentlemen, at meeting again one to whom she became known under very peculiar circumstances; but there is nothing very strange about it, Margaret. I was introduced to Mr. Plowden in Mr. Delmar's office," placing his hand familiarly on the shoulder of the other of his companions, a tall, rather delicate-looking young man—" and we have found out each other's good qualities in a marvelously short space of time, clasped hands in right good fellowship, and I now present him to you as my friend."

He caught Margaret's cold, listless fingers and placed them in Mr. Plowden's warm grasp.

She strove to return the hearty pressure of his hand, and to respond pleasantly to his few low words of regret for having first met her under such distressing circumstances, and his thanks for the favor of this introduction; but she experienced a nameless terror which did not leave her during the whole of the visit.

For Hubert, he seemed indeed to have cast aside his

wretched burden, and to have entered into the spirit of
the hour with all the abandon of a youth just released
from the trammels of college—reminiscences of college
days at which Margaret forced herself to laugh, and
interesting items pertaining to the fashionable world,
and told with a masculine gusto by the delicate-looking
Delmar, were intermingled with the deeper but more
charming conversation of the handsome Plowden.

Before they departed Delmar arranged for the introduction of Margaret to his mother and sister—by
whom, he said, she would be properly *chaperoned* into
society; and on the exchange of a few more friendly
speeches they took their leave.

Annie Corbin, descending from Madame Bernot's
room, met them in the great hall—standing face to face
for a second with Mr. Plowden; if he remembered her
as one of the witnesses whom he had examined, he did
not evince it by either sign or look, but she started
slightly, and hurried to acquaint her fellow-servants.

"What odds, as long as they're good friends?" said
John McNamee, "though its queer that Mr. Hubert
would receive one that was trying to cause his arrest."

But Hannah Moore looked puzzled, and seemed in
deep thought for the rest of the day, saying to herself
when assured that she was alone.

"It can't be that he's doing this to get on the scent
—God help them, if he is!—for he's sharp and cruel."

Hubert had gone to the stoop with his visitors, and
he stood on the marble step exchanging adieus, while
Margaret waited in the parlor doorway. He saw her,
there white and motionless when, having closed the
street door, he turned to ascend to his room; he changed
his course and went into the library instead, motioning
her to follow. She did so, and he did not speak till he
had closed and locked the door; then he turned to her,
his face wearing that same appalling expression of suffering.

"The mask is off now, Margaret. I wore it well

did I not? And now I can be myself—the *murderer* that I am."

He clenched his hands and set his teeth together, while great drops of perspiration stood on his forehead.

Margaret was helpless; she could only look at him in that dumb agony that found no vent even in tears. The pitiful expression of her face seemed to touch him at last, and he said, sorrowfully:

"For the future I must not permit you to witness my agonies; and life will be brighter for you henceforward, so that in time you can forget you have been the murderer's confidant."

"Never, never," she moaned; "and since I cannot relieve your suffering I shall at least try to share it."

He said, sadly; "I believe you, Margaret; and know this, that but for you I think I should have gone mad, the chains I wear are eating so into my vitals—but, knowing that I have dragged you down, I know also that I must undo, as far as I can, what I have done in your life. I must in some way secure your happiness before I go to meet my eternal doom; but seek not after this to know things about me which I would conceal even from your eyes—things which must be known only to my Maker. Be patient, Margaret, and God, if he has no pity on me, will have pity on you."

"But," she burst out almost incoherently, "why inflict so much torture on yourself? why bring home that man to-day when you knew from accounts in the papers how important a part he played on the trial?"

"Ah, Margaret! that was one of my policy strokes. He was in young Delmar's office when I called, and Delmar introduced him to me as his particular friend. Every circumstance of that inquest was revived by Delmar himself, who of course knew of Plowden's connection with it, and the part which my name bore in it; he revived the facts more minutely, I suppose, because it was the first time Delmar had met me since my return from college, and he had but recently made

Plowden's acquaintance; but the friendship between the two was thus warm because of some valuable service which the lawyer had rendered Delmar.

"I had already assumed my mask, and I had so steeled every nerve, that I even entered into close and critical discussions regarding the unknown criminal; I sifted the evidence which had been given at the inquest, and which Delmar with an astonishing memory recalled; I balanced with nice precision the verdict of the astute men who had not penetration enough to discover that they had the murderer just within their grasp, and I concluded by clasping hands with Plowden over Delmar's 'old port,' and vowing a friendship for him as warm as that evinced by my friend. I fancied I was acting grandly—it was, it would be for me admirable training to be often in the presence of this man who was so near to discovery of my secret crime—who would probably even yet weigh my words, and construe my actions. In order to compel his acceptance of my invitation to return home with me, I accompanied him to his hotel, while Delmar went home promising to wait there until we rejoined him. Immediately that Delmar left us I resumed our conversation about the strange murder. Something impelled me to it, to see to what limits I dared go of a subject which was so full of danger for me; but he sought to get away from the topic, and as often as I returned to it he began to talk of something else, I found him pleasant and genial, with a charm about his company which I could not resist.

"Oh, Hubert!" Margaret broke forth, "he will charm you to your ruin; that very fascination will make you betray yourself."

"There is no danger, for when my mask is on I have perfect self-control; and now, Margaret, I shall go to my room for I am tired and need rest."

He opened the door for her, and she went heavily forth to change her dress again and to descend to Madame Bernot.

CHAPTER V.

MARGARET'S introduction to the Delmars was effected, and Mrs. Delmar, a very fashionable widow, expressed her delight to have the opportunity of introducing the beautiful girl to society; while Louise Delmar, or "Louie," as she was familiarly called, a showy girl of twenty-three, showered kisses on Margaret and declared that she would forgive her brother every teasing word since he had given her such a lovely friend.

For sensitive, suffering Margaret, even if she had not been on the rock of constant mental agony, she would have detested the worldliness, the want of heart, which to her was so apparent in the character of mother and daughter; but for Hubert's sake,—Hubert, who through her would be forced also to enter society,—she returned kiss for kiss, responded kindly to Mrs. Delmar's worldly speeches, and compelled herself to maintain an appearance of friendship for the Delmar family.

The son, Eugene, was a good-natured, kindly-mannered young fellow, possessing more force of character than might be supposed by ordinary acquaintances, and he was the only one of his family whose life had anything higher in it than that which was in strict accordance with the maxims of the world.

Miss Delmar insisted on visiting Margaret frequently, and she exacted a punctual return of her visits. Sometimes, fashionable Mrs. Delmar accompanied her daughter, and both would have been delighted to have gratified, by a visit to the room of the invalid, their curiosity regarding Madame Bernot, of whose long and peculiar illness they had heard; but Margaret would as soon have thought of admitting a demon to her aunt, as of permitting so much worldliness within the precincts of that holy sick room.

Miss Delmar further insisted that Margaret should wear gayer attire; and arranged that her own maid—a French importation—should dress Miss Calvert's hair, appealing to Hubert whenever she saw him, for aid in her efforts to enhance Miss Calvert's charms.

The young man answered the appeal by giving to his cousin counsel which sounded to Miss Delmar only like graceful speeches, but to Margaret had a hidden and bitter meaning.

So those two lives of secret suffering went on, at every turn winding into darker and more dreary paths.

During their Sunday walk to church—almost the only time now in which the cousins could be alone—she sometimes ventured to approach the subject of his evident suffering but he always sternly bade her desist. She invariably obeyed, but it was only to walk on in keener, though silent agony by his side. When near the church they continued to separate, he to walk moodily through the least frequented streets, and she to enter the sacred building, miserable, and beset by a thousand vague alarms.

A strange clergyman appeared in the pulpit one Sunday—a man whose fiery eloquence appeared to touch every soul in the vast congregation. He preached on the suffering caused by concealed sin, till Margaret, shuddering, wondered if he knew anything about her. It seemed as if he was preaching to her alone; as if his great luminous eyes had singled out her face. She wanted to cry out aloud in her sympathy with the agony he depicted. She knew it all so well. But after that, he pictured the state of the soul when confession had relieved it of its burden, and Margaret's tears fell fast and plentiful on her prayerbook.

Those of the congregation near her were too much absorbed in their own excited feelings to notice her emotion, and long after the preacher ceased, and the last strain of the sacred music died away, she knelt there unconscious of everything but the tumult which that sermon had caused in her soul.

Hubert met her at the church steps, an expression of impatience on his lips because of her tardiness, but he checked it when he saw the traces of tears on her cheeks.

" Not that way, Hubert ; " she said, as he was about to take their usual route through a frequented thoroughfare, and she led him to one of the by-streets.

She wanted to tell him of the terrible struggle which the sermon had caused in her soul—she *must* tell him, in order to allay her dreadful pangs of conscience ; otherwise, she felt, she would go mad in this war between her sense of duty and what she now deemed to be her sinful love for the criminal.

But, before she could utter one of the words which came up from her overcharged heart, a gentleman turning the corner of the street into which they had just entered, passed them with a rapid, ringing step,—passed so close that he brushed against Margaret's dress.

The sudden unexpected contact drew her attention to him. He turned when a little in advance, raised his hat, bowed to her, and hurried on. Every word of the burning plea which she had intended to make to Hubert seemed to freeze within her heart, and she clutched his arm with both hands, while cheeks and lips blanched to death-like whiteness, " Who is he ? what is the matter with you ? " asked Hubert sternly.

She gasped at last:

" *Roquelare !* "

Forgetting that her cousin knew nothing of the circumstances in which she had been made acquainted with that mysterious name, she was conscious alone of the terror with which the unexpected presence of the strange gentleman inspired her. She remembered his ominous words, and now feared that a new and imminent danger threatened her cousin. Her terror was to receive a new impetus; for immediately that the strange word passed her lips, Hubert turned pale, and violently trembled. His manner showed abject fear. He looked about him in a helpless, frightened way, but the stranger was out of sight. He whispered:

"Come home, Margaret; I am not safe a moment now."

A thousand hurried, frightened questions were on her lips; but at the very first she tried to ask, he said in that same whisper:

"Hush till we get home—there may be ears in the atmosphere."

"He is going mad," Margaret thought, "and I shall go mad, too."

Would that walk never end? The blocks had certainly extended themselves, and was it not for the passers-by Margaret would have quickened her own speed to a run, and have urged Hubert to do the same. As it was, they walked so rapidly that the attention of other pedestrians was attracted to them.

There was a fever in Margaret's veins when at last she ran up the marble steps—a fever that fiercely showed itself in her flaming cheeks and burning eyes, and Hubert's hand was so unsteady that it required three attempts before he could insert his key into the lock. But at last they were safely in the library, and it was painful to witness the abject fear under which the young man still labored, the extreme caution with which he listened for any sound that might betray a surreptitious presence, the tremulous whisper to which his voice sank when addressing Margaret.

"Speak low, Margaret! for there may be ears all about us, and tell me quick what *you* know about ROQUELARE."

She told him hurriedly, in just such a whisper as he had used, adding how he had refused to listen when she had attempted to tell him before.

"I did not dream of this," he answered, "I did not dream that I was tracked. But the card—let me see it quickly, Margaret!"

And while she hastened to get it, he watched, standing in the doorway, and starting at every sound—starting, even when he knew it was only Margaret descending, and trembling violently as he locked the door after her entrance.

He looked at the card for a long time, even when he placed it on the table, resuming his inspection as if there was a fascination about it which he could not resist.

She watched him silently, but with eyes and cheeks as flaming as when she had entered the house. At last she broke forth with:

"Tell me, Hubert, what you know of it—what danger it forbodes to you?"

"Hush!"—lifting his face with a look of terror.

"Remember, there may be ears about us, and we must be very cautious now. You want to know what danger it forbodes to me. Oh, Margaret! there is this danger. "When once *Roquelare* is on the track of a victim, when once *Roquelare* has a single clue to a criminal, track and clue are pursued for years, to the uttermost parts of the earth, until the guilty one is brought to justice. It is the name of a secret society; its existence is known to few beside its own members. I learned of it at college, when a member of my class was tracked by its secret efforts to the very recitation room. *He* had committed a crime—not such as mine —years before, and thought that *one* alone knew his guilt until *Roquelare* began to track him. I have seen him start and shudder, and I have heard him mutter that word while perspiration, just such as covers me now, stood upon his face. He was arrested at last, taken out, handcuffed, and from him in his prison cell I learned what I know of *Roquelare*. It has secret agents everywhere, and it always warns before it begins the work of hunting down. The card that you have received is the warning for me, for the agent knew that you would give it to me.

"All through this dreadful time my chief feeling of security came from the fact that *Roquelare* was not yet pursuing me; but now I am doomed. I know not the hour, nor the minute in which I may become a convicted felon, for Heaven and earth conspire to rob me of my guilty secret."

Great globules of perspiration rolled down his face, but he sat looking rigidly before him as if he saw in the misty space the future shame which awaited him.

The struggle between duty and love had ceased for a time, and love was victorious—the miserable creature was her idol again, and every faculty of her soul was employed in devising means by which to inspire him with renewed hope and courage.

"You are a coward," she said, still speaking in a whisper, but with a firmness of accent in strange contrast to his tremulous tones.

"A Bernot to falter before imaginary evils! Should they track, even should they capture you, there can be no danger unless you through your own cowardice betray yourself. *He* is buried, and with him is buried your secret from the whole world save us two. No one else knows anything; there is no one to betray. For your mother's sake, for the sake of your name on which no stain has ever rested, be a man, Hubert—meet this thing with firmness, and all shall be safe."

Her passionate words seemed to have the desired effect, for, though he continued to tremble, he replied:

"You are right. What cowards crime makes of us! I who once feared nothing am an abject craven now. But I shall steel myself again, and live on until this torture has completed its work."

He shook himself as if he was freeing himself from the fears which yet clung to him, and standing erect before Margaret, he continued:

"You see, I am becoming myself again," with a bitter irony in his tones,—" and now, what is the name of the man who gave you the card?"

"I do not know; I suppose it was given in the papers, but I was too excited and bewildered to think of looking for it at the time. I only know that he was the gentleman who so strongly urged the examination of your mother."

"Ah! then his name is Bertoni. I remember distinctly every name which the papers gave in connection with that investigation, and particularly his; because he was so near to discovering an important clue. Well, thus I dismiss my fears and proclaim myself ready to fight out my existence to the last".

He tore the card to shreds, and flinging the latter on the floor, ground them beneath his heel.

"There, Margaret! fear not for me any more—the dinner bell, I believe. You will hardly have time to change your dress!"

She looked at him in silent astonishment, his tone and demeanor were so changed; his voice loud and firm, his manner fearless and even smiling. He put his finger on his lips when she would have spoken, and unlocking the door, held it open while she passed out.

CHAPTER VI.

ROQUELARE!—the word seemed to have burned itself into Margaret's brain. It started before her at every turn. It peered at her from dim corners. It assumed a startling distinctness even in the noonday glare. It danced fantastically before her when she would have put it farthest from her thoughts. It imprinted itself on the very faces of those to whom she fain would have spoken gayly. It gave her no peace but goaded her from agony to agony till she cried out in utter desolation of soul:

"Oh that I were dead!"

Hubert gave no outward sign of *his* mental suffering, even to Margaret. Again he sternly commanded that no reference should be made to his guilty secret during their Sunday morning walk to church. That walk was not once omitted, and though Hubert and Margaret both, cast keen suspicious glances at every one they passed, he who had given that strange card met them no more.

Charles Plowden became a frequent visitor at the Bernot mansion, and Miss Delmar circulated among her friends that Miss Calvert was the attraction. He did not always see Margaret when he called, owing to her devoted attention in the sick room; an attention which no persuasion from Madame Bernot could induce her to remit.

"Do not press me further, aunt," she said; "I have already gone more into society because you wished it; I go frequently to the Delmars and receive them when they call, and to gratify Hubert, I have promised to accompany them to a fashionable ball next week—do not ask me to do more."

"No! my dear girl, I shall not; nor would I have pressed the subject but that you do not seem well, and yet you refuse to consult a physician."

"I am quite well," she answered, mentally adding, "in body," and then she turned away lest the invalid's anxious gaze might discover her torturing secret.

She was not aware of the report which coupled her name with that of the talented young lawyer who was rapidly winning distinction, but she received Mr. Plowden and exerted herself to be agreeable to him, imagining that such a course of action would prevent him from reviving that, which had been so nearly a charge against her cousin. Alas! her mind held all sorts of fancied terrors now. And Mr. Plowden drank in the tones of her peculiarly sweet voice, and feasted his eyes on her lovely face—lovelier of late than it had ever been, for its very thinness and pallor added much to its spiritual expression, and the look of suffering which forced itself into the eyes at times gave to her whole countenance such an expression as a virgin in the moment of martyrdom might wear.

But the handsome, courtly man was careful to betray neither in his manner, nor by his words aught that could alarm in the least her maidenly reserve.

His attentions while seeking to be devoted, were never warmer than those which might be dictated by the very highest opinion of true womanhood, and the charm of his conversation that drew all within its circle, frequently caught her also, and sometimes even banished from her mind for a second, the ever-present scorching memory of *Roquelare*.

Did Hubert Bernot attend his mother as closely as Margaret did, she would have discovered in him more evidence of failing health—owing to the self-torture which he continued with little intermission—than she discerned in her pale-faced niece. His strength was failing, his breathing frequently labored, and he often placed his hand on his heart as if he suffered from intense pain there; although he rarely evinced it before beholders. Margaret's sharp eyes detected it more than once. She strove to speak to him, to make another appeal to him to have mercy on himself, but he waived her back, and she pressed her hands on her own heart, and cried when alone:

"Lost, lost for all eternity!"

One afternoon, three days before the great ball to which she and Hubert were to accompany the Delmars, her cousin rose from a late dinner without having tasted the tempting viands. To allay Margaret's anxiety he said he had lunched a short time before with Plowden, but she followed him to the dining room door with imploring eyes.

"Don't follow me; I am quite well," he said; but she continued to look until he had ascended the topmost step of the stair. He went slowly and with a stooping gait, pausing once to press his hand heavily on his side.

Margaret, with what calmness she could assume, turned back to attend to some little detail of her daily duties, and then she hurried to her room pausing on the way at his door, for any sound which might form a pretext for her entrance. But everything was still.

She had fancied she would gain repose in her own apartment, but the air seemed to stifle her, and hurriedly donning her out-door costume, she rushed abroad. The sunshiny thoroughfares were little better, and she turned into an unfrequented street, and lifted her veil that the crisp, frosty air might touch her face more brusquely.

A lady approached her—a lady wrapped in costly furs, and with ample velvet skirts sweeping the walk. Margaret turned to effect a rapid retreat, for she recognized Louise Delmar in the extravagantly dressed girl; but Miss Delmar's eyes were as sharp as her own, and in a moment Miss Delmar herself was down on her with a kiss, and, for the street, a too loudly spoken:

"Where in the world are you going my little pale bird?" By a desperate effort Miss Calvert forced back the vexation which was fain to find vent in tears, and she murmured some confused reply about taking a walk.

"Then I shall accompany you," said loud Miss Delmar, "because it isn't often I can have you so entirely to myself."

Margaret sought desperately for some pretext by which she might escape from her provoking companion, but she could find none unless, indeed, she wounded the young lady's feelings; and that, even when agony pressed heaviest on her sore heart, the gentle girl would never consent to do. So the two pursued the same course, and Miss Delmar dropped at once into the light gossip which seemed to form part of her nature.

Margaret wanted to put her fingers in her ears, to cry out, to do anything rather than be compelled to listen to conversation which treated only of silks and laces, and the newest modes for the hair. It was additional torture to be obliged to reply to the frivolous remarks; for Miss Delmar, not content with the music of her own sweet voice, insisted on an answer to each one of her observations, and then she glided into the topic of Margaret's dress for the approaching ball.

"I had a peep at it yesterday, at Madam Dijon's. You cunning thing; not to have told me that it was going to be white *mauve*."

"Indeed, I did not think about it," apologized Margaret, "and I simply chose the first material which suggested itself to my mind."

"That is always the way with you," returned Miss Delmar, "you are the queerest girl I ever met. Do you know, Maggie"—she sometimes employed the diminutive as a mark of particular affection—"that to use one of my old nurse's expressions, I think there is something uncanny about you. You talk to people, and exert yourself to be agreeable to them—anybody can see that—but, then, all the time you look almost as if you didn't belong to this world; and your cousin—while everybody acknowledges him to be delightful, has something so spiritualized and so unfathomable about him, that I never can tell, when he is talking to me, whether he is in earnest or only making fun of me. Then, there is your aunt; all sorts of odd reports are out about her illness. What is the matter with you all, Maggie?—what is the secret which makes you so unlike ordinary mortals?"

For one instant it seemed to Margaret that her heart ceased to beat, and that every drop of blood in her veins rushed in one mad whirl to it, leaving her as cold as though she had been suddenly frozen.

But even in that moment she had sufficient self-control to make no outward sign, and Louise Delmar rattled on, unconscious that the form beside whom she walked was suffering indescribable mental torture.

But after a little, when Margaret became calmer, she felt convinced that it was not any knowledge or suspicion of Hubert's guilt which had prompted Miss Delmar to speak of a secret—that it was simply the impulse of her frivolous thoughts.

"And society says other things about you, Maggie," the voluble young lady continued; "it is breaking its heart to know when your marriage with Mr. Plowden will take place, for it is said that your cousin quite favors the match."

Margaret paused abruptly and looked her companion full in the face—a look of such astonishment that Miss Delmar hastened to say:

"I hope I have not hurt you by repeating this rumor?"

Margaret shook her head.

"What right has society to say such things about me?"

Her voice had taken a slightly indignant tone, and her face had become suddenly flushed.

"Why, Maggie, what a sensitive little thing you are! Society talks because Mr. Plowden is such a constant companion of your cousin, and he has paid you such marked attention. Forgive me if I believed the rumor."

"There is no truth in it," said Margaret, and she turned to resume the walk.

But it was impossible to continue longer with her companion.

Such burning thoughts were crowding upon her, she felt that she must be alone to battle with them. When they reached the corner of a street which wound in an indirect way to Margaret's home, she said to her chatty companion:

"Pardon me if I leave you now; my walk has been sufficently long, and I am anxious to return to my aunt."

"Certainly, my dear; and now I suppose I shall not see you until Thursday. Madam Dijon said your dress would be at our house by seven, so see that you come over early; it will give me a chance to superintend your toilet. *Au revoir!*" Having bestowed a very fond embrace on her inwardly recoiling friend, Miss Delmar swept majestically away.

Margaret darted in an opposite direction, running rather than walking, as if she thought physical exertion might assuage her mental agony. It had been sharper than any pain she had yet endured, to hear that Hubert favored Mr. Plowden's suit, if indeed Mr. Plowden had such a thought. Was Hubert, for whom, and with whom, she had suffered—Hubert, for whom she had forsaken her God—was he willing, nay, anxious, to resign her to another; for if it were not so, how could society discuss this topic so glibly? O God! she was rightly punished. And the fever leaped more fiercely in her veins, and the flush burned more brightly on her cheeks as she continued her way—anywhere; she cared n whither it led her so that it did not bring her *home*. She could not return *there* yet.

The bright afternoon had waned, and the lamps were lit in the streets. But she did not heed the flight of time; she was not even aware of the sharp looks with which passers-by surveyed her.

The strains of an organ floated out from a church which she was in the act of passing. The cross on its spire and surmounting the iron gate which stood open told of the Catholic Faith. The music, slow, solemn, sweet, arrested her steps; for there seemed something in it which echoed the cry that came up from her passionate heart. She entered the building and hurried to an obscure corner where no curious eye might rest on her.

The priest was already on the altar, and the solemn, soothing evening service had begun.

The congregation seemed composed entirely of people in the lower walks of life, but an humble devotion was visible in the demeanor of all. Willingly would Margaret have flung her position in society, her wealth, her beauty, her education, to the winds, and have taken up the life of a menial, could such a renouncement have brought her the peace which was so visible in the faces of the kneeling congregation.

Just before the Benediction the officiating clergyman turned and said a few words of exhortation. Divested of every argument of terror, they *breathed* but the *love* of the Crucified for penitent souls, full of tenderness and pity, for which the speaker's appearance and voice seemed peculiarly fitted. The words opened the floodgates of Margaret's soul, and scalding tears rolled down her cheeks.

"My God! my God!" she murmured, "that I have forsaken so long."

But, beside the image which the clergyman drew of the compassionate Saviour, there would arise another image in Margaret's mind—that of Hubert Bernot.

It thrust itself in front of the Divine face she sought to behold. It extended its hands to her with the despairing cry she had twice heard; it clung to her; it wound itself about her, until, weary and faint from the struggle to resist it, she leaned back in the pew and gave herself up to it.

But even then the struggle did not cease; and when the Benediction had been given, and the last strain had floated solemnly away in the misty distance, Margaret sought to acquire peace by resolving that, on her return home, she would tell Hubert of her desperate struggle with what she deemed to be her duty.

Mr. Plowden was ascending the marble steps as Margaret reached the stoop of her home, and a second glance having assured her of his identity, she turned away to pace the streets until sufficient time should have elapsed for his departure.

She could not meet him in her present excited state.

But the fates were against her that night, for on her return, just as she entered the hall, Mr. Plowden and Hubert were descending the stair, having come from Hubert's room.

She would have hurried to the servants' hall to escape a meeting, but her cousin sternly called her. She shuddered as they approached her, and dropped her eyes.

"You are out late, alone," said Hubert in the same stern voice, while Mr. Plowden extended his hand, and murmured a graceful salutation.

She replied in a confused manner, and felt the blood rushing into her face under their searching look.

"We shall not detain you," resumed Hubert, sternly still, but with a slight touch of sarcasm in his voice.

"No doubt your late errand was an important one," with a peculiar emphasis on the last words, that Margaret sought vainly to understand.

Mr. Plowden again extended his hand with a few more lowly-spoken, graceful words, and turned to the door accompanied by Hubert.

Margaret did not keep on her way to the servants' quarters, but retreated to a part of the hall where the shadows lay deep enough to conceal her from view, and there she waited until the adieus were exchanged, and her cousin turned to ascend to his room.

"Hubert!" she called in a half passionate, half supplicating voice, and he paused as if waiting to hear further.

"I must ask you something to-night. Will you listen to me?"

She had reached his side, and was excitedly whispering the last words into his ear.

"Yes; for I also have a question to ask of you. Come to the library,"

When both were within the apartment, and he had locked the door—an absurd precaution, for no one ever entered without knocking—he said, sternly:

"Mr. Plowden saw you enter a church to-night. Have you gone to confession because at last you have satisfied your conscience by determining to inform upon me?"

She looked at him, startled and amazed; how had he discovered that struggle of which she had been often on the point of telling him, but still had never told? And he, seeing her alarm and amazement and understanding well their cause, said in tones which had quite lost their recent sternness:

"Have you never thought, Margaret, that suffering as sharp as mine is, would enable me to divine your suffering and your struggles—yours have been only too apparent in your face at times—and knowing from our long association how sensitive your conscience is, was it not natural for me to suppose that my secret *must* cause just such a struggle in your soul? It was this supposition that made me extort from you the oath I did; and, watching you when you little dreamed it, I discovered sufficient to tell me that you also absented yourself from confession. But, now, my poor child, I shall not hold you longer to this bond of suffering. I release you from your oath, and if your conscience cannot be otherwise satisfied, denounce me to the authorities. I am so weary of this life of mine, Margaret, that I think I shall thank you for it."

A wild burst of tears answered him.

Alas for her dutiful resolutions!—they were utterly broken before the sight of that pale, grave, suffering face, by the sound of those calm, yet touching tones; had he maintained his sternness, she might have kept her resolution, but his manner now had changed all. His very release from her oath, but bound her the more to keep it and she continued to weep with all the wild abandon of a woe that could know no comfort.

"Why weep?" he continued in those same tones which were like dagger thrusts to her heart, "is it because I have divined your decision a little sooner than you yourself would have told me?"

She found voice to answer him, but it was a voice broken with sobs.

"I have not gone to confession, and be my struggle what it may, it shall never make me denounce you."

He was touched by her grief.

"Forgive me, Margaret; I have judged you too hastily. Mr. Plowden said he saw you enter a church an hour before he came here and that you seemed excited. He would have spoken but you entered before he could reach you. I knew it was unusual for you to go to church save on Sundays and my mind at once reverted to all that I have told you. Then, also, remember, Margaret, the miserable man who speaks to you, and forgive the cruel things he may say, for he is goaded by demons that give him no peace."

She answered:

"And yet you shut me out from your suffering, I who would bear all for you if I could. You give me no help in *my* sorrow. You strive to take from me the only object for which I now live—that object is to allay your pain, to contribute to your happiness."

She covered her face with her hands, for maidenly shame was sending up an indignant protest in the shape of burning blushes for her unmaidenly speech.

Hubert did not answer, as if surprise, or sorrow, or both kept him silent.

And she, after a moment, flinging her hands from her face resumed:

"You trample on the very aid I proffer. You fling *me* to scorn when you favor, as report says you do, Mr. Plowden's suit for my hand."

Her cousin started and then he smiled bitterly:

"So society has already busied itself with our affairs," he said ironically, and then resuming his former tender tone he continued:

"Suppose society is correct in its conjecture, for this report is only the conjecture of fashionable gossip —I think I should be right in so doing. Charles Plowden is a good and gifted man. He loves you as man loves but once in a lifetime. In the shelter of his pure heart you could forget the secret you hold, and fling off forever the burden which a murderer has imposed on you."

A cry, half-smothered, but still so heart-broken, came from her white lips that Hubert shuddered.

It was as if the last chord in her overstrained heart had snapped; and she clasped her hands together and looked at him in a manner which seemed to say:

"Speak on! the last blow has been given. You are powerless to hurt me further."

What emotions were working in his own soul—how he longed to snatch this girl, who was only strong in her passionate love for him, to his breast, and to tell her that every beat of his guilty heart was a beat of love for her! But the bloody image of his murdered victim stalked between, and ROQUELARE in glaring letters danced before his eyes. He had forsworn love, and even the delights of human friendship, so far as he might do; he had promised in the sharp moments of his remorse to deny himself every consolation, that by so doing with the physical torture which he inflicted on himself, he might help to atone for his sin.

What, then, had *he* to do with love? Repressing the passionate impulse which urged him to tell her that even as she loved so was she loved in return, he said calmly, but with an indescribable sadness:

"Margaret, you do not yet comprehend the extent of my suffering. Would you, if the choice were yours, unite your life to one whose course must be always in darkness and agony? Would you have your eyes become accustomed to see the bloody image that is always before mine—your ears to hear the cries and the wrangling of demons which I hear, and which often make me cry out in my sleep? Would you have your heart harrowed by the fear of detection which so constantly harrows mine? would you feel that he to whom you were mated was living continually in some unseen presence which, sooner or later, would lay its iron hand upon him and bring him to justice? Would you be the wife of a murderer, the widow of a felon who was hanged, when another and a happy home is open to you— when a good and pure man is waiting to shelter you in his love? Contrast the pictures well, Margaret, and say which you choose."

He folded his arms and receded a pace as if to contemplate her while she decided.

She did not wait an instant, but rushing forward, she threw herself at his feet, and said, passionately:

"A murderer's agony, a felon's doom, I will gladly share all with you, Hubert."

He stooped and raised her, quivering to press her once, just once, to his aching breast,——the bloody image forbade.

"It may not be, Margaret. I have sworn that no wife shall ever clasp my red right hand; no child shall ever call me father; no love such as you proffer ever bless my existence."

"I do not ask to become your wife," broke forth the trembling girl; "I ask only that you permit me to comfort you as best I may; that you unburden yourself to me when your agony presses so sharp; that you let me enter into your sufferings as closely as I can; that you do not ask me ever to marry another."

"Oh, wonderful depth of woman's love!" Hubert said, and then he averted his head for a longer look into those passionate eyes, into that uplifted pleading face would have drawn from him an avowal as earnest and thrilling as Margaret's own had been.

"Be it so," he said at last, without looking at her; "when my agony is sharpest I shall tell you. I can promise no more now. Good night."

He extended his hand, still without looking at her, and she went mournfully forth.

CHAPTER VII.

THE day broke cold, but clear and bracing, on the night of which was to take place the grand ball that had been the topic of fashionable gossip for weeks.

Margaret leaned from an upper window, that the frosty air might cool the fever in her veins—a fever which had not abated since her last interview with her cousin. Contact with the sharp atmosphere seemed only to increase her wild emotion. Loving hopelessly, resigning her allegiance to the One who alone could strengthen and comfort her for an idol that must sometime be shattered,—living without the expectation of peace in this world, or relief in a future one,—Margaret Calvert continually suffered worse agonies than those of death. She hovered about her aunt almost all day, assuming the servants' duties, hoping thus to obtain at least a temporary repose for her agitated mind.

During lunch, of which she hardly tasted, she said to Hubert:

"You will not fail to come—to be at Mrs. Delmar's before we start?"

"No," he answered, wearily; "but Plowden and I shall go to the club first."

"A club! oh, Hubert! have you joined a club?" in a tone half remonstrance, half entreaty.

He made a warning motion, for the waiter was busy about the table; and dismissing the latter on some pretext, he asked:

"Why this fear? I thought you wished me to court society?"

"It is *Roquelare* which makes me frightened," she answered. "With every new thing I learn about you I imagine it has something to do."

He leaned across the table and whispered:

"Perhaps it has, Margaret. Struggle as I may, I cannot escape my fate. I feel assured of that now, and that every day brings it imminently near.—Would that it were here;—that the time had come for me to fling the wretched thing abroad. It burns so into my vitals. But I have not the courage yet—not yet."

He shuddered and leaned back in his chair, while Margeret replied in a passionate whisper:

"There is no danger, there can be no danger if only you will be firm, and if you will not listen to my weak woman's fears, Oh, Hubert; you shall not, you must not die."

She arose to cross to his side, but the waiter was at the door.

She resumed her seat and the repast was finished in silence.

Miss Calvert, attended by Annie Corbin, went in the carriage to the Delmar Mansion.

On her arrival she found Miss Delmar delightfully excited over her own and Margaret's dress, both of which had just arrived.

She immediately began at least so it seemed to the heart-sick girl—the torture of preparing for the fashionable assembly. Could she have dressed at home, a few minutes would have sufficed for the donning of her costly garb; but owing to Madame Bernot's illness Mrs. Delmar deemed it better that Miss Calvert's toilet should be made in their house, and she had pressed the matter so much that the reluctant girl had at last consented.

Fashionable Mrs. Delmar herself superintended Margaret's toilet. She was indefatigable in assisting to drape the misty lace which was to shroud the girl's fair neck and arms, and in arranging the superb pearls that

Margaret brought in Madame Bernot's old-fashioned jewel-case.

And, certainly, no lovelier sight ever greeted the worldly matron's view than Miss Calvert, when at last, her charming costume completed, she stood up to be surveyed. She was a trifle too pale perhaps; but that only enhanced her spiritual expression, and when Miss Delmar whose toilet was also completed, came rushing into the room looking like some gorgeous flower whose flaming hues surprise more than they please us, she exclaimed with involuntary admiration:

"How lovely!"

Miss Delmar did not envy Margaret Calvert, for she deemed her beauty less attractive than her own showy style, and as rich admirers flocked more numerously to her shrine than to that of her pale lovely friend, she accepted it as sufficient proof that her beauty must be superior. She never imagined that the deficiency in the *number* of admirers was Margaret's own fault; that many who poured insipid flattery into Miss Delmar's willing ears would have gladly transferred their attentions to Miss Calvert, would she have received them. But there was something about the gentle, retired girl which repelled most effectually men who were only such in form and face. So, Miss Delmar understanding nothing of this, could afford, as it were, to patronize Margaret—even to pity her that she could win so few suitors. She deemed the Bernots too strict Catholics for a marriage ever to take place between Margaret and Hubert.

After surveying Miss Calvert for a moment she crossed to her, kissed her and held her at arm's length, as if the lovely face had suddenly been invested with some new charm.

But Margaret turned paler still, for to her distorted imagination, the flaming jewel in Miss Delmar's hair had assumed the appearance of a great quivering bloodstain, and *Roquelare* seemed dancing about it in fiery letters.

"You are not well," said the young lady in an alarmed tone, for it was unmistakable that Miss Calvert was suffering.

"Yes, only a little dizzy," the latter gasped, and she shuddered as she turned her eyes away.

Annie Corbin, who had assisted in the preparation of the toilet, was a witness of Miss Calvert's sudden faintness, and she eagerly noted it that on her return home she might relate it to her fellow-servants.

Mrs. Delmar insisted on the application of *sal-volatile*, and she made hurried search for her own bottle, but Margaret protested and declared she had quite recovered.

There was a sudden bustle in the entrance hall. In a few minutes a servant announced that the gentlemen waited. There was a hurried pinning of last bows, an excited taking of last surveys in the full length mirrors, and then the ladies descended to the parlor.

Margaret had quite recovered, and she was able to hear calmly the low-toned and graceful compliments with which she was met by Mr. Plowden who immediately constituted himself her escort.

Hubert had glanced at her as she entered, but after that one brief look he had turned his eyes away as if he had been stung to the quick. Alas! it was so hard for his poor, guilty heart to relinquish her. Courtesy demanded that he should escort Miss Delmar, and his bitter feelings found vent in the undercurrent of irony that pervaded his talk with her.

She half suspected his sarcasm, but as she was too much in awe of him, and as she lacked the ability to meet him on his own ground, she solaced herself by constantly remembering how eminently becoming was her costume, and how much envy she should excite among the ladies of "her set."

The Bernot carriage, which was more commodious

than the Delmar equipage, carried the young ladies and their escorts; while the young scion of the house, Eugene Delmar, took the family carriage to call for a lady friend whom he had promised to attend to the fashionable assembly.

All that wealth with a lavish hand could bestow was visible in the spendid rooms of Madame Dupret wherein already an aristocratic throng had gathered. Apartment opened into apartment with only a slight curve of fresco work to mark the division, and chandeliers with pendants whose brilliant scintillations almost dazzled the eye, shed a bright and bewildering light over all, while immense mirrors at each end magnified the brilliant scene. Though not the first party, for the Delmars had given two parties which Margaret had attended, it was the largest assembly of the kind at which she had ever been present, its brilliancy for the first hour or two almost banished from her mind the thought of *Roquelare*.

Delmar with his lady friend had joined them, and the three couples apparently formed one of the happiest little groups.

There were numberless introductions to Miss Calvert, and the gentlemen among themselves passed enthusiastic comments on her beauty, while the ladies with true feminine charity endeavored to discover some flaw in her face or dress. She felt relieved when courtesy took Mr. Plowden to another lady, for, knowing now the object of his attentions, and feeling how fruitless all his efforts would be, her womanly heart could not but feel sorrow for what must sooner or later be a bitter disappointment to him. Yet how to avert, or, as in sheer pity she felt tempted to do, to hasten the event, she knew not. Conscious of having treated him with no more warmth than she had done each one of Hubert's friend, she had nothing for which to reproach herself, but maidenly delicacy restrained her from showing any knowledge of his regard for her, while fear (lest in some way Hubert's safety might be affected) prevented her from being more reserved in her manner to him.

Miss Delmar (perfectly at home only in scenes of excitement) was brilliant with a superficial gloss that dazzled shallow minds. In her exuberance of spirits she had somewhat ceased to feel her usual awe of Hubert Bernot's grave demeanor and conversation, and she boldly essayed with him sallies, which grosser and less able minds than his might have accepted as wit. He deemed them worthy only of sarcastic replies, and as she grew bolder, so did his sarcasm become more pointed and telling, till even her coarse nature winced beneath his repeated strokes, and with a deep blush of mortification, she threw herself on the divan beside Margaret, and said pettishly:

"Really, Mr. Bernot, you are the most uncavalier like gentleman I have ever met. I am glad to be relieved from your attentions for a while."

Hubert bowed low and smiled sarcastically for a second; then he turned away with his hand to his heart.

He could have said bitter cutting things to every one of the fashionable company, for all night he had been contrasting their apparent pleasure with his hidden agony. He had been mentally picturing the horror with which the gay throng would shrink from him if his sin should be proclaimed, and more than once he had felt a fierce, wild impulse to shout it out.

These were the times that he had been most sarcastic to Miss Delmar, and these were the times that he had pressed his hand hardest on his heart, and turned excitedly to mingle with the crowd that he might force his guilty secret back.

Margaret's eyes followed him.

A wierd, dreamy waltz struck up from a score of musical instruments and numberless lithe forms began to whirl in a mazy way. He paused near a marble pillar as if to view the dancers, and his face was turned toward Margaret, who was answering Miss Delmar's remarks, but in a listless, abstracted manner which would have provoked that young lady had she not just then been claimed for the dance.

The friend whom young Delmar had brought was also claimed, and as Miss Calvert did not waltz, Plowden at her earnest solicitation had gone in search of another partner; so Margaret was alone and free to watch her cousin without comment. Perhaps it was owing to the fact of being surrounded by so many robust, stalwart young fellows, that he look more than usually pale and emaciated. His skin seemed almost transparent, and even at that distance Margaret fancied she could trace the veins in his forehead.

The waltz grew more dreamy, more weird: the light feet glided, and the lithe forms turned in a more bewildering way; still Hubert looked, and still Margaret continued to see only his white face in all the gay concourse. Sometimes a form floated between them for an instant, and sometimes a portion of flying drapery intervened, but through form and drapery his large dark eyes seemed still to shine, and his white face to look with its bitterly sarcastic expression.

Suddenly she became conscious that he was being watched as intently by another person—a man who slightly leaned against another marble pillar just in the rear of Hubert. She rose in her eagerness to scan the features of that face, and she beheld him who had given the warning of *Roquelare*.

The room swam about her; the whirling faces magnified themselves into hundreds of grim countenances each bearing a likeness to this mysterious agent of a mysterious society; the light grew dim and the music became a dead march. Faint and dizzy she strove to make her way through the dancers to her cousin's side, but the whirling couples surrounded and entangled her.

Plowden who had paused to give his dizzy partner

breath, saw her embarrassing position, and hurriedly securing a seat for the young lady by his side, he came to Margaret's rescue.

"Take me to Hubert," she said faintly, but when they reached him the man who had been watching in his rear had gone.

"Come home, Hubert—I am ill," she said, excitedly, and relinquishing Plowden's arm, she took that of her cousin and leaned heavily against him.

Hubert did not reply. The cord of sympathy which was so strong between those two natures, made him at once divine the cause of her sudden illness. He understood that something had happened to inspire her with new terror for his safety, and his own mind was so constantly possessed by fear that he could not spurn it as a woman's silly fancy. He longed to ask her for an explanation, but he was deterred by Plowden's presence.

"Come home," she cried more excitedly than before.

"Go into the conservatory awhile, Miss Calvert, and you will feel better," said Plowden.

"There!" he continued, "the waltz has stopped; I shall excuse you to Miss Delmar."

And with a puzzled expression in his face he bowed and disappeared amid the couples now looking for seats after the dance.

"Yes, come into the conservatory," whispered Hubert, and the two hurried to an apartment divided from one of the parlors by huge squares of translucent glass and through which shone faintly the color of the foliage within. Other couples seeking change from the heated dancing rooms were also there; but they were lovers, too intent on the recital of their own "sweet tales" to heed the whispered conversation and excited manner of the cousins.

All night long had Hubert imagined if his fate overtook him he would not shrink from it; if his wretched secret should become known through some mysterious means, he would rejoice because it would free him of a burden which of himself he had not the strength to cast away; yet now, at the seeming approach of the doom he courted he was more a coward than ever, and the piteous cry with which he responded to Margaret's hurried narrative, betrayed his craven heart. "Come home," she urged, "you will be safer there."

"Safe nowhere, since *Roquelare* pursues me," he whispered, while his eyes shifted their glances in a wild, unguarded way.

"Look, Margaret, and tell me if I am watched here." But the unsuspicious couples who promenaded in their vicinity did not even glance in their direction, and no eye peered at Margaret from any other quarter.

Hubert grew calmer and bolder.

"To leave now," he said, "would only bring a closer watch on me. No; I shall stay and brave it out. There has been nothing in my conduct to excite suspicion, has there?"

"No; but——"

She stopped suddenly for Miss Delmar escorted by Plowden was approaching.

"Nerve yourself and remain," Hubert had barely time to whisper, before Miss Delmar was down upon them with a volley of anxious expressions about Margaret's sudden indisposition, and reiterated assurances that she knew Miss Calvert was not well since the symptoms of illness which she had manifested when preparing for the ball.

But Margaret declared herself quite recovered, and after a little they all returned to the dancing room.

That his demeanor might in all things conform to that of the gallants about him, Hubert solicited the hand of some fair lady for every dance which succeeded until the announcement of supper. He laughed and chatted just as he saw those about him doing, but all the time his eyes ceaselessly wandered in search of one face.

Margaret fain would have withdraw from every
dancing engagement, and on the plea of having felt
slightly unwell, she might have done so with perfect
propriety, but Hubert had whispered:

"Dance, Margaret; you too may be watched."

So Margaret also formed one of every set, and she
forced herself to be smiling, and in a measure talkative,
while her eyes roamed ceaselessly up and down, and
across the room in search of *one* face.

Intermission came at last and the long procession of
gay ladies with their equally gay cavaliers filed into the
elegantly decorated supper-room. Hubert who was
Miss Delmar's escort was followed by Plowden and Margaret,
after whom came Delmar and his friend. A
smiling waiter met them on their entrance and conducted
them to tables which had been reserved for
them. Miss Delmar and Hubert were seated directly
opposite Margaret and Plowden, while Delmar and his
companion formed portion of a party at another table.

They were among the first in their places and a
laughing crowd surged and swayed about them in the
effort to obtain desirable seats. Margaret half reclining
in her chair was watching eagerly every face that
passed her. She fain would have maintained a constant
survey of the stream of people which flowed on
both sides of her but the rules of good-breeding forbade.

Hubert was talking with apparent gayety to his
companion, but his dark eyes never once withdrew
themselves from the panorama of countenances shifting
before him.

Mirth ran high; the clangor of gay voices and loud
laughter filled the room, and the busy waiters seemed to
be in all directions at once. Margaret drew a long
breath of relief, and for the first time turned her eyes
on the tempting delicacy on her plate.

Suddenly she was thrilled by that mysterious feeling
of being looked at, which most of us sometimes ex-

perience, and she raised her eyes to behold the same mysterious agent of ROQUELARE.

He stood directly behind Hubert, not however looking him but looking intently at her. His right hand was fumbling at his left wrist as if he was arranging the fastening of his cuff; but suddenly from his right hand there depended for an instant, full in Margaret's sight, a pair of steel handcuffs. The whole action was done so quickly, and in such an adroit manner that it attracted no attention save her own. It was an instant of horror to her who so well understood the mysterious transaction—an instant of voiceless horror, during which it seemed as if her heart was rent by a thousand pangs —as if she labored in an agony all the more dreadful because of its very dumbness.

But her white lips opened at last and emitted a scream which brought every one to his or her feet, startled, and well-nigh as pale as was poor Margaret herself.

Immediately on its utterance she lost all consciousness, and but for Plowden's quick support she would have fallen from her chair.

Only two in that assemblage of white faces knew the cause of that startling shriek—the mysterious agent who was now nowhere to be seen, and Hubert, who intuitively felt that it must be owing to the reappearance of the strange secret detective. He looked in a scared way about him even before he hastened to Margaret's assistance, but there was no vestige of ROQUELARE.

The first terrified astonishment of the company over, a score hastened to the assistance of the unconscious girl.

Madame Dupret herself bent her diamond-studded head over the white face and insisted that she should be borne immediately to her own private chamber.

"No; home at once," said Hubert, who feared that when consciousness returned some unguarded word might betray him.

"You are mad, Mr. Bernot," replied stately Madame Dupret, " and unfeeling as well. Your cousin may die on the way."

"Nay, Madame," he replied courteously, but with an air of firmness which could not be gainsayed; "she will recover on the way, and her illness will be better treated at home."

An order was despatched for a carriage, and some one having brought a large soft shawl in which to wrap the unconscious girl, Plowden prepared to carry her.

"Let me have her," said Hubert, almost savagely; and when Plowden, looking at Hubert strangely, resigned to him his light burden, Bernot darted through the surrounding forms as if the life of her he carried depended on his speed.

Ah! his haste was caused by the imaginary pursuit of a score of secret agents of ROQUELARE. And the burden he bore—it was the first time it lay so close to his panting heart; it would probably be the last time, for his doom was coming between them with hurried, unfaltering strides. If he could but rush with it to some spot of the earth where his guilty secret would be safe! But there was no place; for, to his distorted imagination the very air gave birth to voices that had but one cry, and that cry was, "murderer."

His passionate pressure contributed to restore consciousness to Margaret, and she opened her eyes and struggled faintly to free herself.

"Where am I? was it a dream?" she murmured.

Hubert stooped to her and whispered:

"Be silent for my sake."

And though her eyes showed the terror and anxiety under which she labored, she asked no more questions, but let him bear her way without resistance.

Miss Delmar was vehement in her desire to accompany Miss Calvert home.

"She is too ill to be trusted entirely to you," she said to Hubert, but he, firmly, yet without discourtesy, refused to gratify the young lady, and Miss Calvert herself asserted that there was no need of further attention than her cousin could bestow.

She was sufficiently recovered to walk through the entrance hall between Hubert and Plowden to the carriage, and when she was comfortably seated, with her cousin beside her, the young lawyer extended his hand and said with a sadness in his voice utterly foreign to it:

"Good night, or rather, good morning, Miss Calvert" and pressing her cold fingers for an instant he relinguished them to grasp Hubert's hand.

Holding it tightly, he said with the same sadness in his voice:

"Ah, Hubert! we are both drinking of a bitter cup."

And closing the carriage door he turned hurriedly away.

"What did he mean?" gasped Margaret; "surely he does not know?"

"No, no," interrupted Hubert, "unless he also is an agent of 'Roquelare.' I suspect everybody now, for every man's hand is against me; but why did you scream?"

She told him, with her hands tightly holding his, and her shivering form nestling close to his side.

"Oh, God!" he groaned, and then he shrank away from her, and drew his hands out of her clasp, and repulsed her when she would again have drawn near him.

"Is not your suffering mine?" she asked, passionately; "have you not promised to share your agony, when it was sharpest, with me. and yet you repulse me?"

"I dare not," he said, shudderingly; "I must bear my suffering alone now. I have dragged you down too far already, and may have the destruction of two souls to account for instead of my own."

"You think by the little command I evinced of my

feelings to-night that I have betrayed you?" she wailed.

"Nay, Margaret, it is God's justice that is betraying me," and, requesting silence, he leaned back in the carriage, and spoke no more until they had arrived at home.

John McNamee had been ordered to return with the carriage for Hubert and Margaret three hours after midnight, and, as it yet wanted a couple of hours of that time, when it became necessary to take Miss Calvert home, Madame Dupret's own equipage had been placed at their disposal.

The servants of the Bernot household were wont to indulge in merrymakings peculiar to themselves, being favored with an indulgent master in Hubert, and a kindly young mistress in Margaret. To-night, in order that the coachman might not hold his vigil alone, while he waited to return for the cousins, his fellow-servants had arranged a sort of impromptu party. There was a sufficient number of themselves to make it exceedingly pleasant; and, with doors, and hall windows, and entrances to flights of stairs that led above securely closed, not the faintest sound of their mirth could reach the sick room where the patient invalid alternately slumbered and prayed.

Cook had prepared delightfully steaming beverages, and had circulated goodly rounds of home-made cake, shedding over the pleasant cheer the light of her own smiling, good-natured countenance.

Neither the little maid nor McNamee were at home for the first part of the mirth-making, owing to their having accompanied Miss Calvert, but their share of the cheer was reserved and places were maintained for them, side by side, for it was understood that some day not very far distant, Annie Corbin would become Mrs. McNamee.

Margaret, tnougntful for others, even in the midst of her own hidden agony, had desired the coachman after he had set them down at the ball to return to Mrs. Delmar's for Annie, whom he was to convey home in the carriage, and the moment that the little maid was in the midst of her fellow-servants she broke forth into an account of Miss Calvert's sudden faintness which had occurred immediately that she was dressed.

Everybody listened eagerly, but none more eagerly, or with such an expression of concern, as Hannah Moore. She shook her head with some thought peculiar to herself, and cast her eyes down.

"Do you know what it is," said the head-waiter, a pompous man, with side whiskers, and a large square head, "I am of the opinion that neither Miss Calvert nor Mr. Hubert are long for this world; why, they're a wasting before our very eyes."

"It's a fact," replied the under-waiter, a slender, light-whiskered young man, with a very effeminate voice; "they eats just nothing at table, and they never hardly speak to each other, and they look so sad."

"I'll tell you what I'm thinking it is," said McNamee, in his bluff, hearty way, "that Miss Calvert never got properly over the fright it gave her to be on the trial for that man that was murdered."

"Why, surely, John!" chimed in the laundress, "you don't think Miss Calvert was any way concerned in that murder?"

"I'm not saying what I think," replied John, "for it isn't our place, as servants, to think anything about our masters and mistresses, only I revolved it in my mind when Miss Calvert said on that inquest that she had known the murdered man."

There was silence for a few minutes, and then the laundress again spoke.

"There must be some dreadful mystery in it, any way, when Miss Calvert wouldn't tell what she knew about the poor murdered gentleman."

"That's a fact," responded the under-waiter, staring hard into the fuming contents of the glass he held, while with the other hand he affectionately fondled his whiskers.

"I wonder if the man that came here asking all them queer questions about Madame Bernot had anything to do with it?" said the chambermaid, a rosy-cheeked, pleasant-faced girl, who had been assisting cook in preparing a new supply of refreshments.

"Hut, tut," said Hannah Moore, bringing down the knife with which she had been slicing a loaf of homemade cake on the table with a slap, and becoming very red, " sure he was only a poor beggar asking a crust for God's sake. What would he have to do with the like of that?"

"When was this—when did this happen?" asked John McNamee, putting down his glass that he might give the greater attention to the expected reply; and his fellow-help put their glasses down, and disposed themselves also to listen with marked attention.

The rosy-cheeked chambermaid was about to answer—to relate the circumstances, making much of every detail that might heighten its interest, but the cook interrupted with an abrupt and somewhat angrily spoken:

"It's just nothing at all, but one evening long ago, at the time of the inquest over that poor murdered creature, an old beggarman came here to the basement door. Rosie there"—pointing to the somewhat chagrined chambermaid—" and myself were the only ones in the kitchen; Rosie opened the door to him and let him in to have a bite and a sup in God's name. He was tattered and dirty-looking enough, but seemed very thankful for the cup of tea and the bit of cold victuals we gave him, and, by-and-by, while he rested, he asked a few questions about the family. He said he had read of the murder, and how the young lady of the house was mixed up with it someway; and Rosie there answered all the questions he asked; she told him about Madame Bernot and her sickness, and about Miss Calvert and Mr.

Hubert, and sure there was no harm in that, for there was nothing to tell but what the world might know. Now that's all there's in it. The beggar went away, and we never laid eyes on him since, and even Rosie thought no more about it, whatever put it into her head to-night," and the cook resumed her work of slicing the cake with a very self-satisfied air.

Everybody had listened with attention, and now everybody turned to John McNamee, as the tacitly-acknowledged head in the company, to know his opinion of what cook had related.

"I have only one thing to say," he said, taking up his glass slowly and looking round at his companions, "and that is that we trouble ourselves no further about what doesn't concern us. Mr. Hubert Bernot and Miss Margaret Calvert have been a kind master and mistress to us; we'll think only of that and mind nothing else, and, now, here's to their long life and prosperity."

He held his glass aloft, his example being immediately followed by his fellow-servants, and, in a few moments, each one with a right good will, had drained his or her tumbler to the toast proposed.

The cook's good humor shone forth again, and she eagerly seconded the suggestion for a song which the head-waiter pompously made, and, in the midst of a love ditty by the chambermaid, who had quite recovered from her little chagrin of the earlier part of the evening, a carriage stopped before the door. The singer ceased suddenly and the help looked at each other in a bewildered way.

"Something has happened," said McNamee, rising, and that instant the door-bell was violent rung.

"Let me go," interposed Hannah Moore, thrusting herself before the coachman, who was already on his way, and ere he could prevent she was hurrying up the stair which led to the front entrance. They crowded into the passage way, and one or two of the more curious ventured upon the stair, and with strained ears, listened for the slightest sound that might betray what was taking place above. They could distinguish Hubert's voice, and even Margaret's low tones came to them, but that was all; they could make no sense of what was said.

In a few moments the cook returned to them, wearing a grave, sad face.

"Miss Calvert was taken ill," she said, "and they have come home in that French Madame's carriage."

"Then I shall be needed," replied Annie Corbin, hastening to ascend to her mistress.

"No; Miss Calvert said we were not to disturb ourselves, and on no account was she to be disturbed."

So they turned again into the cozy sitting room, waiting while John attended to the horses, and separated only when they had, over another of cook's bumpers, wondered what could be the cause of Miss Calvert's evidently failing health.

CHAPTER VIII.

When Hannah Moore had returned to her fellow-servants, Margaret, clinging to Hubert's arm, whispered:

"I am strong again, Hubert; once more I can bear anything for you."

He did not answer, but suffering her to cling in that wild way to him, ascended heavily to his room. As he reached and unlocked it he turned suddenly and withdrew himself almost fiercely from her hold.

"Despise me, Margaret, hate me—do anything save *love* me as you do," he whispered; "for this love of yours is an added torture. Good God! that I, foul, loathsome thing as I am, should be loved by innocence, and should dare to accept that love. But, no! I shall have none of it; I shall go down to my doom without dragging you further."

And, precipitating himself inside, he closed and locked the door against her piteous cry of:

"Your promise, Hubert, your promise!"

But he was deaf even to her frantic knock and after a moment, during which he seemed to have crossed to the bed and thrown himself on it, not a sound was heard.

When she had listened for some time, she heard the domestics repairing to their rooms.

They were talking in suppressed tones as they ascended the stair, and she hastened to her own apartment lest they should discover her standing at Hubert's door.

But when they had passed, and their respective doors were closed, she came forth again to listen at

Hubert's room. The wildest fears possessed her, and horrible images presented themselves before her. At one moment she was picturing the mysterious agent of "*Roquelare*" obtaining an entrance to the house, and dragging off Hubert in manacles the clank of which she seemed to hear distinctly; at another she saw her cousin a bloody corpse, the victim of his own rash hand. And so she waited, listening in agony, for the slightest sound that might betray what he was doing.

Hannah Moore, who had remained below to attend to some little preliminary of the next day's duties, was now ascending, and Margaret at the first sound of the slightly creaking step, again ran to her room and waited till it had passed.

But Hannah Moore, her mind already whetted by a secret knowledge of something connected with Miss Calvert's suffering, had heard the rustle of the garments and the light tread of the flying feet as they dashed to the room above Hubert's and, instead of retiring, the sympathetic woman left her door ajar and listened for further sounds from Margaret's room.

In a few moments the white, rustling form was abroad again and down at her cousin's door, and the cook, leaning softly over the baluster, watched with bated breath for a realization of her own shrewd conjectures.

Poor, distracted Margaret! she could only stand wedged against the door as if she had been some marble statue set in its arched way, but feeling within her all the fire of a madly-burning fever. Not a sound came from the apartment, and, at last, when the very stillness suggested a score of frightfully alarming things, she began to pace the hall that the sound of her own steps might bring a relief from the dreadful, death-like silence.

Hannah Moore, leaned far over the baluster to watch the white-robed, pacing figure, and when she saw it pause once and press its hands wildly to its head, the kind-hearted woman covered her own face and murmured, inaudibly:

"God help you in your agony this night; it's not sick you are but sore with the secret that's laying heavy on you. God comfort you!"

And then, as if unable to bear longer the sight of the young creature's evident suffering, she turned back to her room.

Alas, for Margaret Calvert; there was no help for her on all earth, and Heaven she herself had shut against her. Turn where she would, only black despair loomed before her. If there was but one to whom she might have told that wretched tale; if there was but one on whose faithful breast she might have sobbed out the grief that was killing her. Under the influence of a wild feeling that impelled her to seek companionship somewhere, without pausing to think even of the propriety of changing her dress, she descended to her aunt's room.

The attendant motioned to signify that Madame Bernot slept, and Margaret, going gently forward, dropped noiselessly on an ottoman just in front of the invalid's chair, so the first object upon which the sick woman's eyes rested when she woke from her light slumber was that white-draped, slender form, with its wealth of curls, amid which yet gleamed the pearls that had been placed there a few hours before.

"Margaret," she said fondly.

The girl caught the old lady's hands, and rested her head on the invalid's lap.

"I am so tired, aunt," she said.

"Then why have you come to me instead of retiring, my dear child?" responded Madame Bernot, who did not know that the return from the ball was earlier than had been intended.

"Because I am so tired of it all," said Margaret, nestling closer to the invalid's lap, "and because you must release me from my promise to go into society any nore. My place is here with you, with suffering and sorrow."

"Margaret!" said Madame Bernot, in tones of sorrowful surprise, and Margaret lifted her head and met the glance of the pitying eyes above her, "you talk strangely for one of your years, and my heart misgives me that there is something the matter with you."

A shudder convulsed the girl's form for a second.

"Long ago, when that deep, black woe came to me, when God's hand was laid heavy on me in affliction, I fancied, by my total severance from the world and its doings, to appease God's future wrath and to satisfy Him for the crime that had been committed; but I fear in doing so I have forgotten other duties—my duty to you. I promised to be a mother to you, but I have not fulfilled my pledge."

"You have more than done so," interposed Margaret, pressing burning kisses on the hands she held.

"Nay, my dear girl, for I have neglected to teach you to give me your confidence."

"Alas! I have no confidence that I can give," wailed Margaret.

The invalid's tones became lower and more earnest.

"I had forgotten, Margaret, that you were young and had youthful aspirations; that you, also, must meet that which comes sometime into every woman's life—love; is it that, my darling? In the society into which you have lately gone has any one won your young heart? Tell me? Remember I hold your dead mother's place."

"No, no, no!" passionately protested Margaret. "I have met no one. I have nothing of the kind to tell. I am free—oh, how free!"

She said the last words bitterly, and buried her face again in her aunt's lap.

Not the shadow of a suspicion of the truth dawned upon the invalid's mind. She deemed the regard which Hubert and Margaret bore for each other but such an intimate brother and sister might have; and, though still not quite satisfied, because of the tone in which her niece had last spoken, she forbore to press further, only said:

"Well, my dear girl, we will not talk of this any longer at present; and now you had better retire, as, Hubert I suppose, has done already."

Margaret left the ottoman and knelt beside the invalid chair:

"Promise me, aunt, that you will seek no more to make me go into society. There is nothing there to satisfy my heart."

Madame Bernot's eyes were on the sacred picture opposite.

"Since you wish it so much,—no; and now, my dear girl, leave me; I shall receive Communion in the morning, and have my meditation to make."

And Margaret went forth slowly,—painfully, listening long at Hubert's door, but there was only the same dread silence. Arrived in her room, she flung off, with feverish impatience, the costume which had excited the envy of more than one belle, and donning a morning robe, she walked the floor till the garish dawn peeped through the half-open blinds.

He who lay upon his couch in the room below, with his face pressed into the pillow and his hands flung wildly above his head, heard the incessant tread above. It worked itself into the startling panorama which his distracted mind was picturing, until it became the tramp of the officers of the law, who were escorting him to the scaffold. It worked itself into the panorama, until it became the tread of a gaping crowd who surged about him on his way to the place of execution. It worked itself into the panorama, till it became the creaking of the very steps of the gallows which he was ascending.

Till the gray, cold dawn peeped into his room he lay, trying to force himself to meet this inevitable doom—to meet it even before it should clutch him in its iron grasp.

But the thought of the dishonor it would bring upon his name, and the blow it would give to his mother, rendered him powerless as a child to give himself up. He thought of flight—of secretly burying himself in some distant corner of the earth—but he knew only too well that God's justice would find him out even there, for his was a secret which earth would not keep. He would have flung down his wretched life gladly, but he could not meet the dishonor which such a sacrifice would entail.

A demon whispered self-destruction; one swift, sure blow which would engender a painless end, but the threats of his religion rose up and drowned the demon's voice.

When at last slumber visited these two suffering souls, it was but to continue the torture of the past waking hours.

On the bright morning which succeeded that miserable night the sun shone into Margaret's room, streaming athwart her face, and waking her up to wonder what it was that lay so heavily upon her heart. She remembered in an instant, and she hastened to make her toilet that she might descend to allay her anxiety about Hubert.

"Who is there?" he asked in response to her knock, and her heart gave a little throb of relief, she had so feared the worst.

"It is I—Margaret."

"Very well," he replied, "I shall be down to breakfast and see you then."

She turned away to her aunt's room, and finding there the clergyman who visited Madame Bernot at regular intervals, withdrew softly till he should take his departure.

Knowing that he would soon leave, she waited in the hall, thinking sadly as she leaned her burning forehead against the cold wall, if she could but pour out her heart in such a confidence as her aunt monthly made,—if she but dared to pour her tale into his priestly ear, now that her anguish was greater than it had been.

He came out suddenly, almost brushing against her, He was an old man, with thick silvery hair, and a face worn with the cares of his sacred calling, but whose expression reflected the patience and charity with which he strove to do his Master's will.

A fierce, overmastering impulse seized the sorrowing girl—an impulse to ask him to hear *her* confession, and the impulse grew stronger when the kindly old man saluted her pleasantly as he passed to the hall-door.

She sped after him, and a trembling "Father" had already issued from her lips when a sound on the stair caused her to look back.

Hubert was descending, and in full view of the clergyman and herself. The words stopped short upon her lips.

"Did you wish to speak to me, my child?" said the priest.

"No," she gasped; and she hurried to open the door.

The clergyman looked at her with an expression half of pity, half of surprise:

"Should you want to see me, you know where to find me," he said, in a whisper; and, with a kindly, good morning, he went his way.

She turned back to the tottering form still descending the stairs. The night's vigil had told more painfully on the wretched young man than on her, for, while she bore only heavy eyes and a weary look, his face was drawn into an expression of suffering that made him look twenty years older, than his age. He clutched the baluster for support, and looked like a man that was groping in the dark.

"You are too ill to have left your room," Margaret said, when she reached his side.

He put out his hand and caught his shoulder, leaning upon it almost too heavily for her slender strength.

"My staff," he whispered, "I can use you for just this once, for in a little time a great, great gulf will be between us. Oh, Margaret! Margaret!"—again that cry, though in subdued tones, for they were nearing the dining-room.

While Margaret sought, in a troubled way, for words with which to reply to him, he had calmed himself and was stern and cold. She watched him closely during the whole of that nearly tasteless meal, but saw only in that white, haggard face the expression of one whom no persuasion, no force could move from a stolid, agonized waiting for his doom.

"Are you going out to-day?" she asked, when he rose from the table and was about to leave the room.

"Perhaps," he replied; "I know not yet."

She repaired to his side, and, when they had reached the hall, closed the dining-room door behind her, that no ears might hear, while she whispered:

"If remarks should be passed about me on my strange conduct last night, what will you say?"

"Oh, a kind of nervousness to which you are sometimes subject," he answered, coldly.

He was breaking from her grasp.

"A moment more, Hubert. You will be careful not to betray yourself?"

He answered, bitterly:

"I am too much of a coward to betray myself." And, wrenching himself from her grasp, he went up to his mother's room. He always studied to conceal from the poor invalid everything that might lead her to suspect his suffering, but this morning she was too absorbed in her meditation on the pious work in which she had been engaged, to do more than smile and bless him.

Two or three hours later brought Louise Delmar

and her fashionable mother with lavish inquiries and sympathetic expressions from which Margaret shrank as much as she did from her own torturing thoughts, but she forced the semblance of a smile to her lips while she carelessly answered them.

"And are you sure, my dear girl, that you are quite well now?" asked Mrs. Delmar, rising at last to depart.

"Quite well," Margaret replied though her face contradicted her tongue.

"You gave us such a fright last night," said Miss Delmar glancing complacently at her reflection in the mirror, "we conjectured all sorts of terrible things about you, but now that you assure us it was only nervousness, we shall feel quite relieved. Of course you will be sufficiently recovered to attend our *coterie* next week."

"Sufficiently recovered, but I shall be unable to attend, nevertheless," replied Margaret; which reply brought a volley of protestations and eager demands to know the reason of such a determination, from both mother and daughter.

"I have no reason save that my nervousness will be better treated by remaining awhile from society," was the response, "so pardon me, my friends if I absent myself even from you, for quiet and solitude are absolutely necessary for me."

She had not intended to say so much but the words forced themselves out of her full heart.

Miss Delmar was shocked. The idea of shutting one's self away from society, which, in her puerile imagination, was the sole thing that made life endurable, seemed to her absurd, while Mrs. Delmar, with an assumption of matronliness which she was incapable of feeling, endeavored to shake Miss Calvert's determination. But the girl was very firm in her quiet way, nor could all the artful and insinuating questions, which the fashionable dame asked, elicit more from Margaret than she

had already told. So, vexed with her own failure, and Miss Calvert's provoking reticence she desisted at last, saying very coldly as she extended her hand in adieu:
"Has your cousin also formed this determination?"

Margaret looked unshrinkingly into the keen gray eyes bent on her, as she answered:

"As he does not suffer from *my* illness the same remedy is not necessary for him; further than that he has said nothing to me about it."

Mrs. Delmar sought to learn no more, and her daughter with such a caress as she might have bestowed on her spaniel, said pityingly:

"I am sorry for you, Maggie,—obliged to immure yourself in this dull house; but may not I invade your solitude some time?"

Miss Calvert muttered a reluctant assent, and the ladies swept out to their carriage. A little later and the fashionable circle in which the Delmars moved had a fresh supply of gossip, for driving directly to the most fashionable of their friends, Miss Calvert and her strange determination were discussed with all the ardor of scandal-loving dispositions. The sage dames of the world formed many conjectures, and offered many opinions of Miss Calvert's character, As much of her life as was known to them was discussed; her connection with the strange murder of eighteen months before revived, and the stream of scandal flowed once more.

"She knew the murdered man," said one; "the papers said that she admitted she did."

"Yes," said another, accompanying her reply with a shrewd shake of the head, "and who can tell what she knew and how she knew it—I am afraid"— with a still more knowing shake,—"that we have been guilty of an imprudence in admitting her to our society."

"That is true," responded a third gentle voice, "and if you remember, I disclaimed against her from the first. There was something about her one could never approach."

Everybody agreed with the last speaker; and then commenced without even the semblance of an effort to spare her, the destruction of Margaret Calvert's character. They did not accuse her of complicity in the murder, they did not even allege against her a knowledge of the perpetrator of the deed, for these "fine ladies" shrank from so coarse and revolting a thing as a bloody crime, but they gave utterance to other and as foul suspicions about the unhappy young creature.

But while they sullied remorselessly *her* fair fame they were equally careful to uphold the character of her cousin—for, was he not immensely wealthy, and did not the heart of many a matron having eligible daughters glow with the hope that in the future the elegant Hubert Bernot might assume a near and dear relation to herself? But Margaret, simply a cousin—a dependant, as it were, of the Bernots—and having already by her beauty and the preference with which the distinguished Mr. Plowden treated her, excited the envy of those less fair and fortunate than herself, *she* was a good mark at which to fire their poison-tipped arrows. They even went so far as to pity the Bernots for having in their house one whose character must certainly be unknown to them, and to censure Plowden for his blind devotion to one so unworthy.

No one imagined that there existed between the cousins more than a cousinly affection; for it was known that the Bernots were strict Catholics, and further, angling mammas did not wish to believe Hubert so far removed from all their baits.

Mrs. Delmar had taken a very warm part in the conference and when at last the exciting topic had well nigh worn itself out, she drew her daughter to her, with:

"We must blame Louise here for having Miss Calvert made so much of. Poor child; her heart is such a generous one it goes out freely to everybody. I only hope, my darling that your acquaintance with her has not injured *your* reputation.

"I think not, mamma," and Miss Delmar glanced complacently at her jeweled fingers.

"And now ladies," concluded the fashionable matron, "since Miss Calvert has voluntarily withdrawn from our circle, I propose that we refuse to accept her when she chooses to return; in short, that in any accidental meeting or intercourse with her, we show by our manner that she is no longer worthy of our favor—my daughter and I shall do so on every occasion."

The proposition was unanimously adopted, the proposition which would inflict upon her, the guiltless one, the full rigor of their jealousy, their envy, their wrath, while he whose heart was black with the guilt of a secret crime, was to continue to be received by the fashionable world with open arms and flattering tongue.

CHAPTER XIX.

WHILE the slanderous conference was going on, its innocent victim was attending to her usual duties but with such listlessness of manner as to convey the impression that she was exceedingly ill,—an impression strongly corroborated by her more than usually pale face and heavy eyes.

Hannah Moore catching an accidental glimpse of the young creature was attacked by her old habit of soliloquy.

"Only she'd think it bold in me I'd spake to her, for even a comforting word might do her good."

The kind-hearted cook's own duties were pressing just then, however, and she turned away with a sigh, while Margaret, little dreaming that any one's sympathy went out to her, sought vainly to turn her thoughts for even a moment from their one painful object.

Hubert did not appear at lunch, and when his cousin sought him to ascertain the cause, he met her on the threshold of his room with a book in his hand from which he did not lift his eyes while he answered her kindly spoken inquiry:

"I am quite well, Margaret, but you annoy me by these constant attentions, I desire to be alone—alone—to have no one watching, or tracking me," and with a rudeness of which he had never before been guilty, he turned abruptly away leaving the door slightly ajar, and resumed the seat he had vacated.

She remained looking at him, but he would not have met those eyes then, even to save his wretched life. He must do something to make her dislike, or hate him for he would not further blacken his soul by linking to it such a pure love as hers.

But, alas! her very presence, the touch of her hand, the sound of her voice, roused with new ardor the love he sought to kill. For this reason he would not meet her look lest his own eyes might be won from the sternness which alone he would have them show, and for this reason he would school himself to be harsh and cold that he might turn her affection from him.

Margaret, far from interpreting aright his rude treatment of her, attributed it solely to the fear of arrest under which she fancied he labored.

"He is so unnerved," she murmured to herself.

She did not censure him; her sorrowful heart accused him of no ingratitude, it only bled for him and longed to comfort him, to throw the whole wealth of its wild passion at his feet, and if such a thing could be, to offer her life in atonement for his crime. She refrained from going to him, judging that he was not in the mood to receive her sympathy, and after that one long, sad look at him she turned silently away.

Later in the day when she heard him descending, she came into the hall and seeing him about to go out she held out her hand saying, softly:

"Be careful, Hubert."

He dashed her hand away and strode on without a reply.

For an instant she was dizzy with mortification and pain; then her woman's love sent up passionate, pleading excuses for him and she murmured:

"Poor fellow! his suffering is so sharp he does not know what he does."

"You are looking very ill, my child!" said Madame Bernot, when Margaret was bathing the poor helpless hands. "I am afraid you need a physician."

"No, no!" protested Margaret, trying immediately to infuse more animation into her countenance and more energy into her manner.

"You have not been out to-day," continued the invalid, "take a walk for my sake."

In obedience to the request Margaret put on her out-door garments and went listlessly forth—walking anywhere, so that strange faces and fanciful shop windows might lull her for a brief while to forgetfulness.

In the middle of a crossing which she was about to pass, a small crowd was collected—some accident had happened to the driver of a vehicle, and men where about to bear the poor fellow to a neighboring drug shop.

A handsome carriage, stopped by the mishap, was drawn up, and the heads of two ladies were thrust from one of its windows. Margaret perceived a slight opening in the swaying throng, and hurrying across found herself directly in front of the occupants of the carriage.

She looked up to meet Mrs. Delmar and her daughter who were only then returning from the charitable conference of which Margaret had been the occasion. The face of the elder lady was set in such a cold, hard expression that it appalled Margaret and checked the salutation already upon her lips; the younger lady withdrew her head and shrank into a corner of the carriage, for, apt scholar though Louise Delmar was in the lessons of fashionable folly which her mother taught her, she had not gone sufficiently far to be able to stifle every impulse of womanliness in her nature; so she withdrew her head that she might spare herself the pain of seeing Margaret's surprise and mortification.

Margaret, imagining that she labored under some strange delusion, recovered her voice and spoke a few kind words of greeting. Her only response was that same cold look during which the gray eyes seemed to dilate in their icy glitter, and then Mrs. Delmar's jeweled hand went up, and the curtain of the carriage window was dropped between the bewildered girl, and the hard stern face.

The crowd was following the injured man, and a way was made for the costly equipage; it drove on, and poor, mortified Margaret stood looking after it like one in a dream.

When her whirling mind recovered its balance her first thought was that Hubert had been arrested, and that the Delmars had refused to recognize her because of her connection with such a criminal, and under the influence of that thought she turned to rush wildly home, but when with flying speed she had gone a block or two, her calmer judgment returned, and suggested the unreasonableness of such a conjecture. Hubert had gone out but a little while before herself, and had such a dread event occurred the Delmars would hardly know it so soon. She walked more slowly and drew a long breath of relief.

"What can it be?" she asked herself; not certainly the decision to withdraw from society, which she had announced to them that morning, for she had given it in the very kindest manner; one calculated to win sympathy rather than anger.

She was too much of a novice in the world's ways to know that the votaries of fashion will tolerate nothing among them which appears in a better mould than themselves—that they gladly seize any opportunity to cast such an one out of their charmed circle. It was due to the patronage of the Delmars that Margaret had been so long acknowledged by the fashionable set, and that patronage was owing to a desire which burned secretly but ardently, in Mrs. Delmar's own heart—a desire to effect the marriage of her daughter with Hubert Bernot, and she regarded Miss Calvert as a very fitting instrument to aid her in the gratification of her wish.

But Margaret's sudden and unexpected withdrawal had demolished her plans—further, she even feared now that Margaret might influence her cousin against Louise, and to afford herself a malicious satisfaction the fashionable woman vented all her spleen on a poor unoffending girl.

Margaret, little dreaming of such an under-current of malice, sought vainly to explain the matter by a charitable course of reasoning with herself. She had been keenly hurt; for though she had found little congeniality in the fashionable world, and had gladly withdrawn herself from it, she was still but a woman, with a woman's natural liking for esteem from all, and this open slight had wounded her to the quick.

She walked on slowly, revolving in the bitterness of her soul the desolation which seemed to surround her. Even Hubert's coldness rose up to taunt her; but she thrust that thought back—she would not entertain an unkind suspicion of him, the idol of her unhappy heart. But the cry of her soul for rest, for sympathy, for a kind look, a kind word from some one, would not be quieted, and while she hesitated whether to prolong that dreary walk, or return home, there came suddenly to her mind the thought of the church she had accidentally entered a few evenings before, and she turned her steps thence —not that she imagined the mere empty form of entering the sacred building would bring her relief, not that she thought to return to those duties of religion which she had so neglected, but that she might rest herself in the sacred awe which pervaded the place, for the very recollection of that solemn quietness seemed to promise something which would soothe her troubled soul.

The iron gate stood ajar as it had done on the previous occasion, and the church door was open, but there was no service going on. There was only the sanctuary lamp softly aflame, and a few kneeling forms around a confessional.

Margaret knelt also, and buried her face in her hands, not through devotion, not even to murmur a wildly distracted prayer, only to seek in a desperate way for a moment's respite from her mental torture.

She could hear the slide as at unequal intervals it moved to admit, or to dismiss a penitent from the curtained recess, and at last she looked up to watch the faces of those who came from the sacred tribunal.

Hard, weather-beaten countenances, some of them were, but the lines of sin and care were softened in the peace with which they shone, and Margaret from the very depths of her sick soul envied the poorest one there.

She turned her eyes to the life-size picture of the crucifixion above the altar. The waning daylight seemed to have concentrated all its fading beams on the painting. It stood out the one distinctly visible thing in the gathering gloom, and as Margaret looked, it seemed as if the divine eyes were turned upon her in compassion and love.

One person alone remained to be heard, and Margaret, fearing that she too might be considered a penitent, rose to depart. The eyes in the picture haunted her; she turned for another look, and influenced by some strange, resistless impulse which sprang out of that second glance, she knelt again.

The last penitent was heard, and the priest, lifting his curtain, discerned the outlines of another kneeling form. He dropped it quickly, and Margaret knew that he waited for her. Oh the sharp, sharp struggle of that minute—at once impelled to go, and to flee! She looked up at the picture, and the eyes seemed to be piercing her soul. Rising hurriedly, she crossed to the curtained recess, but in the very act of entering, her cousin's image rose before her, pleading with extended hands, and that passionate cry. She would have turned back, but the priest had drawn the slide, and was waiting for her to kneel.

The secret which had been kept so long was told at last; the burden that had pressed so sore and heavily was flung down, and when the slide was again drawn, and the curtain lifted, there came forth another person than she who had entered—a being who could have cried out in the exuberance of her joy, and whose trembling feet could scarcely steady themselves sufficiently to bear her to the chancel rail, there to pour out her thanksgiving, and her joy to Him whom she had so long forsaken.

Everything had been told in that sacred confidence, and the result was, not to be a denouncing Hubert, not even to be a lessening of the love and care which she had hitherto given him; instead, the confessor had taught her to so direct her love and care that God might be served instead of the creature, alone. And she had received such consolation that, she felt, did the very worst of her fears become a reality she should be supported by an unfailing strength. Prayer, to which she had so long been a stranger, ascended from her heart with burning fervor—not for herself now, but for unhappy Hubert, that he too might be inspired to confess his crime.

How lightly she flew home, and with what different feelings she entered her aunt's room—not that her fears for Hubert were less, but that her trust in God's providence had returned! She could lift her eyes above the ignominy and sorrow and pain of a few short years here, to the peace and bliss and glory of a hereafter! she could storm Heaven with her prayers for Hubert, and at the last, if the law should exact from him his own life for the life he had taken, she could unite her grief with that of the "Mother of Sorrows" who had given her only son for the world; and should the blow not kill Madame Bernot as, she feared it would do, she would minister to her with increased devotion, and thus giving the remainder of her life to sacrifice and prayer, she would offer all up, that Hubert's soul might find favor with its offended God.

These were the thoughts which brought her such peace as she had not known for eighteen long months, and which so transfigured her face as to bring forth from Madame Bernot:

"You seem much better, child; I think your walk did you good."

"Much good," answered Margaret, and she busied herself in arranging the invalid's slight evening repast.

Hubert, accompanied by Mr. Plowden, had come in directly after Margaret's return; in a little while she was summoned to the parlor to meet the guest.

He looked pale and seemed slightly embarrassed as he rose to greet her.

"I rejoice to find you so much better," he said, after a little apparently painful hesitation on his part, and then with an abruptness entirely foreign to his usual quiet and graceful manner, he told her the purpose for which he had desired to see her. He poured out in impassioned language the tale of a love which had grown day by day till now at maddening heat it would leave him no peace until he should secure its object.

It was impossible not to believe him, and it was cruel not to pity him—this proud, distinguished man of the world who was laying bare before a frail girl the secret workings of a haughty and ambitious soul. His voice trembled with subdued eagerness, and his eyes looked wild and troubled.

"I have made your cousin my confidant," he said, in conclusion, "and I have his sanction, nay, his wish, expressed even this evening, to speak as I have done."

Margaret's heart gave a throb of pain—it was like a cruel shock for a moment to learn that Hubert could thus cooly dispose of her, despite the promise he had given; but it did not weaken her devotion to him; no shock however cruel could do that; her care because of his very guilt and her love for him should not fail—were he not a sin-burdened man her heart would have broken ere it should have betrayed by word or sign that he was the object of its love.

She answered Plowden kindly, even tenderly, but with a frankness which told him at once that his suit, was fruitless. She had not even hinted that her heart was pre-engaged, but the keen lawyer detected much more than she had told, and he said, when she had concluded:

"I understand you, Miss Calvert, and had I known before what I think I know now, I should not have subjected either of us to this ordeal."

"Know now;" she repeated, "I have told you nothing."

Fear, lest she had unconsciously betrayed Hubert, made her tones tremulous.

"No, you have told me nothing; but I understand now, much that before this was unintelligible to me," and he looked gloomily at the floor.

Margaret's face blanched. Had he been all along suspecting Hubert's guilt, and had she unconsciously supplied a clew. She laid her hand on Plowden's arm and said, with piteous entreaty in her tones:

"You have seemed to be Hubert's most devoted friend; do not let this come between you—be his friend still for sake of the affection you say you bear me."

He answered sadly:

"Do not fear; I shall be the same to him that I have been—for the present, farewell!"

He caught her hands and held them so tightly for a moment that they ached from the pressure; then dropping them as suddenly as he had seized them, he hurriedly departed.

CHAPTER X.

MARGARET did not see her cousin after her interview with Plowden, until they met at breakfast the next morning, and Hubert's manner was as repellant as it had been on the previous day; but she, recalling the counsels of her confessor, strove not to be affected by it, and she put into *her* manner such affectionate kindness as well-nigh destroyed his self-erected barrier of coldness. It was the same when they met at lunch, and at dinner, immediately after which he came down dressed to go out.

"Shall you remain out late?" asked Margaret, following him to the door.

"Yes; I am going to the club," and without looking at her he hurried forth.

She looked after him, watching until he had turned the corner, and then her eyes sought the clear evening sky, and her lips moved in prayer. She could pray now—she could turn for relief and hope to one unfailing source.

She busied herself in the sick room all the evening until Madame insisted on her retiring, and then she ascended to her own apartment to watch for Hubert. She could not rest while he was out; now that *Roquelare* seemed to be so closely upon his track.

Midnight struck and he had not returned; it was not his custom to remain so late at the club. Her heart beat wildly and her breath came thick and hard.

Kneeling by the open window, regardless of the

frosty air which blew sharply against her face, she mingled prayers and tears for the poor unhappy criminal.

A form was coming down the street, a form erect and lithe like Hubert's but with a much more rapid step than he was wont to have of late. It turned to ascend the stoop, but without waiting to see further she flew below, and was in time to open the door just as the stranger's hand had sought the bell.

It was Plowden—Plowden strangely agitated, and looking frightfully pale as he came into the light of the hall.

"Something has happened to Hubert," she gasped, "tell me quickly."

"Calm yourself," he whispered, "and for your aunt's sake, take me where there can be no fear of eavesdroppers."

She led him to the darkened parlor; he left the door partly open that the light from the hall might enter, and gave her a scrap of paper whispering:

"Read, but for your aunt's sake, make no outcry."

She read with burning eyes:

"I have cast my burden down at last—'Roquelare' has seized me—come to me in the morning; Plowden will conduct you, but keep everything from my mother until it can be gently broken to her.   HUBERT."

She made no outcry; she only stood holding the paper fast and looking at Plowden in a helpless, bewildered way, as if she were utterly broken by the intelligence he had brought. She had fancied she was strong. Since her confession she had repeated to herself that should the worst happen she was prepared to meet it; but now at the mere tidings of that which she had daily feared she was as weak as an infant. How could she give him up? How could she endure to have him pay the penalty of his crime even though that penalty should be a long imprisonment instead of death? And then arose within her all the cruel fancies which had so tortured her during the past eighteen months.

She reeled and would have fallen but for Plowden's timely grasp.

He supported her to a chair and waited until she seemed to have become better; then he whispered:

"You had better retire, Miss Calvert; you are not strong enough to hear any more now, and I shall escort you to him early to-morrow."

"No, no!" she replied in the same whisper, and clutching his coat as if she feared that he might leave her despite her remonstrance.

The light from the hall shone sufficiently into the room to reveal plainly her pale suffering face and pleading eyes.

Plowden thrilled with a compassion and tenderness he had never felt but for one being before, and, for an instant there rose within him a fierce overmastering impulse to right the wrong which had come between and was blasting these two young lives. But after that moment in which he had almost yielded, he thrust the impulse back, and answered quietly:

"Do you wish to know how it happened? Are you strong enough to hear? I was present and saw all."

She bowed her head in assent, and he resumed:

"Hubert and I went together to the club and at the supper which followed the business of the evening, conviviality reigned,—toasts were proposed, anecdotes told; glasses clinked and mirth seemed to run high in every breast; even Hubert appeared unusually gay till one story was told, one toast was proposed. Can you guess what it was, Miss Calvert?"

He bent low to that pale, uplifted face and looked piercingly into those dry burning eyes.

"No, no! I cannot," she gasped; "but tell me quickly," and she tightened her hold upon his coat as if by that convulsive clasp she might ward off the faintness which was coming upon her.

"A gentleman began a tale—a gentleman who joined the club shortly after your cousin, and who had been a regular attendant.

"He was always in his place, always punctual, and his courtly, yet unobtrusive manner won for him universal regard. The first time I saw him, and heard him speak, his face and voice recalled some one I had seen and heard before. Every subsequent meeting confirmed the impression, but strive as I would, I could not recall where. Last night—for it is morning now—when he began to speak, this strange impression of mine pressed painfully on me. He told a tale of murder—"

Margaret started, and Plowden paused as if he feared to proceed.

"Go on," she whispered hoarsely.

"Of murder, where the victim being left to die on the street was found cold and stark in the chill dawn of an autumn morning—Of a girl who came on that same day to look at the body as it lay in the *morgue* and from whose manner and reluctant admission sufficient was gained to put one man on the track of him who had done the deed—of a girl who for eighteen months had kept the secret of the murderer with devoted care—of the murderer himself who was tracked to every resort by the hidden agent of 'Roquelare'—of the murderers' secret which was gnawing the heart of both the criminal and his confidante, and having told all these things he added that he wished to propose for their next toast this faithful, suffering girl who had borne so well the murderer's burden.

"The tale had riveted us all, but Hubert, beside whom I sat, visibly started at times, and once he half rose as if to contradict, or defy the speaker; but the speaker had so engrossed the attention of all, that Hubert's motion was unperceived save by me.

"I pulled him back into his seat, and whispered him to be careful."

During the tale the speaker's eyes had not once turned to Hubert, but when he had concluded he bent a full penetrating look upon him. In the awed silence which followed that strange tale and before I could suspect what your cousin might do, before I could try to prevent his action, he had risen, and, extending his hand over the table, he said slowly and distinctly:

"*I* am the murderer of whom the gentleman has spoken—I, Hubert Bernot, confess myself to be the murderer of Cecil Clare."

Plowden again paused, for that white face lifted to his, frightened him—it was so white, so rigid; but the pale lips motioned rather than said:

"Go on!" and he resumed:

"That unexpected confession seemed to have paralyzed everybody but him who had drawn it forth. He rose, and standing directly opposite to Hubert, said, looking round at the startled faces about him:

"I am Bertoni the lawyer, and one of the secret detectives of *Roquelare*. Many of you will recognize me better in a few moments," and removing a thick, black curling wig, and beard and whiskers of the same hue he stood fully revealed as the lawyer with whom I had been connected in the investigation of the murder of Cecil Clare.

"Hubert, as if overcome by some reaction of feeling, sank into his chair, and Bertoni, pointing to him, said:

"You have made a confession; there are a score of witnesses to testify to that confession. You cannot escape your doom now."

He signaled to one of the members of the club who hastily left the room.

"I saw the signal and the ready obedience it obtained, and I knew that Bertoni was not the only agent of *Roquelare* in the club, for that society has its members everywhere—members who are pledged to assist each other in the pursuit and arrest of any criminal.

"There was a scene of wild excitement. All had started to their feet, and one or two of those nearest to Hubert had drawn aloof from him as if they feared the proximity might bring danger to themselves. Others crowded about him asking an explanation, and tendering their sympathy; he made no answer, only sat looking straight before him till he who had been despatched from the room returned, accompanied by two officers.

"Then Hubert rose and said he was ready to accompany the officers, asking only to be permitted to write the message which I have brought to you.

"Bertoni would not lose sight of him for a moment —he accompanied him in the carriage which was hastily summoned, and Delmar and I equally anxious to learn all that we could, jumped into a hack and followed.

"At the prison gate we were allowed a parting word. Hubert pressed my hand hard and said:

"'Tell my cousin to have no anxiety about me, but to give all her care to my mother'—that is all, Miss Calvert."

All! was it not as much as earth had to offer her of anguish? She released his coat from her convulsive clasp, and pressed her hands over her burning eyes. He waited, hoping and expecting that tears would come to her relief, but when she looked up at him again there was not a trace of moisture in the large bright eyes. She rose, steadying herself against the chair, and said with such a passionate wail in her voice that it smote the proud, ambitious man by her side like a knife applied to a festering sore.

"What shall I do? what can I do to help him? I have no friends I know not to whom to apply.".

Plowden seemed to labor under some intense excitement; he replied, almost wildly:

"Margaret—Miss Calvert, will you not regard me as your friend? My services, my"— he would have said life but the word died in his throat—" are at your command; only command me and I shall be happy. I ask no reward—I ask only the permission to serve you. Do you think that I have been blind all these months —do you think that I have not read the secret which was eating into your cousin's life and your own? His unguarded admissions would have told me as much even had I not divined it in the very first instance. It was this knowledge which made me keep so close to him; which made me work myself into his confidence without asking it. I did it that I might guard him from betraying himself for he was *your* relative, *you* whom I love as I have never loved woman before. I might have kept this passion of mine within severe bounds had I discovered one fact earlier than I have done—the fact that, cousins though you were, you loved each other."

Margaret started.

"Pardon me, Miss Calvert, if I touch upon delicate topics, but having begun, I must speak on. I discovered Hubert's passionate love for you three nights ago when you fainted at the ball. It was that discovery which drew from me at the carriage door the remark that both he and I were drinking of a bitter cup—he, loving you as he did and prevented by a wrong from possessing you; I loving you as madly, and—but no matter."

He stopped suddenly passing his hand over his face as if he would hide its expression; then he abruptly resumed:

"When Hubert savagely demanded to bear you himself to the carriage I discovered in that moment that his secret crime came between you. My discovery was confirmed the next day when I spoke with him. He would not admit his love, but he reiterated that your hand was far beyond his reach, and that all time would not suffice for him to attain it, and then in his turn he asked me plain questions about *my* love. I answered him as frankly, as I afterward made my avowal to you. He besought me by the friendship we bore each other to press my suit. He affirmed that I could do him no wrong, but, on the contrary, the greatest service man could render to him, as you were his near relative and he was your only protector. My own heart only too eagerly impelled me to gratify him,—with what success you already know; but on *that* occasion I learned, not from any admission of yours, for you were very guarded, but from something about you which I can hardly explain, that your heart was already in possession of another, and *that* other your cousin. I might have told you all this then, Miss Calvert, but I forbore because you were afraid of me—you feared that I held some dangerous knowledge of your cousin and that I might use that knowledge—you fancied that you had given me some clew when I spoke of much being plain to me that before had been unintelligible; you did not know that I meant by that your love for Hubert, your generous unselfish love which makes you more sensitive to every thought of harm for him than the certainty of immediate death for yourself could do.

"If any doubt had remained upon my mind, if any hope that the attachment was not mutual, and that but cousinly affection made you warm and tender to this unhappy Hubert, the closing portion of my last interview with you would have dissipated all. You did not intend, Miss Calvert, to let me read you; you strove hard to show me only a smooth, cold upper surface, beneath which it would be impossible for me to strike; but I penetrated the crust, and saw not only a love faithful unto death, but a record of the struggles and hidden agony of eighteen long months. I knew then how far beyond *my* reach you were, not only for time, but for all eternity; so I forbore to speak as I have spoken to night. I felt that the time would come when I could so speak; for, from the wild and unguarded remarks which your cousin sometimes made, I learned that "Roquelare" was in pursuit of him, and I knew what *that* meant.

"Now that you are aware how much I know, will you trust me—trust me fully, knowing that I ask no reward, that I claim not a particle of the affection you have given to your cousin?"

She extended her hands, trying to speak the burning words of gratitude which came up from her full heart, but the tears which had refused to come before choked her utterance.

"You knew, and yet have not betrayed!" she said, brokenly, at last.

"Betrayed! sooner would I have cut my tongue out."

For a moment he seemed to labor under some fierce excitement. He trembled violently and his hands clasped Margaret's with a painful pressure.

A clock in an adjoining room struck three—three o'clock Sunday morning. The sound seemed to calm Plowden. He said, quietly:

"We both need rest; you to recruit your energies that you may bring something like comfort to that poor fellow a few hours hence, and I that I may think how I can best help him. My position has made for me many and powerful friends—all that their interest can do shall be brought to bear on Hubert's case. Also it will be necessary to make some arrangements before I see you again, in order that you may be admitted to to him without delay. So, for the present, farewell, and be of good cheer."

He pressed her hands respectfully and went cautiously forth, Margaret accompanying him to the door.

"At nine," he whispered, "I can scarcely be here before." She bowed her head, and he departed.

When she had closed and locked the door as noiselessly as she had opened it, she paused, lookingly carefully about her, and listening for any sound. Nothing disturbed the grave-like stillness save the ominous ticking of an upper hall clock, and she went forward again smiling bitterly as she remembered the little need of caution now.

The secret had been flung abroad and the name of Hubert Bernot coupled with the epithet of *murderer* would soon be in every mouth. And then all the anguish born of that thought came again upon her. It required an hour of cruel wrestling with gaunt doubts and fears that sprang up like giants in the mind of the grief-stricken creature—an hour of prayers during which her heart sent up such fiery petitions to Heaven for strength and help that her whole form was convulsed with their fervor, before she became sufficiently calm to think collectively of her duties in this sad emergency.

At last, exhausted by the excitement she had undergone, she rested her head against the *prie-dieu* on which she knelt, and slumbered soundly until the bright light of the morning woke her.

Oh, the wretched awaking to what at first seemed but an ugly, ugly dream; the sharp and rapid recollection of the anguish already undergone;—the cruel realization of the anguish that was yet to come! It was almost insupportable, and she felt that if she were still a renegade from her religious duties, despair would have paralyzed every faculty. As it was, her suffering, while keen, was not hopeless; for though hope might die here, it would surely bloom hereafter.

The breakfast bell sounded, and directly after there was a knock at her door.

It was Annie Corbin.

"I knocked before, Miss Margaret, when it seemed as if you didn't hear the first bell, but you didn't answer; and I knocked at Mr. Hubert's door, but he didn't answer either, and it frightened us a little."

"Did you alarm my aunt?" asked Margaret hurriedly.

"No, Miss; we thought it better not to, until we'd know further."

Margaret gave a little sigh of relief and pressed her hand to her forehead.

Sooner or later the servants would learn about Hubert either through the papers or otherwise; still she deemed it better to try to conceal all from them until some plan could be made with regard to her aunt, lest she might by any accident receive untimely news of Hubert's imprisonment.

So she said, quietly:

"Mr. Bernot spent last evening with some friends and he has not returned."

On her way to the breakfast room she entered Madame Bernot's apartment.

When the affectionate salutations were exchanged, which always passed between the invalid and her niece, Margaret said:

"Hubert was called away unexpectedly, last evening, and he will be obliged to remain away for a few days; he desired me to bear his apology to you, and his affectionate remembrance; he felt that you would exempt him from all charge of neglect of you, since it was duty which enforced his hurried departure."

"And he was right, my own dear boy; great as my affection is for him, greater still is the pleasure, indeed I might say the triumph, it affords me to know, that not even his mother whom he loves so dearly, comes between him and duty."

She lifted her eyes to the picture.

"I thank you, O my God! for having given me such a son."

Margaret bent her head to hide the blush of shame at the cruel deceit which she was practicing on this saint-like mother, and she sought the first opportunity of hurrying from the invalid's presence. Her solitary, cheerless, and well-nigh untasted breakfast, was scarcely finished, when Plowden was announced.

"I thought you would prefer not to take your own carriage;" he said, "so I have taken the liberty of ordering the cab, which brought me, to remain."

"You were right," she said, gratefully, " for that

would have spread the news at once among the servants," and waiting only to put on her bonnet and cloak, she hurried out with him, utterly unconscious that the very fact of accompanying a gentleman in a strange conveyance and that gentleman Plowden, was sufficient of itself to create perplexity and suspicion among the domestics.

John McNamee scratched his head in troubled thought, and Hannah Moore dropped the spoon with which she had been basting a huge piece of venison, and gazed abstractedly into the fire. The other servants had gone about their usual avocations, so the pair were alone in the kitchen.

"I don't like the looks of things," said the coachman—"I feel queer, somehow, for something tells me Mr. Hubert's in trouble."

"What kind of trouble?" asked the cook, sharply, rising from her low position in front of the fire.

"I don't exactly know," was the reply, "only it looks queer to see Miss Calvert going out in a common hack. It can't be to church they're going, for sure he's no Catholic."

"He *is* a Catholic," burst suddenly from Hannah More, then she became very red in the face, and as if to hide her confusion she turned hastily to attend to some culinary duty.

McNamee looked at her with an expression of wonder, and he continued to look as if surprise had deprived him of speech.

"What's the matter with you, John?" she asked, stooping before the fire again, and resuming her basting.

"This is the matter with me," he said, crossing to her, and laying his hand on her shoulder. "I'm thinking that you know something more than the rest of us. Just now it flashed on me what you said at the inquest, over a year ago, to that same Mr. Plowden when he was examining you, that maybe if he pressed you too far, you'd tell things about other people, and now you seem to know he's a Catholic. I'm only putting this and that together, Hannah, and thinking that if you know anything that isn't good about him, you ought to put that young creature on her guard. Sure it's plain he's paying his addresses to her."

The cook was crying.

"Oh! John, John!" she said, rising again, and wiping her face with her apron, "I *do* know something, but I promised at a death-bed never to tell it. There is something that is not his fault, and there is something bitter and cruel that rests on his soul. But perhaps he's repented, and will make Miss Calvert a good husband. Don't tell any of the others what I've been saying, and maybe I can think of a way to put her on her guard, without breaking my word to the dead."

She turned sadly to her work, while John, wearing very grave face, repaired slowly to the carriage-house.

CHAPTER XI.

A PRISON! Margaret shuddered when the hack stopped before the dark, massive front of the city jail.

She had never been within such a place before, and she clung tightly to Plowden's arm as they ascended the stone steps, and treaded the stone floors of long, cheerless corridors.

Bertoni, almost at the very head of his profession, and supported by the mysterious influence of "Roquelare," had little difficulty in having Hubert Bernot consigned immediately to close imprisonment. Indeed the secret agent of "Roquelare" had seemed to exhibit a savage bitterness toward Hubert as if in revenge for the long delay of his capture—causing him to be searched, and his pocket knife taken from him lest the unhappy criminal might attempt self-destruction.

So Hubert Bernot, the aristocratic-born, the tenderly-reared, the once high-spirited youth, the cultured gentleman, was securely fastened in a murderer's cell.

It was a bare, desolate place enough, and the officer, whose duty it was to give admission to the cells, and who preceded Plowden and his companion, glanced back at Margaret as if he was curious to note the effect on one so lovely, and apparently so refined.

But beyond a trembling eagerness which was visible in her manner, and an intense anxiety that displayed itself in her eyes, there was nothing to betray the various emotions which were struggling in her soul.

The iron door of a dim narrow apartment was flung back, and something arose from a low pallet in the corner—something, for Margaret's vision was blurred by sudden weakness and it seemed as if she saw through a mist, arms extended, and as if she heard from afar, a voice crying:

"We are free at last, Margaret!"

Heedless of the presence of others she went forward with a husky, stifled cry to throw herself into those arms, to sob out on his breast the love which was as true to him now and as tender, as it was in the first days of his guilty secret. But he caught her and held her at arm's length, whispering:

"No nearer, Margaret; the gulf between us is as impassable as ever."

Plowden who remained in the doorway jealously, fiercely watching, saw that it cost Hubert a mighty struggle not to fold to his breast the panting, eager girl, and for the first time since his manhood the courtly man of the world was attacked by something very like a woman's weakness. He was sick of the ghastly wrong which separated those two young hearts, and disgusted with his own base part in life. He turned away and joined the officer who was waiting without.

"Though your crime is known," said Margaret, between choking sobs, "your punishment, your disgrace is none the less mine. I suffer for you, with you, as keenly as I have ever done. I would comfort you as much as it is in my power to do. I would show you how, when a poor, frail creature like me loves you so much that your very sin and its penalty beget only new tenderness, what God's compassion, God's love, must be for you."

Hubert, continuing to hold her from him, and to look mournfully down into her eyes, shook his head.

"It is for innocence like yours to talk and feel in this manner; but, for a murderer like me there is only to suffer for my crime with what courage I may."

"There is more, Hubert!"— she wrenched herself

from his grasp and knelt before him—" there is your peace to make with an offended God; there is your return to your religious duties to effect. You have made a public acknowledgment of your crime, make now a private one to God's minister, and then, and not till then, will you be prepared to bear the punishment of your sin."

"It would be a mockery, Margaret—confession to a priest now, when I have flung my secret abroad—but *you* are released; *you* can kneel at the tribunal of penance once more."

"I have already done so; I flung *my* burden down two days ago;"

And lowering her voice though her manner became more impassioned, more thrillingly earnest, she whispered the counsels which her confessor had given her for the poor, unhappy criminal.

He listened like one under the influence of a spell until for one brief moment there came back to him the peaceful happiness of the past before he had imbrued his hands in a fellow creature's blood. But it quickly fled and left him only more vile and loathsome in his own eyes.

He started from her.

"Listen to more, Hubert," she said; and he sank on the bed with a groan.

Approaching him until she was sufficiently near to seize his hands, and to fix his eyes with the tender, earnest, and seemingly inspired look of her own, she resumed: and never did mother pleading for an only offspring at the feet of a relentless judge, nor devoted wife imploring mercy for a condemned husband, plead more powerfully, or use more touching arguments than Margaret in her entreaties to Hubert to have mercy on his poor sin-stained soul. Love made her eloquent; love sent up from her heart words with which to paint such a picture of God's pardon and tenderness for the penitent sinner, that the unhappy criminal drew his hands from her clasp, and covering his face with them, said:

"But this is not for me."

"For you, for you," she answered: "and now I shall bring a priest to you to-morrow."

He neither assented nor refused, but remained with his face buried in his hands.

He looked up at last, and motioning her to a seat beside him on the pallet, he asked about his mother and what excuse had been made for his absence, answering when she had told him:

"It is well—but how shall we continue to conceal it from her? Sometime she must know it."

His head sank on his breast in anguish at the thought.

Margaret replied slowly, as if she were deliberating the plan in her own mind:

"I think Father Germain, who is your mother's spiritual director, will break it to her, after he has visited you, and when he shall deem it best—that is, if you request him to do so."

"My helper in difficulty, my comforter in adversity," burst from Hubert impulsively, and then he continued in the same impetuous way:

"Last night when that terrible story was told—the story of my crime, of your faithfulness—when the piteous picture was drawn of your wretched burden, a thousand devils seemed to pluck the guilty secret out of my heart; but I could have kept them at bay, I could have fought them down, and I could still have retained the horrid thing which had been my companion so long, but for you—the proclamation of my crime would set you free; would keep you no longer the murderer's confidante. Faithful, faithful Margaret!"

He put his arm suddenly about her as if to draw her to him, but he as suddenly took it away saying, with a shudder:

"Never, never must we embrace—as I told you before, the gulf is just as impassable, for the blood of my victim swells it high and wide. Come often to me if you will, with such comforting words as you have spoken this morning; continue to attend my poor, broken-down mother as you have done for years, and when the end comes, if the last prayer of a soul that has suffered hell's torture for eighteen months will be heard, if the dying sigh of a man whose life was blasted by *one* crime will be received, then shall Heaven bestow on you its most cherished reward."

Plowden's form darkened the doorway.

"Shall I intrude if I enter?" he asked. "The time is almost up."

"No, come;" said Hubert, and rising he extended his hand to the lawyer. Then, turning to Margaret he continued:

"This is my faithful friend who also knew my secret and yet never betrayed me. I discovered that for the first time last night, when he tried to prevent the confession I made."

A vivid flush darted into the lawyer's cheeks, but it disappeared as suddenly, and he immediately changed the conversation to the plans he had been devising for Hubert's safety.

He spoke low, but still with no fear of being overheard, for his tact had disposed of the eavesdropping officer before he re-entered the cell.

"I saw Delmar this morning," he said, "and a few other friends, Hubert, and they all agree in pronouncing this confession of yours to be a mental illusion—the vagary of a mind unsettled by too close application to study. Your case shall be conducted on this ground; and since all that 'Roquelare' can do will be able to *prove*, absolutely *prove* nothing against you, we shall defeat its designs and you shall escape."

"No;" almost shouted Hubert, "that would be to doom myself again to the living death I have already endured. I have sinned, I shall undergo its punishment, and now I am only impatient to proclaim my crime in open court that my sentence may be immediately passed."

Plowden became furious. "You are mad, man; you would kill yourself," and then with a somewhat calmer aspect, he turned to Margaret, saying:

"Speak to him, Miss Calvert. Beg of this poor lunatic to have some mercy on himself."

She would have pleaded with him, but he waved her back repeating more earnestly than before:

"My determination is fixed "—he folded his arms and drew himself up—" I tell you the blood of my victim is crying for this atonement; a life for a life: "

He looked as if he saw another presence than that of Margaret and Plowden, and he made no reply when then lawyer said, passionately:

"Then we must save you from yourself."

Margaret burst into tears when she approached to take her leave.

"You will die here," she said, "in this desolate place with no companion, no friend near you."

"No, Margaret;" and for the first time that morning something like a smile crossed his features, "but I shall be less desolate, less friendless than I have been for eighteen months. My guilty secret kept me an outcast from all my kind. The mask I compelled myself to wear banned me from fellowship with any, but now that I am known, that I need play a false part no longer, this cell has more of peace and happiness, mockery though it be for me to use such words, than my own home has had since the commission of my crime."

The officer was at the door announcing that every minute of the time had expired. A hurried leave was taken, Plowden promising that his influence should break through prison discipline sufficiently to permit a daily visit from Margaret and himself.

In the hack the lawyer seemed absorbed in troubled

thought and Margaret also painfully abstracted. Not a word was spoken, until Margaret, as if suddenly remembering something, said with a start:

"Please stop at St. M——'s Church—I shall be in time for the last service."

A curious expression came into Plowden's face—a dark, ominous look, succeeded in a moment by one so sorrowful and tender that it seemed to change his whole countenance.

He bowed assent, regretted that it would be impossible for him to accompany her into the church, but proposed that the hack should wait for her; or, if she preferred, he would stop at her home on his way and send her own carriage for her. She declined both his proffers, saying that she always walked to and from church, and there was silence again until they arrived at the church.

The service had already commenced. Plowden walked with her to the porch of the church holding her hand as if he feared that she might break from him. He whispered:

"When you enter you will pray for your cousin?"

"Certainly," she answered, her tone expressing the surprise which she felt at such a question—every breath of hers was well-nigh a prayer for him whom she loved dearer than life.

Plowden whispered again: "May I ask you when you pray for him to pray also for another unhappy soul—one whose torture is as great as that which your cousin has endured?"

She bowed her head, and with a hurried adieu he turned away. Why she should pause and look back in the very act of entering the church she could hardly explain to herself unless it was owing to the lawyer's inexplicable words. She could neither understand them, nor the emotions they roused within her—mingled emotions of pity, dislike, and fear for him who had uttered them.

He, having descended the steps, was standing with his hat in his hand looking toward the open door of the edifice.

Margaret Calvert never forgot the expression of his face—Hubert's countenance when it showed his suffering most, never wore such an appalling look as this was.

He turned away, replaced his hat, and quickly entered the hack, while she went up the aisle, feeling like one just aroused from an ugly dream.

Many times during the day that look presented itself to her unbidden—unwished, it came before her; she sought no solution of it, for its cause was utterly beyond her comprehension. It was something about which she could ask no explanation, and though in a puzzling, tormenting way it would associate itself with every thought of Hubert, she could give no definite place to it in her fears for her cousin.

All that bright, mild Sabbath a certain inexplicable heaviness seemed to oppress the whole Bernot household; even the invalid seemed to be affected by unusual langor and weakness, so that Margaret feared to leave her, though she was most eager to see Father Germain in order to tell him about Hubert.

Late in the afternoon, however, Madame Bernot sank into one of her child-like slumbers, and her niece seized the opportunity to hurry forth on her anxious errand.

The good old clergyman was somewhat surprised to be summoned from the reading of his sacred Office to meet the young girl.

"Is your aunt worse? Does she require me!" he asked hurriedly.

"No, Father; but Hubert does, and I have come to tell you about it."

He conducted her into his study and prepared to listen, his face expressing the greatest concern and attention.

It was almost a repetition of the sacred confidence she had given in the confessional two or three days before, but this time there was no mention of herself. It was a simple recital of Hubert's suffering—of Hubert's remorse; but the clergyman's keen penetration discovered much that she had left unsaid.

He said. softly, when she had finished:

"Your cousin was not alone in his suffering—you, poor child have sorrowed with him—you also have borne his secret—is it not so?"

She averted her face, for tears which the tenderness of his tones, had called up, were rolling down her cheeks.

"I knew you were troubled about something," the kind voice resumed; "on the morning of my recent visit to your aunt when you met me at the door. You seemed to wish to speak to me, but something prevented; it was to tell me this unhappy secret, was it not?"

She bowed her head, still keeping her face averted, for the tears were coming faster.

Her sensitive heart could not as yet receive the tenderness and sympathy from which it had been debarred so long without being overcome by grateful emotion.

The priest waited until she grew calm.

I shall visit Hubert to-morrow and consult with him what to do about your aunt. By all means keep the news of this unhappy affair from her for the present—it will require the greatest care and tact to break it to her."

His face became very grave and sad, as if the hardest and most mournful part of the whole wretched affair would be the telling to Madame Bernot that her only child was a murderer.

"The servants," said Margaret, "will learn of it through the daily papers, and they may perhaps betray it to the attendant who waits upon my aunt, or they may speak of Hubert in such a manner as to cause his mother to suspect something."

"Tell them," said the priest, "tell them to-night before you retire, briefly what has happened; eighteen months ago when the papers were full of this case, and they themselves played important parts in it, they were careful at your desire to keep everything pertaining to it from your aunt. Surely you can trust them again."

And mingling a blessing and encouraging words with his kind adieu, the old clergyman saw her depart.

The evening had passed heavily in the servants' hall of the Bernot household. Some of the domestics according to their Sunday wont, had gone to church, or to visit their friends; but all had returned by a certain hour in order to be in time for a brief season of festivity which was according to their nightly custom.

Margaret, aware of this practice, waited until the hour arrived; then she rang for Annie Corbin and announced her desire to speak to the assembled help.

"Faith, I am afeerd there's something bad up," said McNamee when he heard the order, and Hannah Moore stood as if she had been suddenly paralyzed. A chorus of exclamations, and questions, and surmises burst from the others, in the midst of which the door opened and the young mistress entered.

Silence instantly reigned, and every face wore an expression of sympathy.

She approached slowly, as if she were not sure of how her communication would be received, and pausing when she reached the centre of the room she looked about her. Every eye was riveted upon her with something more than respectful attention—with a kind of sorrowful tenderness as if her fair, fragile appearance had struck at once the kindest chords in their warm Irish hearts.

Some one in respectful silence had placed a chair for her, but she waved it back with a smile, and as if the survey of their faces had given her confidence, she began:

"Eighteen months ago all of you were summoned

to give evidence on a sad and peculiar murder case. There were circumstances connected with that affair sufficient to arouse not only your curiosity but your suspicion; yet you forbore to wound me with either. I asked you at that time to aid me in keeping from my aunt all knowledge of it—you faithfully did so, I have come to night to make a similar request. Your master, —your kind, young master,—lies in a prison cell accused of the murder of this man who was found dead on the street eighteen months ago."

She paused as if she was startled by the sudden blanching of the faces about her; then, recovering herself she resumed:

"The papers to-morrow will probably contain full, though not strictly correct, accounts of the manner in which his arrest was affected, and all of you may be summoned again to give evidence. You may even hear a strange confession from Hubert's own lips, but may I ask, for his sake who was always a kind master to you, that whatever you may read, however startling the rumors you may hear, you will faithfully keep every syllable from reaching my aunt. It will be necessary to tell her sometime, but she must not know yet, perhaps not for some days. A single unguarded word uttered in her presence might cause her instant death. I know I have your sympathy my good, faithful people, shall I have your promise as well—your promise to aid me in keeping this unhappy affair from my aunt? Give no hint of it to her attendant, and as she does not read English, and has no friends in the city whom she can visit, she will learn nothing about it."

The help looked at McNamee as if they expected him to answer for them. Either because of the fearless, genuine honesty with which he always gave his opinion, or the true kindliness of his frank nature which won for him popularity wherever he went, or, maybe, both, the coachman was looked up to by his fellow-help, and on any occasion where leadership became necessary,

John was assigned the prominent position. On this occasion he understood what was required of him, and stepping slightly forward while a blush dyed his face, he began in his simple, hearty way to thank Miss Calvert in the name of his fellow-servants for the confidence she had again given them, and which he promised in the name of them all, should be sacredly kept, adding as the continued sound of his own voice made him less abashed:

"If we should be summoned again, we have only the same evidence to give that we gave before; whatever any of us think, whatever any of us *know*"—his eyes rested on Hannah Moore's face—" we have only to tell what we told before."

"Thank you, my kind friend," said Margaret, and she extended her hand to Mc Namee.

"Thank you all," she repeated, bowing to the others, and then with a kind "good-night" she retired.

Mc Namee's words, "whatever any of us *know*," had caused her heart to beat quickly, and as she ascended the stair she tried to think what it might be that any of them *could* know. She hurriedly reviewed every incident of the past eighteen months, back to the terrible night, or rather morning, when Hubert first told her of his crime. She felt certain that no one of the servants had seen or heard anything at that time which might cause suspicion. Then, what *could* they know? But, remembering in a moment that Hubert intended to accuse himself in open court,—that, as he had said to her, he would tell everything, she thought how little difference it made whether the help had become possessed of any of the facts or not.

Two sad to retire, she sat listlessly at her dressing table trying to look into the dark and impenetrable future.

A timid knock sounded and to her invitation to enter, Hannah Moore presented herself her face flushed and her eyes red from weeping.

Margaret kindly pointed to a chair, and the cook sank into it.

"You seem unwell," said Miss Calvert, gently, "what is the matter?"

"I'm trying to get courage to speak to you," answered Hannah with a burst of tears," knowing what you'll think of me after, and you so kind and considerate yourself."

"It is not that you intend to leave us?" asked Margaret with a sort of wail in her tones; for the thought flashed upon her, that perhaps the very servants would refuse to remain in a house, the master of which was charged with murder, and that this was but the foreshadowing of how all Hubert's friends would eventually desert him.

"God forbid, Miss, that I'd want to leave a home where I've had more happiness than ever I had since I left the ould country. It's not that, thank God, but it's something that will make you think me bold and impertinent, and stepping out of me place; but it's lain heavily on my heart this many a day, and it'll give me no peace till I tell you."

Margaret Calvert's face grew whiter. Was it something connected with Hubert's crime that she was going to tell, something which must be told when he should be brought to trial?

"It's about Mr. Plowden," resumed Hannah. "He comes to see you, and you seem to think kindly of him; and sure that's none of my business, only to bid you be careful. Don't trust him further than you can see, for he's deep and smart, an', maybe, he's only laying a trap to take your cousin in, the poor dear boy, that didn't do the deed at all,"

Margaret sprung terrified from her seat.

"What do you mean? what do you know about my cousin?"

Poor girl! the rapid succession of alarming events had totally unnerved her. Every moment she was forgetting that Hubert was bent on bringing himself to justice, and she was as wild with fear at the thought of still another possessing his secret, as though he had not already revealed that secret.

"Calm yourself, Miss, for God's sake!" exclaimed the cook, as she rose, terrified also at Miss Calvert's wild manner.

"God knows," she continued, "I didn't mean to speak of your cousin, but in my trouble it slipped from me."

"Tell me what you know about him," said Margaret, and she spoke with such trembling eagerness that the words came forth brokenly.

"Oh, Miss, it's only the night that he came back after we thought he had gone away to travel. I couldn't sleep that night with my rheumatism pains, and I was up when the door bell rang. I thought to answer it, that maybe your aunt was taken worse and a doctor had been sent for; but on my way down I heard the door opened, and I heard some one come in. I listened, for I was anxious about Madame Bernot, but I could hear nothing more. I waited in the hall that Mr. Hubert's room opens from, and in a little while I heard some one coming up. It was so dark I knew I couldn't be seen, and I thought it would be better to stay there till whoever it was should pass, for fear it might seem queer to find me in that place at such a time. I could tell by the sound of the steps there were two persons coming up, and by the rustling of a dress that one of them anyway, was a woman; I heard whispering, but I couldn't understand what was said, till they came so close that it was only by wedging myself into the niche in the wall, that I saved myself from being found out, and then I heard one of them whisper:

"'Don't ask me what has happened.'

They passed on, and I heard some door softly opened and closed. I went back to my own room, thinking queer things of what I had heard, and dreaming of it when I went to sleep. I didn't speak of it next day, for I feared you'd hear it, and that perhaps you wouldn't believe how I came to be listening at such a time of the night. Afterward, when we came to know that you were held as a witness, and saw in the papers all about that case, I kept thinking of what I had heard that night; but I didn't think anything about Mr. Hubert. I didn't think one of the whispering voices was his, though I was almost sure the rustling dress belonged to you. I didn't speak of it, for, somehow, there was a great fear on me that if I did it might injure you. I didn't think of Mr Hubert at all, for I believed as all the help did, that he was far away then. But when Mr. Plowden examined me in the court—when he asked me if there was ever anything to make me think your actions strange, or to suspect Mr. Hubert hadn't left home at all—you looked at me, and somehow in a minute, it all came into my mind. I knew then that one of the whispering voices was Mr. Hubert's; that what had happened was this murder, and that you knew all about it. But I'd have cut my tongue out before I'd have told it there, or told it anywhere. My heart ached for you, and many a time since, when I've seen you sad and sick, and heard the rest of the help remarking on the ill looks of yourself and your cousin, I knew it was the secret that was killing you both.

"I'd have tried to comfort you in my humble way, but I feared you'd be frightened at my knowing so much, or that you'd be angry at my presumption. I never spoke of it to the others, and I tried to keep down the suspicions that would come in their minds sometimes.

"When I saw Mr. Plowden coming here so regular, and the warm way yourself and Mr. Hubert seemed to take to him, my heart misgave me, for I knew what his nature was. I'm bound by a promise to the dead—*his* dead—not to speak, so I can't tell you something which would make you distrust him too. I didn't know him in the court at first, for I didn't look at him much till it came my turn to be examined by him, but then I knew him, and he knew me; he couldn't help but know me, and I saw he did by the look in his eyes. Oh, why was Mr. Hubert mixed up with this case at all! Why did he have anything to do with the murdered man lying in his cold grave this night, and I not able to tell you what I know!"

And Hannah Moore flung her apron over her head, and sobbed bitterly.

Margaret was as white and motionless as a statue. She could make no attempt to bring order out of the chaos of thoughts caused by this strange communication. Her imagination was too wild and too swift in its erratic resolution to succumb to her will now, so she could only wait as one on a rack might do, not for relief, but for change of torture.

Hannah lowered her apron, and resumed:

"I wanted to tell you many a time to be careful how you'd trust the smart lawyer; I feared he'd ferret Mr. Hubert's secret out, and use all his means to bring the poor young man to punishment, for the sake of getting himself a fine name. I thought of trying to see him in some secret way, when I'd let him know that I was watching his actions, and that perhaps *I'd* tell something in the long run if he mean't any harm to Mr. Hubert; but I didn't know how to manage a secret meeting with him, so I only kept on fretting to myself, and worrying, when I saw you two young things sinking under the secret you thought no one else knew anything about.

"Sometimes the help would talk of Mr. Plowden's attentions to you, and to-day when you went out with him it was said that he was really paying his addresses to you; then, I couldn't rest, knowing what I do about him. When you came down stairs to-night and told us of Mr. Hubert's arrest my heart jumped into my throat, for I thought it might be through Mr. Plowden he was taken, and then I resolved that I'd tell you all that I could, without breaking my promise to the dead. Maybe he's different now; maybe he's sorry for the poor heart he wouldn't comfort before its death, and maybe he's very good; but be careful of him, Miss Calvert,—don't trust him too much, and forgive me my boldness in telling you this."

And again she covered her face with her apron and sobbed bitterly.

It seemed to be little use for Margaret to seek light out of the thick darkness which was settling upon her.

More perplexing and more numerous were the mysteries which appeared to grow out of this one sin. If Hannah Moore could but tell what she knew of Plowden, but to stop short, just where doubt and conjecture became absolute pain, seemed so cruel. All that the cook related might after all, be only the vagaries of a suspicious mind which had been too ready to build huge piles of evidence on slightest foundations; but Plowden's inexplicable look of the morning rose before her: as if to strengthen the testimony just given.

There was something, nay, there was a good deal in what Hannah Moore had just told, and there was much in that appalling look.

Did it mean that he had been hunting Hubert to his doom, that his passionate avowal of love to her, his affection for Hubert, his expressed determination to save him, were but so many masks to hide his base object—was it possible that he had been working with " Roquelare " ? At that stage of her wild conjectures there swept into her soul such a flood of bitterness as she had experienced never before even in her moments of sharpest agony.

Trust betrayed; and such a trust! Winning friendship and affection only that he might effect a base purpose—truly in the past hour, the world had turned upside down to her and left her drifting hopelessly out to an unknown, bleak shore.

Hardest of all was the search for her own line of conduct, amid so much broken trust and cruel deception. Since Hubert's arrest she had clung to Plowden as the one mutual friend whose legal skill, whose powerful influence was to bring some degree of light out of the great darkness. Now, if this was to be no more, if she must discard him herself, and warn Hubert against him, what would be left? Nothing; no one—for in all the vast city Margaret could think of no friend whose influence would assist in this case, or whose sympathy could support her, and amid Hubert's friends there were none who possessed the skill, or influence of Plowden.

The warm-hearted cook had only made the lot of her young mistress harder to bear, and had she not been too absorbed in her own tears, she might have seen more suffering in Miss Calvert's face than she had seen there ever before.

Sorrow makes the best of us selfish in some degree. Margaret, absorbed in her own wild thoughts, forgot for a few moments the presence of the faithful domestic and the effort she had made to do that she deemed to be her duty; but it flashed on her suddenly, and she held out both hands to the weeping woman, and said softly:

"How can I thank you, my faithful friend? You, to whom no confidence was given, have kept what you knew, so well."

"Don't speak of it, Miss. I'd do far more if it was in my power, and I'm only fearing that I spoke too late about Mr. Plowden. Perhaps he's worked harm already to Mr. Hubert."

"I don't know—I hope not," and Margaret's lips grew white with mental anguish.

"He seems to be Hubert's best friend now, and mine, so far as helping my cousin is concerned. Hubert gave himself up, publicly confessed his crime, and he intends to make the same confession when he is brought to trial."

"The poor boy; may the Lord help him!" ejaculated Hannah Moore.

Margaret continued: "It is due to your faithfulness to tell you this much. My cousin did not intend to commit murder; he was maddened to it, and there are circumstances connected with that murdered man which, if made known, will do much to lessen my cousin's guilt. The whole dreadful case will be revived again I suppose. All of us may be examined over——"

"Faith, they'll get nothing out of me but what they got before, if they examine me fifty times," interrupted the cook.

But Margaret, without heeding the interruption, continued. "And through all the trying time I shall have but one friend to turn to—Mr. Plowden. I must trust him still; I must lean on him, be he what he may, until this trial is over. If he be our enemy instead of our friend, then God help him and pity us!"

"Amen;" ejaculated the cook. And then, with painful hesitation in her manner, she said:

"Maybe it'll be better not to tell Mr. Plowden that I've said anything to you. He knows how I am bound by oath never to speak of what I know, and it might make him fiercer like, if he knew I had been trying to put you on your guard."

Margaret faintly smiled.

"For Hubert's sake I shall be sure to conceal every suspicion from Mr. Plowden—I shall endeavor to treat him as I have already done—so have no fear."

"Thank you, Miss! and now have you entirely forgiven my boldness in speaking as I did?"

"There is nothing to forgive." Margaret replied, "but there is cause for great gratitude on my part."

She wrung the cook's hand to reassure her, and said a kind good night.

Hannah Moore, as she passed through the hall, still wiping her eyes, murmured to herself:

"Thanks be to God, there's a great load lifted from my mind."

A load lifted from her only to be added to the burden of doubt and fear and anguish, which her young Mistress carried.

CHAPTER XII.

NEVER were exertions more vigorous for the attainment of an object than were those made by Plowden in behalf of young Bernot.

But at every step he was opposed by the agencies of "Roquelare." Like Freemasonry it seemed to have its members where one would least expect to find them, and to live in a labyrinth of grips, and passwords, and signs. The aid that otherwise would have been volunteered to the criminal was shudderingly withheld when it was known that he was hounded by "Roquelare," and the theory that he was suffering from a mental hallucination was generally abandoned when it was known that his arrest had been made through its instrumentality.

Plowden cursed through his teeth and worked the harder to discover what proofs of the crime, if any, Bertoni had collected; but in that particular instance his skill was of no avail—the detectives of "Roquelare" did their work too well.

Once they met on the street—Plowden and Bertoni—the former on his way to Hubert's prison, the latter returning from court. The men lifted their hats and smiled; Bertoni's a smile of malicious triumph, Plowden's an ironical grin. Plowden turned when Bertoni had passed and hissed through his set teeth:

"Curse you; I'll foil you yet, if I have to—"

He stopped suddenly, and went hurriedly on his way with the unfinished sentence sticking in his throat. It stuck there till he reached the prison, bringing out great globules of perspiration on his forehead with every step, and then it sank slowly and chokingly back, for he lacked courage to send it further.

Father Germain had visited Hubert, and to Margaret, who saw him directly after, he said:

"Poor fellow! it is a sad case——all the sadder because he holds exaggerated ideas of his sin, and while he is so anxious to plead guilty in court, he is just as determined not to disclose anterior circumstances which might put the matter in a very different light."

"I know," said Margaret sorrowfully, "in talking to me he has said that neither he nor I could break the promise given to his mother, that he would not break it, even to save his life, and he has made me make the same promise."

The priest shook his head.

"There is but one thing that will relieve his scruples, when his mother knows all she will release you both from your promise, and she will command him to declare everything connected with this unhappy affair."

"Yes; but, Father; when can she be told?" and Margaret's voice grew piteous. "She was unusually worse last night, so that we were obliged to summon the physician. He came again early this morning, and said that she must have absolute quiet."

Her voice became broken from tears.

"My poor child! you forget that it is all in God's hands."

In God's hands! There was a dreary sort of comfort in the thought, but still there was comfort, and Margaret dried her tears, and went forth, if not cheerfully, at least with so calm an aspect, that few meeting her would have dreamed of the aching heart she bore.

Days passed—miserable, montonous days that dawned and set on the same sorrow, on the same anxiety. Rumor had it that Bernot's trial was postponed to afford Bertoni an opportunity of producing important witnesses who would testify against the prisoner, and rumor also circulated that the young man was daily sinking under prison discipline. The discipline had been made comparatively light for him, owing to the influence of the feminine portion of fashionable society, who had longed to make Bernot an idol and now exalted him into a hero.

His crime, the curious and romantic way in which it had become known, was just the sensation for which their frivolous minds craved, and despite the remonstrances of their callous brothers, and the commands of their practical fathers, gushing fair ones would persist in giving vent to their friendship and sympathy in daily gifts of flowers and books, and choice delicacies.

"He was so handsome," said one, languishingly.

"And so *distingue*," repeated a second.

"And so talented," added a third.

But no one spoke of Margaret.

The world, according to its wont, extended its arms to the guilty one, because of his wealth and his position, but for her who was supposed to have neither, and whose faithfulness and devotion should, at least, have awakened pity, it had only silence, or scorn. Fashionable Mrs. Delmar was full of matronly sympathy and tenderness for the unfortunate criminal. The peculiar turn which events had taken, discovered to her scheming mind an entirely new source through which she might make Hubert fit into her own private plans. She had never supposed for one moment the existence of a more than cousinly attachment between Hubert and Margaret, and had she done so the report of Miss Calvert's betrothal to Plowden—a report which was generally believed—would have disabused her mind of that idea. Fashionable society had declared young Bernot to be "fancy free" without even a passing preference for any of his fair friends, unless indeed his frequent visits to the Delmar residence, and his friendly courtesy to Miss Delmar when they met at public assemblies, might be taken as proofs of a contrary fact. But the gossips had intimated that these intentions were rather owing to the warm friendship which existed between the young men, and Louise herself had not been anxious for the circulation of a rumor which she knew was entirely devoid of truth.

Now, however, that the young man was in prison on a charge of murder—in a position in which it was reasonable to suppose that former friends and acquaintances would neglect him—Mrs. Delmar fancied that she had a grand opportunity of showing him the constancy of *her* friendship; an excuse, as it were, to let him know the ardor of her daughter's affection for him. The feeling on the part of Louise was not as ardent as the wise mother desired it to be, but she trusted in her own ability to raise it to a white heat when necessary.

She was deterred from her purpose by no fastidiousness regarding Hubert's crime; that she considered a mere youthful indiscretion arising from his natural impetuosity—a crime, if crime it was, which, at the very worst, the law would punish only by imprisonment which could be very much shortened by influence. She frequently pictured to herself, young Bernot, on his release, hastening to her and pouring out his grati- for her kindness to him in his dark days, and what more natural than that her long-cherished hope of marriage between him and Louise should then be realized? Not that her matronly heart yearned to call Hubert "son" because of his own intrinsic worth, but because her matronly prudence coveted his wealth.

His wealth, or that of some other equally rich son-in-law would be necessary to continue the fashionable extravagance without which Mrs. Delmar could scarcely exist; and Eugene had already protested against the frequent calls on him when the ladies' own ample incomes were expended, and he had more than once threatened to moderate their style of living.

The diplomatic woman would have brought her tactics to bear on some other of the wealthy admirers who appeared to flutter about her daughter's shrine, but there Eugene himself interfered. He jealously guarded his sister, and discountenanced so sternly any but mere passing attentions from the gentlemen of her acquaintance that she rarely attempted more than a brief flirtation.

To Louise, this strict guardianship made little difference. So long as she was permitted the winter's round of balls and parties, and the summer's stay at watering places, she was content—as much of her heart as had not been warped by her mother's example and instruction, or hardened by the lessons of fashionable folly which she had begun to learn from her very infancy, and which she had continued to learn for over a score of years, never had been very seriously touched. Perhaps the nearest approach to it had been affected, by Hubert Bernot; for, mingled with her intense fear of him—a fear approaching to awe—was a feeling such as no other man had ever roused in her heart. She could not understand it, and she tried to forget it; but possibly it was the existence of that feeling which prompted her to agree with her brother when he was wont to say in reply to his mother's oft expressed wish for Louise's marriage:

"There is sufficient time; she is young yet, and it would cause such a break in our home."

Good-natured fellow as he was, he little dreamed, even while he wondered that his mother should evince so much anxiety and sympathy for Hubert, of the real object of that solicitude and tenderness.

Margaret Calvert rarely entered into the wise lady's calculations. She had settled it satisfactorily in her own mind that the young girl would be married to Plowden as soon as the ceremony could be performed with propriety, and she relied on her own kindness to Hubert to counteract any influence which his cousin might exert. Should she in the future be reproached by Bernot for her neglect of Margaret, she could very easily throw all the blame on Margaret's self, and also impute to her the more serious charge of openly rejecting every offer of friendship made by herself and her daughter.

Thus shrewd Mrs. Delmar laid her plans, and having sufficiently instructed her daughter, Hubert was treated to an unbroken series of what the fashionable woman was pleased to term " comforting visits." How he bore the inflictions—for they were nothing else—was attested by the relieved expression which came into his face the instant that the cell door closed after the elegantly attired ladies.

Mrs. Delmar spared no pains to avoid coming in contact with Margaret Calvert. She entertained a nervous dread of meeting the girl,—particularly of meeting her in Hubert's cell, where she feared Margaret's presence might frustrate the execution of her own little private plans, and owing to that dread, she at length grew to hate Margaret with a hatred all the more bitter *because* of the inoffensiveness of its victim.

Her first inquiry of the grim-faced warden whose duty was to admit visitors to the prisoner, was invariably to learn whether Miss Calvert was in the cell—Margaret, from her frequent visits, was well known, to every official —when informed that Margaret was there, under pretence of not disturbing the cousins' interview, she would withdraw with her daughter, and the Delmar carriage would roll away, to return at another hour.

But little as the fashionable woman suspected, or would have believed it had she been told, it was due to the influence of the girl whom she so causelessly hated that Hubert Bernot received her and her daughter with a show of affability. Not through Margaret's direct influence, for she was not even aware of the ladies' regular visits. Hubert rarely spoke of them; for these two divided hearts—and yet hearts that were so closely knit by the bond of a mutual love—had so many other things about which to think and speak. He, with all

his worldly lore, his brilliant mind, found he had much
to learn from this simple girl, who was rich only in
natural virtues and the grace that comes from prayer.
Step by step she led him up from the miry path where
his feet would slip and his garments trail in the slough
of crime, to heights where the fresh breezes of a new
life, evoked out of his own penitence, blew upon him,
and gave him renewed vigor for his rugged journey.

Father Germain doubted that his influence or
counsels, or even consolations, would have been of any
use if the way had not been first prepared by the teachings of this Heaven-inspired girl. Her whole heart,
her life was in this task, of bringing Hubert's soul
entirely back to its God.

That her efforts were not without avail his changed
demeanor showed. He was no longer wild and turbulent as he was wont to be at times in his interviews
with Margaret during the first days of his imprisonment
fiercely denouncing himself, and passionately importunate for the time of his trial. He had grown strangely
calm, promised Father Germain he would do nothing
rashly, but let the law quietly take its course, and he
had even acquiesced in some directions given by
Plowden.

An unusual gentleness characterized his manner—
as if Margaret Calvert had been imparting some of her
unselfishness, her own thoughtful consideration for
others to him, and in that lay the secret of his kindly
reception of Mrs. Delmar and her daughter. Not divining the motive which prompted the visits, he fancied
he ought to be grateful for them, and he strove to smile
and seem cheerful, even when his soul was vexed and
writhed in torture at the prolonged interviews.

Thus Louise Delmar saw him as he had never
appeared to her before—he was never cynical now; he
no longer talked at her from heights which made her
dizzy to approach; he brought himself down to her own
low level—"making himself agreeable," as she called

it—and alas, in so doing, took undisputed possession of her frivolous heart. Had Hubert dreamed of the effect of what he intended to be simply courteous conduct, he would have recoiled from the Delmars as he used to do from the fancied visions of his murdered victim; but he did not dream of it, and so continued, at every visit, making the poor girl's heart flutter more and more painfully.

Mrs. Delmar knew it, however, and rejoiced. She mistook Hubert's changed demeanor for a growing attachment to her daughter, and fed her willing mind with her own ambitious hopes.

Eugene Delmar, good meaning fellow that he was, always paid his visits to the prison on foot. His mother carefully refrained from asking him to accompany herself and Louise on these errands. He was "so stupidly good," she said to herself, that he would be more likely to counteract her schemes, if he knew them, than to aid them, by any influence he might possess.

The poor patient invalid—her illness had taken a more severe form. There was more acute suffering and a greater duration of it every day than hitherto; but her eyes never failed to wander to the thorn-crowned head or her lips to murmur "Thy will be done!"

Perchance it was in that room, by the side of that sick chair, that Margaret herself learned the lessons which she so successfully taught to Hubert, for many a time when she saw the invalid's face contract with pain, and a death-like hue from very agony spread over it, and yet heard the white lips murmur the sentence which was so perpetually upon them, "Thy will be done," had she herself fallen on her knees and murmured, with a heart broken with sorrow, "Thy will be done!"

A physician came every day now, not with the expectation or hope of being able to effect even a partial cure, but to give such transient relief as skill might afford to extreme pain.

And Father Germain came every day, not so much

to minister to her spiritual wants as to learn when her state of health would permit her hearing the truth about Hubert.

But every day the physician shook his head to the priest's inquiry, declaring she must not be told yet in any circumstances, and every day Margaret's heart sunk when she had to say no, to Hubert's eager question:

"*Does my mother know yet?*"

Madame Bernot had continually inquired for him, wondering, after the first few days, why he did not write, and Dr. Durant called Margaret aside and told her it would be necessary to have Hubert write letters of some sort to his mother, as the suspense and anxiety occasioned by his fancied silence were aggravating her disease.

So Hubert wrote, dating his letters from the little country place on the Hudson whence he had started on the traveling tour he had taken in company with a college mate over a year and a half before. He put no invented descriptions in the missives—he filled them with no invented incidents; he could not have done that; but he wrote pages with that peculiarly devoted affection which seems only to exist between a widowed mother and an only son. They were boyish from their very simplicity—they were almost holy from the depth of religious feeling which pervaded them.

He gradually began to speak of another as occupying the position in which he himself was placed a prisoner for the murder of a fellow-being months before. He described the fictitious criminal as having a widowed mother, loving and patient like his own, and he conveyed the impression that he was helping the poor condemned to bear manfully the punishment of his sin. This plan afforded him full opportunity for laying bare his own remorse and penitence to his mother's eye, and had it not been for Margaret's vigilant care, he would have written, in the heat of his emotions, more than sufficient to betray that it was his own state he was describing.

Madame Bernot listened to those letters as she had never listened before to any others—even his. In one of them, he wrote:

"Tell me, mother, words to say to this poor sinner —you who have suffered so long, whose suffering came upon you in one fell blow, who forgave even when your untimely dead were mutely imploring vengeance from their coffins, who made others forgive when home and hearts were miserably broken; you who have shut yourself away from all the world to pray and suffer in silence must know how to comfort this poor sin-burdened soul. Impart this comfort to me that I may in turn transmit it to him, that I may speak words of consolation to his broken-hearted mother."

The invalid requested Margaret to read this passage again, and when her niece had obeyed she signified that she wished her hands placed together for prayer, and then her clear, sweet voice, which no suffering seemed to have power to weaken, lifted itself with such fervor in its tones as could only be born of years of self-sacrifice and suffering:

"Oh, my God, Thou hast taken all but him! Thou hast cut off one in the midst of a sin, but Thou makest this one, whom Thou hast spared, that which I prayed to see him! Thou hast made him dutiful and mindful of Thee, and now Thou makest him 'Comforter of the afflicted'! Make me suffer—increase my torture; but, oh, my God! pardon him who has gone, and preserve the innocence of this only child Thou hast left me."

Then she said to Margaret:

"Tell him in your answer that out of the abundance of his own heart will he find words of consolation for his grief-stricken friends. He places too high a value on my poor sufferings; he forgets that I am only a poor, feeble mother who has been striving to bring her sorrows to the foot of Calvary, but is yet only wrestling with the fears and agony of Gethsemane. But tell him also, Margaret, that my heart is flooded with joy at the thought of the help he is trying to afford these sorrowing people ; tell him to remain with them, to be a son to this poor afflicted mother, to lead her—as from his letters he must know how to do—to Calvary's height, and God's blessing and mine will be his work."

It seemed to Margaret as if her heart would burst. To continue this deception was harder than anything else connected with this sad affair; and when Father Germain paid his visit that day she found an opportunity of secretly telling him her trouble. He knew that Hubert wrote letters to his mother, and, from Margaret, had learned something of their contents; but she gave him this one to read. A bright hopeful look spread over the priest's face when he had read it.

"It seems like an inspiration from Almighty God, my dear child, to have him write in this manner," he said. "It is the very best method that could be taken to prepare her mind, and it will do so without any consciousness on her part, or any interference or assistance from those who may be about her. When the time comes to tell her, there will be far less danger to herself to apprehend; so now, my dear child, remember it is all in God's hands, and you have nothing to do but perform your duty as you have already faithfully done."

But that duty grew harder every day, and nothing but the firm faith and hope in God's care, with which she had fortified herself, would have borne poor Margaret through.

"It is His will," she murmured, when, seeing her aunt's fearful paroxysms of pain, she thought of the anguish yet in store for the poor suffering creature.

"It is His will," she murmured again, when she beheld Hubert's evidently failing health, and thought, with a sudden icy pressure round her heart, that in any case her cousin's days in this world were numbered.

The report which said the young man's health was

failing was true; but the rumor that added "failing under prison discipline," was not the fact.

It was the sudden and entire loosening of the severe mental strain which he had kept up for eighteen long months; it was the influence of the spiritual over the material—in a word, it was his soul, beautified as it was, by humble, holy penitence, and filled with a rush of exquisite feelings, the like of which he had never experienced before, that had gained such complete ascendency over his body as to make it daily grow weaker and more spiritual.

He was not without a physician's care, for, from the first day of his imprisonment, he was regularly visited by two medical gentlemen who ranked high in the profession. Their visits were paid by order of Bertoni, that on the day of trial their testimony might prove Hubert Bernot to be of perfectly sane mind. Plowden smiled bitterly when he first became aware of that, and muttered savagely to himself:

"He thinks he is securely closing every loophole; but, by Heaven! I'll foil him yet."

If Hubert was himself conscious of this daily decline in his health, he made no allusion to it, and when questioned by anxious Margaret, or sympathetic Father Germain, smiled and answered that he would be quite well as soon as his trial should be finished and his sentence passed. But for all that, and despite the visits of the strange physicians, whom Margaret looked upon with a sort of terror, because they came through order of that mysterious agent of "Roquelare," his cousin would have Dr. Durant visit him, and even prescribe, which that physician did to quiet her fears, though he well knew the inefficacy of his prescriptions to restore a constitution that was being undermined in the peculiar way in which Hubert's was.

Mrs. Delmar was also frightened at the increasing transparency of the young man's countenance and the supernatural lustre of his eyes—frightened lest death should step in and frustrate her plans, and insisted upon sending her own physician to attend him till assured by Hubert that he had already the services of three very excellent medical men.

Plowden still pursued his indefatigable labors in Hubert's behalf; and Margaret, when she saw his earnestness, as she could not help but see it, and the almost painful intensity with which he applied himself to collect the merest fragments that might be turned to testimony in Hubert's favor, reproached herself for having entertained any suspicions of the friendship he professed for herself and her cousin.

But still, his look at the foot of the church-steps came back to her, and in company with what Hannah Moore had said; she wished a hundred times she had neither seen the one nor heard the other.

She had confided it all to Father Germain—her doubts and fears, and perhaps unkind suspicions of the lawyer; but the priest's advice was to pursue the course she had already begun, as there was no alternative but to continue to trust Plowden till something more definite about him could be learned. So she strove to make her demeanor such as it had been before any suspicion entered her mind; and though she was not at all times as successful as she would wish to be, she was sufficiently so to prevent Plowden from observing any change.

CHAPTER XIII.

The under-waiter in the Bernot household had a weakness for musical clubs, and carried that weakness so far as to become a member of one himself, and to undertake a few lessons on the banjo from an amateur performer on that instrument. But either the teacher failed to work rightly on the musical genius of his pupil, or the pupil himself lacked ability to profit by the lessons of his tutor, for the persevering efforts of three evenings a week for many months had failed to make the under-waiter bring forth a single tune from his much abused instrument.

Hannah Moore had borne the excruciating discord in her kitchen, and John McNamee had endured it in the carriage-house, whither the under-waiter was accustomed to go in his leisure moments during the day, that he might learn from John what he thought of his musical progress; but both cook and coachman at last protested against the torture, and the cook assuming a motherly sort of patronage toward the effeminate-looking little fellow, had seriously advised him not to be making a fool of himself any longer with the provoking thing, "but just be sensible, like other people."

And the little under-waiter tired of the labor that was bringing no reward, ruefully adopted her counsel, and sold his banjo. But he couldn't give up his visits to the club, where at least he could pretend, by his applause, that he understood and valued good music with the best of them.

Yet the little man's heart had been secretly gladdened some months before, and his ambition to be considered a connoissieur in music very suddenly re-kindled. Among the occasional new-comers which the club admitted to membership had been one who was apparently a skilled performer on the violin—a genial, jolly fellow. He easily won the friendship of all, but seemed especially to attach himself to Samuel Lewis, the little under-waiter. When he learned (and he was not long in making the discovery) that "Little Sam," as Lewis was dubbed by his fellow-servants, had a weakness, and that weakness was to be able to play something on some instrument, he graciously favored the whim. He talked music at the little man—played music for him, pretending that his fine musical ear could detect beauties of harmony inaudible to any one else, and at length proposed to give Lewis instructions on the instrument for a trifling consideration.

Lewis was in ecstacies. He forgot his former failure or remembered it only as the fault of an incompetent teacher, and, availing himself of the proffer, determined to keep these lessons secret from his fellow-servants till he could astonish them with an unmistakable evidence of his musical ability. Somehow, the much desired result was as slow and difficult in coming as it had been before, but the teacher was as earnest and hopeful as he had been at first, and the little man believed his repeated failures were only what every beginner had to experience.

They hob-nobbed together—teacher and pupil—in restaurants, over tempting little treats provided by Lewis in grateful acknowledgment for the teacher's cheap terms, and, under the influence of stimulants, which the tutor insisted on providing, the little man was wont to grow very communicative. He had frequently invited the tutor to call on him, when he would have been delighted to introduce him to his fellow-servants; but jolly Mr. Liverspin always declined the invitation.

"I know you, my dear fellow," he would say, "and that is sufficient" and then he would artfully question "Little Sam" on the kind of " Boss " with whom he lived, and, as Hubert's and Margaret's indulgence to their domestics was a theme upon which the little under-waiter easily waxed eloquent, cunning Mr. Liverspin grew wise very speedily. He used to seem affected when " Little Sam" described the apparent ill-health of Hubert and Margaret, and would shake his head in a lugubrious manner while Lewis recounted all the gossip about the Bernots that took place among the Bernot servants.

When Hubert was arrested, and " Little Sam " told Mr. Liverspin all about how Miss Calvert informed the help of that sad affair, the tutor seemed so affected that it required several applications of his handkerchief to his face before he could ask a single question. The sight of this evidently sincere emotion increased little Sam's desire to be more communicative, and so Mr. Liverspin found himself as fully enlightened upon every point connected with that particular occurrence as though he had been present when Miss Calvert made her request of the servants.

Though the little man was somewhat "in his cups," still, after that chat, he had an uncomfortable feeling that he had been talking too much; perhaps it was owing to Liverspin, who, being slightly off his guard for a moment, had permitted his face to wear a different expression from his wont. Be that as it may, Lewis determined not to let his fellow-help know that he had been saying so much to Liverspin, especially Hannah Moore, who, on "Little Sam's " representations, had been anxious to see the new acquaintance, but, when she learned that Mr. Liverspin refused all invitations to come to the house, delivered as her indignant opinion :

" Them that keeps company with servants out of doors and are above coming to see them in their master's place ain't fit acquaintances for nobody."

So the little man set his teeth hard that no impulsive communications regarding Liverspin might find their way to the ears of his fellow-help, and when he felt compelled to make some reply to their observations, he was careful to use only his stereotyped expression "that's a fact."

Generous John McNamee was constantly on the alert to learn all he could regarding the impending trial, retailing the slightest fragment to Hannah Moore, between whom and himself a warm friendship existed —a friendship begotten of their mutual sympathy for imprisoned Hubert and unhappy Margaret. And both the unselfish domestics so constantly exhorted the others to be careful and watchful of everything pertaining to their young master's interest, that when they were served with subpœnas which compelled their attendance a second time in court, Hubert Bernot had no truer friends than that little circle of warm-hearted, faithful Irish domestics. They prayed in their fervent way for him and devoted Margaret; and on the evening previous to the day appointed for the trial they remained together late, consulting about and arranging their statements for the morrow.

The evening before the day of trial, Plowden, by great effort, had obtained permission for Margaret to see Hubert again.

She had been with him in the morning in company with Father Germain, and both had entreated him to permit the circumstances of the past which led to his crime to be told in court, but he was as flint to every appeal, answering:

"It is part of the atonement I am trying to make to permit nothing to be told save the crime itself. I will have nothing said that will tend to extenuate my guilt, and I cannot and shall not break the promise given to my mother; It is cruel to persist in asking me to do otherwise."

And the priest and Margaret desisted from further efforts, and, for the first time since Hubert's incarceration, his cousin's heart swelled with a rebellious indignation, and an impatient murmur rose to her lips. It was almost as if she had said:

"Why is God so cruel? Why does he not make my aunt well enough to be told that she may release Hubert from his promise?"

But, with the very first word of the reply which Father Germain made to her sorrowful repining, when both had reached the sun-shiny street, her poor crushed heart regained resignation, and she murmured, while the scalding tears ran down her cheeks:

"Thy will be done."

"It is somewhat singular," said the priest, "that Mr. Plowden has never requested Hubert or you to tell him what you formerly knew of this poor murdered man. Surely it would be necessary to help the defence of your cousin; however he seems so devoted to the case and so thoroughly understands his business, that there is little danger of his neglecting so important a point."

Margaret made no reply to that, but, in a few minutes referred to the command Hubert had enjoined upon her of giving as her testimony in court every word of the confidence with which he had entrusted her so many weary months ago.

"It will be helping to criminate him," she said, with a fresh burst of tears.

"Nay, my poor child," answered the priest," it will make him neither more nor less than what he is in the sight of God; neither will it definitely prove his crime in the eyes of men; and since his peace of mind here, and perhaps his salvation hereafter, depends upon acceding to his wish, there is no alternative for you but to drink the bitter cup."

She had not promised obedience to Hubert's command, but possibly the prisoner had construed her silence into assent. However, when she returned that evening, accompanied by Plowden, Hubert at once repeated his request of the morning.

Plowden had left the cell to walk in the corridor—he invariably did when the cousins were together. His quick tread, and the restless look in his eyes betrayed the anxiety, and even nervousness, under which he labored.

Hubert besought Margaret, by her love for his soul—her earthly love for him—her affection for her aunt, to grant this, his one earnest wish.

"Why do you hesitate?" he asked. "You prayed for pardon and peace for me; you begged to suffer that my mental torture might be lessened. You have won for me a reconciliation with my Maker; now will you hinder the completion of such atonement as is in my power? You kept my secret for me, and I suffered the more because of your very faithfulness. I bid you fling it away forever now, to make it as public as you have hitherto kept it secret, and I shall be free. Oh, Margaret! why keep away the peace which will come to me when you have done this?"

He spoke in a calm, even, low tone, without a trace of passion, and his face lit up with some strange feeling that riveted Margaret's eyes upon it.

"I will try to do what you request," she answered, quiveringly, "But I also have a favor to ask of you. By the love you bear your mother, promise that you will plead not guilty, to-morrow in court. Of that mercy, at least, you may avail yourself without scruple, and for the sake of your mother, Hubert, I beg you to do so."

"Be it so," he replied sadly; "I shall plead 'not guilty.'"

"And I," she answered, "shall do what you ask, though my heart should break in the effort."

Plowden, entering the cell to announce that the time was up, heard Margaret's reply, and he averted his head that he might not see the suffering depicted in her face. When she had taken her tearful leave of Hubert, and thrown herself back in the carriage to weep unrestrainedly, Plowden said, abruptly:

"May I ask what request Hubert has been imposing on you, the granting of which seemed to cost you so much?"

She told him, adding:

"This morning was the first time he desired me to do so; I had thought it would be sufficient to give only the evidence I had given before."

"So it would be," said Plowden, hurriedly; "nor could they force you to tell more; but Hubert is mad, and the promise is not binding,"

He knew even while he spoke how little Margaret would concur in such an opinion, but he was not prepared for the passionate manner in which she proclaimed her duty to Hubert.

"But think, Miss Calvert," said the lawyer, slowly, and as if he were trying to stifle some impulse which urged him to speak as passionately as his companion had done, "your evidence may do much to weaken the defence—may frustrate every chance of acquittal, and may tend to make the sentence a long imprisonment."

"But it will bring peace to his soul: a peace that will sweeten even a life-long imprisonment," she answered.

It was too dark for either to see the other's face, and Plowden was glad, for he felt that he could not have controled the expression which swept into his countenance, and which, if Margaret had beheld it, would have aroused anew her wonder and alarm.

"Suppose," he said, after a pause, "that your evidence would be sufficient to commit him—would cause him to be sentenced to death, would you still give it?"

"If his soul's salvation—if his peace of mind were at stake, I would."

"And yet this man, whom you would deliver up to death, is dear to you?"

Plowden spoke in a half curious, half scornful tone.

"Dear to me?"—her voice quivered pitifully—"I had to trample on my heart to make myself give him that promise to-night; and to-morrow, if I have strength to fulfil it, it will seem like plucking my heart out and flinging it down for others to trample upon."

Plowden did not answer, and silence was maintained till they arrived at Margaret's home. He accompanied her up the steps as he always did, and waited with his courtly manner till she had been admitted to the house, not descending even when, having promised to call for her on the morrow in order to accompany her to court, he bade her good-night and the massive door had closed between them.

Once his hand was on the bell, as if about to pull it, but he withdrew his fingers before they had time to do their work, muttering:

"I cannot—not yet; till every chance is lost!"

He bounded down the steps and into the hack, as if he was flying from some imaginary pursuer.

CHAPTER XIV.

THE day of trial came at last. Aristocratic circles were in a quiver of excitement. The fair creatures who had been so assiduous in their attentions to Hubert were anxious lest brothers and fathers should not succeed in obtaining for them good places from which they might see and hear all the sensation that the affair should afford.

Lawyers who had attained pre-eminence in the profession, and shysters who fancied that legal skill could be obtained with little effort and less brains, shouldered each other on their rapid way to the court-room. Sensation seekers and idle spectators, who had little else to do with their day, were numerous, and thus all classes were represented in the crowded court-room.

Fashionable Mrs. Delmar and her daughter were there, under the espionage of Eugene. The elder lady's face had been subdued into an expression of the most tender melancholy, ready to be turned upon the prisoner the moment he should appear.

The interest and sympathy of all the fair creatures were concentrated on Hubert—every eye was turned to the place where he was expected to present himself, so that when the heavily-veiled, slender-formed lady entered, leaning on Plowden's arm, and quietly took a seat near the witness stand, she attracted but little attention. Many recognized her, for there was a peculiar gracefulness about Margaret Calvert which no costume could conceal, but her former fashionable friends had neither sympathy nor interest to spare for merely a dependant in the Bernot household.

Perhaps she had never been so keenly conscious of

her want of female friends, as at that moment when she took her seat in the great crowded court-room. Oh! for a mother who might whisper hope and courage to her—for some one whose hand she might press under cover of her cloak.

She looked over at the domestics, who had taken their places a moment before her entrance, and read in their faces only the kindliest sympathy. Little Sam Lewis in close proximity to Hannah Moore, as if conscious of some power in her which might help him to do his duty, looked restlessly about him in search of Liverspin, who on the previous day had said to the little man, with the usual application of his handkerchief:

"I'll be present to-morrow, my dear fellow, though it will be a severe trial to my feelings."

Little Sam, firmly believing in the sincerity of Liverspin's emotion, thought it would not be amiss to tell the good-natured cook how fully Mr. Liverspin sympathized with Mr. Hubert and Miss Calvert; but Hannah was slightly incredulous.

"No good man would ever be above visiting servants in their master's house," she said, "but I'll be able to tell better when I see what he's like;" and she frequently stooped to Sam to know if his friend had yet made his appearance.

There was a sudden buzz and rustle of silken garments, as several ladies rose that they might have a better view, for the prisoner had entered. He looked neither to the right nor left, but walked with a steady, erect gait, and took his seat as naturally and quietly as though he had been long familiar with his strange position. For a second after he had taken his seat, he shaded his eyes with his hand, as if to shut out the multitude of stares directed at him; then, removing it, he sat erect, and slowly glanced about him till his eyes rested on the veiled face almost directly opposite.

He knew the countenance the friendly screen concealed, and an expression of intense scorn swept over his

features, as he marked the isolation, as it were, of her
position. There was no lady in immediate proximity
to her, no friend save Plowden, who was busy with
some papers.

Hubert glanced away to the Delmars, and met the
elder lady's look of tender, melancholy interest. He
did not divine the motive of the fashionable woman's
extreme kindness to him, but at that instant, he intuitively guessed how his cousin had been treated by her
fashionable friends.

Mrs. Delmar was so delighted that he had favored
her with a particular glance, that she could almost forgive Eugene his harsh reprimand to herself and Louise,
for so unkindly remaining aloof from poor, forlorn
Margaret. The good-natured fellow had besought his
mother, even before they had left home that morning,
to call for Miss Calvert, and accompany her to the court;
but the elegant lady was attacked with hysteria at the
very idea of such a request, and Eugene was fain to desist, though not without having said some sharp words
to both his mother and sister.

On Hubert's entrance, Margaret forgot the awkwardness and loneliness of her position. With his pale face,
so strangely like his mother's in its spiritual expression,
to contemplate, she saw nothing else; with his slight
form—slight now almost to emaciation—before her, she
could think only of the long years of imprisonment
which possibly awaited him.

Plowden had told her that, in any case, the verdict
would not be murder in the first degree.

The dread proceedings began. A jury was im-
paneled, and Margaret's heart gave a terrified bound
when she heard some one behind her whisper to a companion:

"There are members of Roquelare on that jury."

She looked at Plowden, who also must have heard
the whispered remark, throwing her veil partially aside
in her alarm.

His forehead was gathered into a heavy frown, and great beads of perspiration stood on his face, but he bent over the paper he held as if to avoid meeting her eyes.

She held her breath as the prisoner, true to his promise to her, pleaded with a firmness which she feared he would be incapable of assuming, "Not guilty," and her breath came in labored gasps when Bertoni, the prosecuting counsel rose to make the opening speech. The intense silence that reigned was almost painful, and the stern, heavy face of the great lawyer wore an expression of triumph as it turned itself to the dense crowd.

He seemed to revel in the suspense in which he kept all waiting for his first words, and when he did begin he burst upon them with a sudden, almost fierce loudness that made many in the crowd start. Over their heads, in a perfect volume of sound, the words rang from his iron throat; brief, clear, pithy sentences that carried their point and did their damaging work as they went. Like a man who is sure of his power and uses it fearlessly, Bertoni struck out boldly and swept on with masterly strokes until his goal was reached, and then the prisoner's chances of acquittal were meagre indeed.

He reviewed the case from the first; brought distinctly to the minds of his hearers each incident of the investigation that had occurred twenty-one months before; dwelt on Miss Calvert's visit to the *morgue* as the first clew that had been obtained to the murderer; on the examination that followed; and then he referred sarcastically to the position Mr. Plowden had occupied on the trial; Mr. Plowden's disinterestedness at first; his eager proffer to work up the case that the untimely end of the deceased might be avenged; the sudden diminishing of his interest; his neglect to seize an important clew; and his evident anxiety to bring the examination to a close.

"What inference can be drawn from all this?" he thundered; "only one—that the might which wealth and influence possess over comparative poverty and obscurity purchased this able lawyer for the service of a wealthy criminal."

Plowden set his teeth hard, and clenched the papers fiercely in his grasp but he exhibited no other sign of the passion which Bertoni's words had roused.

Hubert's face wore an indignant flush, and his eyes sparkled angrily; but the lawyer continued:

"Every event that has occurred since, tends to prove my indictment of this high-minded, legal gentleman. He has been the friend and constant companion of this self-proclaimed murderer. He is here to day as the counsel of the accused. He will attempt to erect a defence on a very carefully, but yet very weakly, laid foundation of mental delusion; but when evidence shall be given to show that when the examination of this case was last conducted, when subpœnas were served on the servants in the Bernot household, the presence of one domestic in that house was purposely concealed—when further testimony will prove that Miss Calvert, at the time of her visit to the *morgue*, possessed the murderer's confidence, and must have connived at the escape of the murderer herself—when it shall be still further shown that Mr. Hubert Bernot was here in this city on the night of the murder, though report placed him nearly a hundred miles away, and when it shall be proved that he was of perfectly sane mind at the time he proclaimed himself a murderer in the presence of over a score of witnesses, I think the fabric which my honorable opponent has erected will fall very speedily to the ground."

For one instant his eyes met Plowden's flaming gaze, but he continued in the same triumphant tone:

"The murderer's confidante gave the first clew. On her visit to the *morgue* she betrayed her fear and anxiety; it was enough for any member of 'Roquelare.'

"A certain agent of that society watched and discovered sufficient to feel sure that he knew the murderer of Cecil Clare. But the clew had to be followed cautiously, for in these times there are many quibbles in the law by which criminals escape. 'Roquelare,' gave its warning, as it always does,—gave it to the criminal's confidante, for the criminal himself was at that time in a distant country, and one of the secret agents of 'Roquelare' watched for his return, tracked him when he did return, ascertained his pursuits, marked the places which he visited, and became familiar with some of his very companions. In this way he discovered the devotion with which the murderer's confidante guarded the murderer's secret."

Here Bertoni slightly lowered his voice and spoke more slowly, glancing at the veiled face whose owner had sat like a statue from the beginning of his speech; resuming in that slow, lowered tone when he described the agent of "Roquelare" suspending the handcuffs over Hubert's head, and Margaret, who alone had perceived the action, fainting at the sight.

There was a half suppressed murmur from some of the ladies; for many who were Bertoni's auditors, had been present at the scene which the lawyer described, and had wondered at Miss Calvert's sudden swoon; but Bertoni, regardless of the interruption, proceeded to detail the circumstances that had led to Bernot's self-accusation of murder.

"This agent of 'Roquelare,'" he said, "who had been on the criminal's track so long, sought for an opportunity of joining the club to which the murderer belonged; he did so, and no one save other agents of 'Roquelare' who subsequently also joined the club, penetrated the disguise he had assumed. Then he had an opportunity of studying every motion of the accused, of discovering how to play upon his fears, and of waking into bitter being, by stray words, his remorse for his crime. The agent did not intend to bring him to justice so soon; he meant to wait till further and more positive proof could be collected, and he told the story which elicited that confession only to make its effect on the accused; he did not think it would goad him to a confession, but since it did, 'Roquelare' at once fulfilled its part."

Bertoni paused for an instant as if to mark himself the impressive silence which waited upon his words, then he proceeded to briefly review certain points of the former evidence which promised to have an important bearing on the testimony that should be presently elicited, and with a glance at the prisoner that conveyed as plainly as if he had spoken how repugnant was the task.

The next step was the proving of Hubert's sanity and for this purpose the two physicians who had attended him by Bertoni's order were summoned in succession to the stand. Their evidence went to show that not only was the prisoner of perfectly sane mind at the time that he made his strange admission, but that at no previous period in his life had there ever been even a slight mental derangement; and to corroborate this testimony Dr. Durant was called.

Margaret knew he had been subpœnaed as a witness, for he himself had told her, but she was not prepared to hear him catechized on his treatment of her aunt. He was obliged to tell on his oath all that he knew of Madame Bernot's disease; of the origin of the latter he could only say, as other medical men had already done, that it had resulted from some severe mental shock whose cause was utterly unknown to him—that the consequences of that shock had been a painful illness of over eight years in duration. His further testimony showed that neither had Madame Bernot's mind ever maintained any but its proper balance, and then, in reply to a last question by Bertoni, he described her present condition, her utter ignorance of what had happened to her son, and the imminent danger to her life which there would be in acquainting her with it.

Little Sam Lewis had been divided between watching and listening to the witnesses, looking around for Liverspin, and replying to remarks on his tardiness by Hannah Moore.

"Perhaps he was afraid the scene would affect him too much," whispered the little man, when his eyes ached from their painful straining in every direction.

"Perhaps no," answered Hannah Moore dryly; and she disposed herself to listen more comfortably to the testimony of the next witness who should be summoned.

"Magnus Liverspin!" called the judge.

Everybody in the vicinity of the little under-waiter thought it was to him the pretentious cognomen belonged, from the electrical manner in which he started to his feet at the sound. But he made no attempt to move from his place; only stood there with open mouth and such a look of ludicrous bewilderment in his round, staring eyes, that the attention of the people about him was attracted.

"Sit down, you fool, and don't be gaping in that unmannerly fashion," whispered Hannah Moore, as, with a very ungentle tug, she placed him suddenly in his seat.

"But it's him—it's Liverspin, that I was telling you about," responded little Sam, in a very excited whisper; and thereupon Hannah Moore slightly elevated herself to obtain a clear view of the witness. She could see but the back of his form and his profile; the former was straight, tall, and somewhat portly; the latter was overspread with a deep, florid hue.

Bertoni was asking some preliminary and apparently unimportant questions; but, in a few moments he launched into inquiries that brought out Liverspin's testimony to such facts as his acquaintance with a servant in the Bernot household, his learning from that acquaintanceship Miss Calvert's anxiety to have Mr. Bernot's imprisonment kept not only from her aunt, but from the special attendant upon her aunt, the determination of the servants to tell, should they be a second time subpœnaed, only what they had told at their former examination, and the injunction of one particular domestic to abide by that determination whatever any of their number might think, or even know.

"Do you know how long this special attendant of Madame Bernot's has occupied her position?" questioned Bertoni.

"She had been in attendance on Madame Bernot before that lady left the South," was the reply.

Bertoni glanced at Plowden, as if to note whether he was cognizant of the point just gained; but Plowden, waiting to begin the cross-examination, was watching the witness.

"When did you first see this domestic of the Bernot household, whose acquaintance you seem to have so assiduously and successfully courted?" questioned Plowden, at the last, when it was evident that he was nearly through with the witness.

The man answered promptly.

"When did you first make his acquaintance?" queried Plowden again.

Liverspin answered as promptly as before.

"What motive prompted you to become a member of that club in particular?"

Bertoni interposed, alleging that the question was not a pertinent one, and need not be answered.

Plowden, darting a look of scorn at his opponent, said, ironically:

"The honorable gentleman seems afraid to have motives too closely scrutinized, lest so doing should discover mean mercenary things about the agents even of this immaculate 'Roquelare'; lest, if we go too deep we may discover that it is not the desire for justice, the burning love of equality of rights for rich and poor alike, that actuate each member of this justice-loving society, but a desire and burning love for fame and honor as well. The conviction and sentence of yonder hunted prisoner will cover my legal opponent, who is the secret agent of whom he himself has spoken, with fame and glory enough to last a lifetime. He hoped for and expected this, and has worked accordingly. I say hoped, not expected: he could not with certainly expect, for the few who comprise the heads of that society hold out no rewards to stimulate the energies of their members; neither do they award every work of justice that is done by their secret agents—as a man's life is discovered to be just, as the motives with which he has hunted down any criminal are thought to be simply those of justice, in proportion does 'Roquelare' dispense its awards. If then my honorable opponent fears not scrutiny into his motives, if justice animates his dealings as prosecuting counsel, why will he not permit an impartial examination of every witness? The justice which 'Roquelare' seeks, demands this."

The irony with which Plowden had begun had given way to a passionate earnestness under whose influence his very face seemed to soften. Bertoni's heavy countenance darkened, but he gave no other sign that the speech had aroused him to a white heat of passion; even his voice, when he replied, did not betray by a tremor his inward excitement. That he might not be supposed, he said, to have any reluctance to refute the malicious and unfounded charge of his honorable opponent, he would withdraw his objection and leave the counsel for the defence at perfect liberty to put any question he chose, to the witness.

Bertoni slowly resumed his seat, as if desirous to show by his very calmness how false was the imputation cast upon his honor as a member of "Roquelare."

Plowden repeated his last question to the witness. The witness glanced at Bertoni, as if seeking in his face some cue which might help him to mould his answer, and Plowden seeing that, turned directly round and faced the opposing counsel. It was a bitter, malignant expression which shone for a moment on the countenances of both lawyers, and then Plowden turned back and looked at the witness, while the latter gave his answer in a bungling, evasive manner.

"Did you, or did you not, enter that particular club solely to cultivate the acquaintance of this domestic of the Bernot household?" asked Plowden.

The witness was a full minute in bringing forth his reply, and then it was as if the riveting glance of the lawyer's keen eyes had compelled him to speak the brief affirmative.

"How did you first become aware that this domestic was a member of that particular club?"

It was evident that the witness was growing uncomfortable—that some secret fear was influencing his evidence—as if he were not sure how much truth he ought to tell, and yet was not equal to the task of inventing falsehoods which might answer the purpose.

His reply was long in coming, and people bent forward to watch Plowden's face because of its curious expression, rather than to hear the reply of the witness; but the witness at length, with a sort of bravado, as if defiant of consequences, answered:

"I learned it by inquiring from other servants who reside in the same street with him."

"And you made those inquiries at the instigation of, of another?" said Plowden.

"I did," answered the witness, with a little hesitation.

"That other, being a master whom you served in this particular instance because of a promised reward?" continued Plowden.

"Yes," again hesitatingly answered the witness.

"In what business were you engaged before you begun to play the part of spy on the servants of the Bernot household?"

"Traveling comedian."

"How did you come to obtain this last position, which you have filled with such credit to yourself and such honor to your employer?"—speaking with a bitter sarcasm.

"Through an advertisement in one of the daily papers for an energetic, shrewd man, who was capable of playing parts."

"You applied in person?"

"I did."

"What was the result of that application?"

The manner of the witness had grown a little more confident, as if he were treading on more certain ground, and he answered with less hesitation.

"After being asked several questions about myself, I was told that my business would be to ingratiate myself with the Bernot servants, and learn what I could from them of the private life of Mr. Hubert Bernot and Miss Calvert."

"Did your employer suggest to you in what manner you were to accomplish this?"

"No; I was left to the invention of my own wits."

"And what did your wits suggest?"

"To introduce myself to the servants of other families in the street as a poor fiddler who was soliciting pupils for a livelihood. From them I learned that the only one who might be likely to need my services was a servant in the Bernot family, who already belonged to a musical club. That information gave me a plan upon which to act. I joined that club, and worked myself into the favor of Mr. Samuel Lewis."

"Why did you not visit the servants of the Bernot family in the first instance?"

"Because I thought it better to learn at first something of them from others rather than from themselves."

"Why did you confine yourself to the acquaintanceship of only one of these servants?"

"Because he was enough for my purpose. He was

soft on the subject of music, and I obtained all the information I wanted from him."

"You kept accurate reports of every communication obtained from this victimized domestic, and faithfully transmitted them to your employer?"

"I did."

"You knew, or suspected, at the time of your being thus strangely employed, or shortly afterward, the ultimate purpose for which you had been hired: to assist in hunting down a suspected criminal?"

"I did."

"You were paid regular day wages apart from a promised reward should your efforts aid in accomplishing the aim of your employer?"

"Yes."

"Mention the promised reward."

There was a start from Bertoni—an impulsive, uncontrolable start, which almost brought him to his feet and turned upon him the wondering glances of all about him. The witness looked also; and Plowden, seeing the direction of the witness's eyes, turned and again directly faced the prosecuting counsel.

During the whole of the cross-examination it seemed to many—even those who were somewhat versed in the practices and technicalities of the law—as if the whole court was out of order—as if Plowden was permitted to continue his most unusual cross-examination, and one apparently bearing little on the case in hand, because of some secret influence, which had, perhaps, more at heart the vindication of "Roquelare" than even the prosecution of the prisoner.

Plowden turned back and fastened his eyes more eagerly on the witness, compelling an answer from the latter as if by the magnetism of his glance.

"When all should succeed as my employer wished, I was to receive a large sum of money."

"Did he at no time stimulate you efforts by promising that you should become a member of 'Roquelare?'"

There were half-smothered exclamations from certain masculine throats, wondering, almost frightened looks on certain masculine faces, and even the judge's rigid countenance became clouded and threatening; but Plowden, apparently heedless of the excitement his question had caused, waited for the answer of the witness. Again it was evident that the latter was very uncomfortable—that he was more uncertain than ever what reply to make, but while he hesitated Bertoni rose and objected to any answer being returned to the last question.

Plowden smiled, well knowing the objection would have little weight, Bertoni was caught in his own trap, since the judge and some of the jury were members of "Roquelare," the question would have to be answered, that the character of one of that mysterious body might be proved honorable or otherwise. And the question was answered and in the affirmative.

"Only one question more," said the triumphant Plowden.

"The name of the gentleman who so hired you and promised this munificent reward?"

The witness had seemed to recover what was evidently his natural manner, a sort of swaggering, independent bravado—as if he had come to the mental conclusion that his evidence had already accomplished the worst for himself, and his best course was to brave the consequences as he had already braved many a buffet of fortune before. So he answered promptly:

"That's him sitting on the right hand side of the judge—Mr. Bertoni."

"That will do, Mr. Liverspin," and Plowden, making no effort to control the triumph in his face, begun in earnest, almost impetuous tones:

"For the honor of 'Roquelare,' whose principles, whose aim I, though no member, revere, it was necessary to be sure that its secret agents had violated no rules.

had pursued their work with no unworthy motives. One of the stringent regulations of this mysterious society is that no member hold out to any man, as inducement or reward, the promise to procure for him membership in that great body. No member can ask any man to join the society; no member can tell to any man who is not a member, the secret influence for prosperity which membership of this society exerts upon individual lives; yet it is evident that the counsel for the prosecution has done these things. If he had not showed the benefit which must accrue from being a member of 'Roquelare,' why would this traveling comedian feel himself incited to new efforts because of such a promise? All this I hope those who ere long may have the life of my unhappy client in their hands will bear carefully in mind; remember that the secret agent of 'Roquelare' who has hunted the accused to his present position, has not pursued his work according to the honorable precepts of 'Roquelare' itself; that as he has erred in this respect he may also err in his present work; and when justice has been meted to yonder prisoner, I hope justice also will be meted to this unworthy member of 'Roquelare.' "

Plowden sat down, wiping his face, for the perspiration lay in thick heavy beads upon it. Bertoni's countenance was as stolid and heavy as it had been at the beginning of the trial. From the time he had given that sudden start, he had seemed to have perfect control of himself, evincing neither by change of color, nor the expression in his eyes, how every word of his legal antagonist was rankling in his heart like a barbed arrow. He bent forward to the judge, as calm, apparently, as if he was not the centre of a sort of terrified interest to the breathless crowd, and said something in an inaudible tone, the result of which was an adjournment of the case until that same day in the ensuing week.

If any one in the miscellaneous throng which immediately, on the adjournment, began to pour forth to the street, deserved pity, it was poor, little, victimized Samuel Lewis. He had listened to the cross-examination of his pretended friend, Liverspin, with an expression of face like one who was suffering from a horrible nightmare. Hannah Moore's indignation toward, and scorn for, the little man, had been too deep for words. She was bursting with wrath, and with violent impatience waited for an opportunity, when she could unrestrainedly pour the vials of her anger on his head.

The other servants were shocked, indignant, and contemptuous also, and darted in turn fiery, scornful looks at him.

They hardly waited to be properly in the street before one and all launched indignant epithets at him, and Hannah Hoore, with her face burning from anger, which had been rendered none the less violent by her efforts to extricate herself from the crowd, began:

"I don't know how to keep my hands off of you—traitor that you are—your friend, Mr. Liverspin, indeed—he's a divilspin—that's what he is."

It was only the attention which her angry speech, and angrier demeanor were attracting, that caused her to desist at last, and let the little man, who walked by her side with a most dejected gait, continue his way in silence.

He made no reply to any one of their scornful sallies —indeed, he seemed as if he had not yet recovered from the first emotions which the appearance of Liverspin as a witness had excited, and he maintained his melancholy silence till the Bernot residence was reached.

"I can't go in," he said, thrusting his hands into his pockets, and looking ruefully down the area steps. "I've gone and done a bad thing for everybody as well as myself; I didn't go to do it, but it's done—I'll send after my clothes and things, and tell Miss Calvert that I didn't mean to hurt her—that I——."

The little man's emotions overpowered him, and the

rest of his sentence was lost in the handkerchief which he hurriedly put to his eyes.

Hannah Moore, whose indignation was wont to be as quickly subdued as it could be easily kindled, and whose most violent resentment was never proof against the sight of real emotion, was in a moment all sympathy and compassion for the little under-waiter; but she deemed it better policy not to let the change in her feelings become too apparent; so, with a rough kindness, she jerked "Little Sam" down the steps, and into the house, saying as she did so:

"Don't be making a bigger fool of yourself than you are already, and face the consequences of what you've done like a man. I only wish I had Divilspin here. Faith I'd teach him not to play the spy anymore."

CHAPTER XV.

ALMOST everybody, save the members of "Roquelare," were surprised and disappointed at the adjournment of the case after so brief a session; none more so than the prisoner himself. He was impatiently eager for Margaret's examination that she might make public the confidence with which he had entrusted her—that despite his own plea of "not guilty," his crime might be speedily proved. He was almost angry with Plowden for drifting away from the case, as the latter seemed to have done in his cross-examination; he could not understand what the crafty lawyer had gained by so doing, and, if he had understood, he would not have been pleased, for he desired nothing for himself but the most rigorous justice.

Mrs. Delmar, however, was exultant, and kept nodding her head in the exuberance of her satisfaction, till the crimson plume in her hat acquired a fashion of nodding also, and kept perfect time to the stately dame's motions.

"Depend upon it, my dear," she said to her daughter, when Eugene had gone to see that their carriage was in waiting, "Mr. Plowden has made a very strong point somewhere; he is very sharp, and his sharpness will carry Hubert safely through all this, and then——"

Louise Delmar's face brightened, and faintly blushed.

"You need not color," resumed the fashionable mother, playfully tapping the girl's cheek; "you understand what I have left unsaid," and the stately lady drew herself up, and looked at her daughter with a very self-satisfied smile.

It was pardonable in her maternal heart to swell with complacency since she had a daughter so obedient to her precepts—since untoward events seemed of themselves to conspire in the fulfilment of her hopes.

"I would go over and speak to Mr. Plowden," she continued, looking in the direction of the lawyer, "but he is engaged with that odious Margaret Calvert."

Eugene returned to accompany them to the carriage.

"Surely, mother," he said, "you will go and speak a word to that poor girl—not one of her lady friends has so much as bowed to her all the morning."

Mrs. Delmar drew herself up, and cast a look of contempt on the daring pleader; then taking Louise's arm, swept in scornful silence to the door.

Eugene, burning with an indignation which he could scarcely control, followed; and assisted them to their seats in the carriage.

"Where are you going?" asked his mother, seeing no disposition on his part to enter.

"To tender to that poor, deserted girl, the sympathy and friendship which my mother and sister refuse," and he slammed the carriage door, and walked angrily away, while his mother, since he would not be present to witness it, refrained from her usual attack of hysteria, and contented herself with saying:

"I do wish Eugene was as sensible and obedient as you are, my dear."

If her son had not the common sense and obedience which his fashionable mother supposed to be consistent with filial affection, that he had unusually refined feelings of sympathy, and a singularly unselfish kindness of heart, the few low words he spoke to Margaret, proved.

She was waiting while Plowden arranged some details of legal business, and she turned gladly to Delmar when he approached, as a relief from the feeling that she was an object of curiosity to the loiterers who still remained.

The young man would fain excuse the absence of his mother and sister, feeling that Miss Calvert must be aware of their presence but a short time before, but, somehow, looking into that pale, gentle face, he could not utter the apologies that rose to his lips. Perhaps Miss Calvert suspected the truth, for she seemed studiously to avoid speaking of them.

Plowden joined them, and, on their way to the hack, which Margaret preferred to use on all occasions now —Delmar said:

"What possible bearing could that cross-examination of yours have on Bernot's case?"

Plowden glanced hurriedly about him before he answered.

"Accompany Miss Calvert and me and I will tell you. There are too many eaves-droppers about to speak it here."

"Well?" asked Delmar, impatiently, when they were seated in the hack and the driver had received his order.

"That cross-examination was to prove a suspicion that suddenly entered my mind while Liverspin was giving his evidence. If I could prove my suspicion to be correct, I would gain one strong point in Hubert's favor. The suspicion was, that Bertoni might have violated one of the rules of 'Roquelare.' If I could prove that, the strong point gained would be this: disappointing Bertoni in the aim for which he was working; that aim was the reward that 'Roquelare' gives to those who work in strict accordance with its rules. Bertoni is high now in the legal profession—in worldly prosperity; but if he were to succeed in this case, with the purity of his motives unsuspected, with his violation of the rules of 'Roquelare' unknown, he would be elevated to the head circle in that society, and his very name be a signal for such homage as should never be paid to man. I studied Bertoni when I first met him on this same case, and learned then what has been corroborated to-day. He is unscrupulously ambitious—power is his god. His desire for the power which success in this case would give him, made him forget to be cautious, and when he promised his tool to make him a member of 'Roquelare,' he probably imagined that he himself would be at that time in a condition to initiate Mr. Liverspin into the mysteries, and could teach the latter what reply to make when he should be asked if anyone had ever requested or induced him to become a member of that society. If he feared, in the event of non-success, that Mr. Liverspin would tell of the promise that had once been held out to him, he thought probably that it would make little difference, as it is not often a chance of 'Roquelarian' work occurs, and it is only when a member is engaged in such, that they make a rigid scrutiny of his motives. Knowing that I was not a member of 'Roquelare,' he did not suspect that I knew of its secret workings; hence his neglect to tutor Mr. Liverspin for my cross-examination. He did not dream the turn my questions would take, and Liverspin chanced to be sufficiently ignorant of court-etiquette, and possessed of just sufficient conscientiousness to regard his oath, to give me the very evidence I wanted. The case was adjourned because Bertoni was totally unable to continue it. He knew he would be summoned before a secret conclave of 'Roquelare' before many hours, where the charge that I have made against him will be investigated, and its truth or falsehood substantiated; if the former, they will expel him from the society, and the disgrace of that expulsion will follow him through all his after life. Knowing this—knowing the reward for which he has worked cannot be his, and that to continue his prosecution of Bernot will only bring his name and himself in a disagreeably prominent light before the members of 'Roquelare,' he may abandon the case, and in his bitter disappointment betake himself to some obscure path in life. This is my hope: to have Bertoni no longer as prosecuting counsel. His skill is more subtle and dangerous than any other in the profession. With another in his place, I could successfully plead Hubert's case. That is all. Do you understand it, Delmar?"

Delmar had listened with wondering eyes and almost bated breath, and he answered slowly:

"Yes, I understand it; but where did you get your intimate knowledge of 'Roquelare'?"

A peculiar expression came into Plowden's face—a softened look that changed the whole of that dark countenance into the tenderness of a woman's gaze; he answered in a low, sad tone:

"I have my knowledge from a relative who once stood high on its annals. Something made it necessary for him to withdraw from the society; he caused his death to be published among the members,—a death at sea, which precluded the possibility of honors to his body—and shut himself away from all worldly fellowship."

"Is it not against their rules to have as much knowledge of them as you possess, generally known?" asked Delmar.

"Yes; were they aware of just how much I know my life would not be safe a moment; but I was careful to mention only rules which regulate the outer circle of 'Roquelare'—a knowledge of such, though known to scarcely any outside the members, is not punishable; they will probably dog me to discover, if possible, the extent of what I know. But I think I am sharp enough even for 'Roquelare'."

The hack stopped suddenly with a lurch that started Margaret from her seat and sent her almost into Plowden's arms.

"It's a quarrel of some sort," said Delmar, who looked from the window to ascertain the cause of the unexpected stop. Plowden thrust his head forth also, while Margaret looked from the opposite window. Children, and even women, attracted by the noise of the *melee*, crowded round the combatants; an excited throng blocked the passage-way for every vehicle. The driver of the hack had whipped his horses up, hoping to force a way through the curious people, but some nma, with an oath, had caught the beasts and thrown them violently back on their haunches.

Because of the constant swaying of the crowd it was difficult to tell who were the principal actors in the fight; and not till an accidental opening occurred was there presented to the view of the occupants of the hack two men, whose stained and torn clothes and red and perspiring faces bore severe evidences of the contest in which they were yet engaged. Nearer and nearer to the hack they worked themselves, the crowd giving way before them to close up in their rear and urge them on with loud, crazy cries, struggling with a desperation that made Margaret shudder and shut her eyes to the sight.

Plowden leaned further forth to catch a better view of one of the bloody countenances. "Look!" he said to Delmar, "is not that Liverspin—the one this way?"

But, without waiting for a reply, and evidently forgetting the presence of Margaret, he opened the door and descended from the vehicle, and, having paused an instant to give some direction to the driver, hastily mingled with the crowd; and at that instant the excited cries of the people suddenly ceased, for the guardians of the peace had made their appearance. Both combatants were taken into custody, one surrendering himself quietly and seeming to take the whole affair as a matter of course; but Liverspin loudly and angrily protested; vociferating that he had not provoked the quarrel, and that his arrest was a flagrant piece of injustice. They hurried him away, however, and the crowd began to disperse. Plowden returned to his place, vouchsafing no explanation till the hack was again on its way.

"It is as I expected," he said, slowly. "Liverspin's arrest is 'Roquelare's' work. I knew they would be constantly on his track from the time he would leave the court, because his presence will be needed in the secret conclave that will judge Bertoni. But I hardly thought they would take possession of him in this manner."

"How do you know that they have?" asked Delmar, who was beginning to feel an uncomfortable awe of the lawyer.

"My mingling with the crowd discovered that fact," was the reply. "By so doing I obtained a close view of the man with whom Liverspin was fighting, and I saw the peculiar mark that stamps a member of 'Roquelare'. You heard Liverspin say that he did not provoke the quarrel; he was right—he did not. I learned on inquiry that, while he was quietly drinking at some bar, a stranger accosted him, and goaded him by scornful imputations on his calling and character, that this fight was the result. The law will keep him safely till 'Roquelare' needs him."

"And then?" asked Delmar, breathlessly.

"When 'Roquelare' has no further need of him, and has assured itself that he possesses no dangerous knowledge of the society, he will be given his liberty."

"And the cause for which he has been arrested will not be tried—neither he nor his companion in the fight suffer the consequences of their rashness?" asked Delmar.

Plowden smiled, almost as if in contempt for the childishness of the young man's understanding which could not comprehend the selfish policy of "Roquelare."

"Have you not already suspected," he said "that 'Roquelare,' though assuming to work only for justice, sacrifices even justice when its own interests are at stake. Not having its principles based upon what is commonly termed a universal brotherhood, its policy must at times be selfish; it has an opportunity to be so, since its influence, in a great measure, controls the very law."

Delmar said no more till the hack had turned into his own street in order to drop him at his own door; then, extending his hand to Plowden, as if some very kindly thought of the young man suddenly banished his uncomfortable awe, he said:

"I thank you for the voluntary confidence you have given me; you have requested no pledge from me not to betray it, but, nevertheless, what I have heard is as sacred as though I had sworn never to reveal it."

Plowden pressed the hand he held, as if in grateful thanks, and replied quickly:

"To gain that for which I am working I would be willing to suffer even the merciless vengeance of 'Roquelare.'"

Delmar fancied he knew the end for which the lawyer was working, and he replied quietly, but with the evidence of a heart-felt sincerity in his tones:

"You have my best wishes, my dear fellow, for your success."

For an instant his eyes wandered to the pale, sad-faced girl opposite, and Plowden, seeing the look, read the thought that was in the young man's mind. He smiled bitterly, knowing how immeasurably beyond his reach was the hand of Margaret Calvert, even though her heart had not been given to Hubert Bernot; but he replied gracefully, as was his wont; and, when the hack stopped to let Delmar alight, he pressed the young fellow's hand warmly and gratefully. Margaret bowed her adieu, and leaned back again to relapse into the melancholy silence upon which Plowden's own mental disquietude prevented him from intruding.

Since the previous evening, when it had cost her so much to give Hubert the promise he desired, she had been, as it were, stretched on a rack of mental torture, at one moment fancying that, perhaps, after all, to give the confidence with which he had entrusted her to the public would be unnecessary, that God did not require it, and that so doing would, as Plowden said, but render more sure Hubert's chances for a long imprisonment, without rendering him any material spiritual good. It was only by calling to mind Father Germain's counsel, and Hubert's own assurance of the inward peace her compliance with his desire would give him, by frequent and earnest prayers for strength to fulfil this terrible duty, that she had been enabled to go calmly to the court that morning—to sit there, though with a frightfully palpitating heart, as she realized how each minute brought nearer the dreadful summons which would compel her testimony; and then when it was only by such desperate efforts that she had fortified herself for the ordeal, to have that ordeal postponed—to have another week of suspense and heart-breaking anxiety thrust upon her—it brought a sickening feeling, that partook almost of despair. Fain would she have turned from the world and laid herself down to die anywhere, so that death would but quickly come. Though taking no part in the conversation between Plowden and Delmar, every word of it made an indelible mark on her mind; the more indelible because her mental faculties were so sharpened by suffering.

Who and what was Plowden, to possess so much, and such dangerous knowledge of 'Roquelare'? if he were not a member of that body, and Margaret, regarding all secret societies as opposed to the teachings of her Church, held an involuntary abhorrence of the members of such, especially when they called themselves Catholics. Thus her fear of, and dislike to Plowden increased, depite her efforts to the contrary—despite the trust she wanted to repose in him for Hubert's sake.

The very mystery which seemed to hang heavily about the trial was making her ill—the very thought of the dread influence of "Roquelare," which seemed to penetrate into all places and at all times, made her shiver with an undefined fear. Oh, the bitter consequences that came from that one sin! And then her mind went back to a former wrong—the wrong that had caused Madame Bernot years of suffering; that was the antecedent of Hubert's crime, and she wondered how much more of sorrow that was consequent upon that first evil, was to come. Forgetting the presence of Plowden, she buried her face in her hands, and murmured aloud.

"How long, O Lord, how long before Thou wilt be appeased—before Thou wilt forgive?"

Plowden started from his train of anxious thought and looked at his companion, his face softening, as if at the sight of her misery, and his lips twice opening as if trying to speak reluctant words; but he did not say them, he thrust them back just as they were on the very point of leaping forth, and perceiving that they had arrived at Margaret's residence, he prepared to assist her out with as calm a mien as though his soul was not writhing in an agony all the more desperate because it was so hidden.

CHAPTER XVI.

That week—that long, horrible week—smiling faces, and fragments of merry conversations which Margaret sometimes met and heard on her hurried way to the prison or the church, the only visits that she paid, had for her such a strangely unfamiliar look and sound, as if they were part of years before. Never would smiles like the olden ones, ere another's sin had blighted her, brighten her face again; never more would the light, happy words that came from a guileless youth be on her lips.

She had told Father Germain, her unfailing sympathizer and counselor the whole of the dark, troubled time, all that Plowden had said of "Roquelare," describing the effect which that conversation had upon her own feelings for the lawyer.

The priest's brow slightly darkened, and he bowed his head, as if in troubled thought; but he raised it in a moment, answering with a sudden brightening of his features: "God's finger is distinctly traceable in all this—Plowden is shrewd and subtle; and it is a little mysterious how he could have obtained so much knowledge of 'Roquelare' without being, as you say, a member of that society—however, that is no proof that he is not still Hubert's friend—the very manner in which he has begun the defense proves not only his ability, but his earnest desire to serve his client; I think you may trust him entirely. Do not trouble yourself about any motive from which he may work; God alone must be the judge of that, and the unexpected and peculiar turn that the case has already taken is but one of the many ways in which God's ends are served—remember this, my child, and remember also that He is watching and taking care of it all."

Yes, she constantly remembered that, but her heart would sometimes flag and faint under its heavy burden.

To have seven days rise and set on a monotonous routine of suffering—to rise in the morning with a suffocating pain round her heart and a blur before her heavy eyes that darkened the very sunshine streaming into her room; to descend to her aunt's apartment and perform the numberless, nameless, little loving services which were her daily wont, and perform them with a calm face, and to talk in calm tones, when her very soul was writhing to show by some outward sign its agony—to meet the physician morning after morning, only to hear the same hopeless answer, "she must not know yet;" to attend to the routine of household care which devolved upon her, and which she could not very well resign to one of the domestics; to have kind, assuring words for poor little Sam Lewis for whom the cook had obtained a ready forgiveness from Margaret, and a desire that he should on no account think of leaving his place; to visit Hubert and to help him bear the torturing suspense occasioned by the postponement of his trial, and then to go wearily homeward and wonder if over another household in the vast city the bird of sorrow brooded so ominously—such was the experience of that miserable week to Margaret Calvert.

Perhaps the happiest time, if ought in that sorrowful period could be called happy, was that which she passed with Hubert; it was exquisite bliss to be near him, and yet it was heart-rending torture to know that no view of the future would satisfy him unless it embraced the most rigid austerity—the absolute denial of earthly mercy for himself. He demanded almost passionately of Plowden why he had pursued such an unexpected course on the day of the trial; and when the lawyer half smilingly explained, he answered mournfully:

"You are not my friend after all, Charlie; I want to escape through no quibbles of the law, I want my defence conducted on no fine points and technicalities which take not a single jot from my crime, I tell you," growing hot with sudden feeling, "I murdered Cecil Clare. I left him *dead* on the side-walk, and all your nice turns, and all your professional skill cannot alter that fact. I am a *murderer*, and as such I want to be tried —as such I await my punishment."

Margaret was present, listening quietly as she always listened, but holding her heart lest she should betray by any sign that which would make Hubert anxious about her.

Plowden laid his hand on Bernot's shoulder, and pointed with the other to the pale, silent girl.

"Hubert, do you think of that other life so closely twined with your own? Do you think that this punishment for which you are so madly importunate will not lay its heavy weight upon her? You compelled her to bear the burden of your secret; for eighteen long months you made her share your hidden suffering. Will you inflict further torture upon her, the innocent one? Will you make her suffer also the consequences of *your* crime? or will you, listening to the dictates of prudence submit your case unquestioned to me, and if you should be acquitted, will you reward her for her faithful devotion? She has earned it—you *owe* it to her."

He had spoken slowly and distinctly though in a low tone, and his last words were uttered with a peculiar solemnity which seemed strangely to subdue the prisoner.

Who shall describe the effect of his words on Margaret—the vista of happiness which he opened to her view—the infinite rest implied by his speech? Hubert free, fearful no more of his doom finding him out, and she his wife twining about him all the love and tenderness of her happy heart—such she knew was the signification of Plowden's words. Sudden color flashed into her face, her eyes brightened, her whole countenance looked as it had never looked to Plowden before.

Hubert, strangely silent, strangely drooping since the lawyer had spoken, raised his head and saw Margaret's changed face. As if the sight of her instantly completed some half formed determination, he held out his hands and said in tones so passionate and yet so mournful that it seemed as if a dual being were speaking in him:

"He is right; I do owe to you all that could be in mortal's power to repay. But you have taught me how to make my very sin a claim on God's mercy, a plea for God's love, and now, I would give the remainder of my life to Him whom you have taught me to know so well. But it shall be as *you* say, Margaret—for your months of devotion, for your love which has been the same through all the changes in my fate, the decision shall lie with you. Come here and tell me which it shall be—if I should be acquitted, our union"—for an instant there broke over his face an expression as if he saw some glowing vista—" or even in that case, the remnant of my poor life given only to Him who died for me? Which shall it be, Margaret?"

He continued to extend his hands, but with an expression of passionate entreaty upon his face:

Plowden watched the scene with as intense and painful an interest as that which was felt by his two unhappy companions. He read in Margaret's face the emotions which struggled in her soul—the wild desire to throw herself into those extended arms and decide for Hubert's and her own earthly happiness—to claim him by the suffering she had borne for him—by the very love which was part of her being; but she did not move from her place, she did not extend *her* hands. The color died out of her countenance, her eyes resumed their mournful expression, and she answered, while her indescribable voice grew more sad and yet more sweet with every word:

"I would not come between you and your God; if you deem this sacrifice of yourself to be a necessary atonement, I would be the last to make you forego it. As I have shared your secret suffering, so I can share your voluntary penance. I shall not be less generous than you are, and when God beholds our two hearts severed from each other for His sake—severed for all time, and offering to Him all the sorrow that such a severance must entail, surely He will forgive more completely——He will love more dearly. I have no claim upon you, He has all; you are God's, Hubert, now and always."

"Oh, Margaret, Margaret! truer, more faithful in this hour even than thou hast yet been," Hubert answered, with that strange blending of passion and sadness in his voice, and then his hands dropped to his sides, and he turned suddenly to Plowden.

"You hear," he said, almost fiercely, "she who loves me, and whom I love, counsels me to continue in the way I have begun; while you, who have only friendship to sacrifice, would keep me in the slough my sin has made. When I tell you that my remorse can alone be allayed by an utter renouncing of every thing that is dear to me, why do you refuse to help me? —why seek for loopholes of escape for me when the soul of that murdered man continues to cry for vengeance on the murderer?"

He covered his face with his hands, for an instant, as if to shut out some terrible vision; and when he uncovered his countenance, and resumed, his voice was lower, sadder, but more entreating and more earnest.

"Oh, Charlie, by the friendship you bear me, by the confidence I unconsciously gave you, and which you refuse to betray, by your love for yonder faithful girl"—growing suddenly excited—"I implore you to help me to bring peace to my tortured conscience."

He grasped Plowden's hands, and looked into his eyes, as if his life or death were to be decided by the lawyer's answer.

Plowden—ah! how his dark soul leaped fiercely up to answer that heart-cry—how the question of life or death tugged at his own heart strings, and mercilessly swayed him in a very storm of agony—how Right smiled and beckoned, and lured him on; but Wrong with threatening aspect stepped between, and thrust him back to his cowardly fears.

Brave, and able, and skilful as he was, the talented lawyer lacked moral courage—he would have given worlds to be able to strike down the Wrong which separated these two young lives, but worldly sensibilities had paralyzed his arm. He broke from Hubert's grasp, and turned away to conceal the workings of his countenance; he knew the same expression was upon it as Margaret Calvert had seen at the church door.

Hubert and Margaret waited for his answer—Margaret wondering if it would be an assent to Hubert's wish, and if that assent would imply a relaxation of efforts in the prisoner's behalf, so that the full rigor of the law would be administered, and that *might* be death. Her poor, fluttering heart turned sick at the thought—surely God did not require Hubert's life—was not his sacrifice of all things dear, enough? Alas! poor quivering creature, she could give him up whom she loved better than life itself, and continue to live, knowing that the same world yet held them both, the same sky canopied both; but to press the coffin-lid upon him would be to bury in the same grave more of her than would remain on the then desolate earth!

There was no such thought in Hubert's mind. He had learned how to thrust back all yearning for the ties which make life so sweet, and having resolved on a complete immolation of himself as the only means of true atonement within his power, he would have no mercy —he would relent on no consideration, no power short of Heaven's own decree. *He* waited to hear, that he might press with a lightened heart on his penitential way.

Plowden turned to the two silent ones, turned slowly, and spoke as if he was struggling with himself for power to utter the words:

"Trust me Hubert—till the end—nothing pertaining to the murder shall be concealed, and if I proceed in untoward ways which you cannot understand, have faith in me still—justice shall be done to all."

He seemed to linger over the last word, and to say it bitterly.

"That is all I can promise; are you satisfied?"

But Hubert turned away with evident dissatisfaction, and threw himself face downward on the pallet; Margaret's sad voice bidding him adieu roused him.

He pressed her hand hard, looking at the same time as if it was only by some desperate effort he prevented himself from drawing her to him, while he said passionately:

"Oh, Margaret! you alone of all the wide, wide world are *true*."

She bent to him and whispered:

"Your mother?"

He started up.

"Yes, Margaret, but she does not *know*. When she has learned what I have become, will she be then as she is now—now she thinks I am all that a mother covets in a son; *then* will not her pure soul shrink, my mother though she is, from the murderer? You did not shrink —you have been the same through every change, and how does the world regard you for it? Do you think that I did not notice the respectable distance "—his voice took an accent of intense scorn—" your former friends maintained from you on the day of the trial? And this, Margaret, is only a portion of the reward which the world will give you. What has your love for me so far brought you? What will it bring to you in the end?

only a bitter separation. Will you still cling to it?"

"Always."

Her answer was low, scarcely more than a whisper, but Plowden standing gloomily at the cell door, heard it; he purposely kept his eyes on the ground, that he might not see the unhappy pair, but he heard—heard with a painful distinctness—every word of the soothing sentences which Margaret spoke.

He was tempted to curse her calmness, his own heart was such a raging fire, but just then his eyes involuntarily lifted, and rested on her pure, sad face.

As if the calming effect which her words were already producing on Hubert, extended to the lawyer, he too grew strangely calm, and listened, while the memory of one who had pleaded with him as Margaret was pleading with Hubert, stole softly back.

The simple virtues of Margaret Calvert were exerting a more potent influence than all the great and mysterious power of " Roquelare."

They went out together, the lawyer and the sad, silent girl, leaving Hubert still in that sort of unearthly calm which her words had produced—they went out together from the shadow of the prison walls into the sunny streets where life was so busy, the lawyer still under the spell of memory which Margaret had unconsciously caused, the girl communing with her heart so sore from suffering and sacrifice.

Silently and slowly they walked, because both were so preoccupied, until a form, having hurriedly passed them stopped, turned, and stood directly in their way. Both looked up, and both started, for Bertoni's heavy face smiled scornfully at them. He raised his left arm— raised it high as if purposely to show the blood-red bandage which encircled his wrist, then dropped it, and hissed:

"Now, more than ever; for *revenge* is the motive."

He turned and went rapidly on, darting into the first cross-street he reached.

The spell which had wrapped Plowden's faculties was dissolved. He turned quickly to Margaret:

"This is incomprehensible to you; but I—I, too bitterly understand it. 'Roquelare' has expelled him; instead, however, of abandoning Hubert's case, and burying himself in obscurity, as I had hoped he would do, he means to continue the prosecution that he may have revenge for what I have done to him. He will work desperately now, and I also shall have to be desperate in order to save your cousin—to save him from the most fatal consequences of that crime."

His face was covered with perspiration, and yet he shuddered.

Margaret did not answer—she could not. The cruel maze in which this sudden, and startling intrusion of "Roquelare" placed her, left her powerless to frame a word. Plowden walked on, wiping his face and muttering indistinct sentences between his teeth. He paused at the corner of the street at which it was Margaret's custom to leave him after their prison visits.

"I know why you never let me accompany you further," he said abruptly, "because you do not go directly home; you stop on the way to enter a church —is it not?"

She scarcely heard him, for her heart was repeating:

"'And I also shall have to be desperate in order to save your cousin from the most fatal consequences of that crime.'"

The lawyer, without waiting for her answer, continued moodily:

"When you go there to-day, Miss Calvert, pray as you have never done before; for all that Faith and Hope and Love of divine things can give you, you will need, should Bertoni triumph in this case."

He turned away suddenly without even an adieu, and walked rapidly in an opposite direction.

The wretched girl also pursued her way, but it was with slow and painful steps, for all the fears and doubts which she had struggled so heroically to suppress were upon her with tenfold fury. From the lawyer's last words she augured death for Hubert, and with all her self-abnegation, her heart—her whole soul—still shrank from *that* ordeal.

Father Germain entering the church on his return from a sick call, turned to look a second time at the white uplifted face of a girl who knelt before a statue of the Blessed Virgin—it wore so holy, so inspired an expression—it seemed so far from everything earthly. Recognizing the person, and thinking that she might desire to speak to him on the conclusion of her prayer, he waited at the vestry door. But that colloquy with Heaven, that petition to the dear patroness who never fails to use her intercession for those who fervently implores it, had been too sacred, too real, for the soul that had been so engaged, to descend immediately to earthly cares. She rose and passed quietly out, with the weight on her heart as heavy, with the sorrow within it as bitter, but with resignation to **endure calmly every trial God might send.**

CHAPTER XVII.

AGAIN came the day of trial, and the sun shone as brightly as it had done on that same day a week ago, but interest and expectation were more violent, and feminine hearts palpitated quicker with hope and desire that the prisoner, through his counsel might defeat the law.

Mrs. Delmar and Louise, both in the very brightest of summer attire, were early in their places; the elder lady in an agony lest the pearl powder, with which she had plentifully overlaid her complexion in order to give a pale, interesting look to her features, should lose its effect in the crowded court-room, was vigorously fanning herself. The younger, paler than it was her wont to be, though not by artificial means, was absorbed in thoughts of the visits she had made to the prison during the week.

She had gone daily, always accompanied by her mother, and Hubert had not submitted to the infliction with his former graciousness. He had not, it is true, openly wounded their sensitiveness; he had not rebuked them for their unkindness to Margaret, but it was only for Eugene's sake he had refrained—simple, frank, generous Eugene, who made daily visits also, and each time showed a friendship so deep, so sincere, that more than once Hubert caught the young fellow's hand, and murmured:

"What have I done to merit this?"

Between the young men, the subject of Margaret's treatment by Mrs. Delmar and her daughter was silently but mutually tabooed. Eugene shrank from making excuses for it, the falsity of which apologies he knew would be so apparent, and Hubert forebore to speak of that which he knew to be beyond Eugene's control, or influence.

But though he restrained the scathing rebuke which rose hotly to his lips when Mrs. Delmar paraded her affectionate interest in him, he was cynical and sarcastic in his conversation to her and Louise; he talked *at* the young lady, not *to* her any more, and when they prolonged their interview he became taciturn, and almost morose.

"It is anxiety about his trial that makes him so unlike himself," said Mrs. Delmar, "but once that terror is past we shall have him more charming in his manner than ever."

Perhaps her daughter's heart did not credit that prophecy, for love is attended by so many fears that hope itself is often dashed,—and alas! for the happiness, for the peace of Louis Delmar's future life, her mother's lessons had been but too well learned. She loved Hubert Bernot with all the uncontrolable passion of her warped and shallow nature. His cynicism, his sarcasm, the very observations he launched at her from summits so far above her mental grasp, were but as chains binding her to the heights on which he stood, but chains that would never draw her from her own level—they would only hold her in a hopeless, weary, broken-hearted bondage.

Yet, with that strange passion, there came to her, perhaps for the first time in her life, desires for a different life from the one she was living—softened, chastened feelings that made her turn impatiently from the constant parade of her mother's vanity, and which might, if properly guided, have made her a better, truer woman for the future. She even felt kindly to Margaret Calvert. There was no jealousy of her, for she supposed, in common with the fashionable world, that

Margaret was betrothed to Plowden, and was she not deterred by a certain awe of her mother, she would have proffered, even at that late day, her sympathy to Hubert's cousin.

Margaret sat alone, and a little apart from a group of severe-looking ladies, whose comments were sometimes so loud as to violate the laws of good-breeding. They were often distinctly audible to the motionless girl, but if their petty malice called painful blushes to her cheeks, or caused her bosom to heave with throes of wounded feeling, the thick veil screened the one, and the large loose folds of the friendly cloak, concealed the other.

"She is so forward," said a modern-looking Diana, knitting her brows, and darting a glance of scornful indignation at Margaret.

"It is certainly very bold and unfeeling in her to sit there so calm when her cousin's life is perhaps in imminent danger," said another elegant fair one, to whom Margaret, because of Mr. Plowden's attentions, had long been an object of sore envy.

"That is true," replied a third with a fashionable lisp, "and it proves how just was dear Mrs. Delmar's decision regarding Miss Calvert's readmission into our society. How glad I am that she caused us to decide then not to readmit her under any circumstances; now, of course, she has forfeited all right."

"Certainly," responded the modern-looking Diana, "but we should have remembered in the first place, her obscure condition—that she has no fortune in her own right—absolutely nothing but what her aunt and cousin choose to give her."

There were hotter blushes on the veiled face, and a quicker beating of the sad heart under the friendly cloak.

It was true that Margaret had only what her aunt and cousin choose to give, but, owing to Madame Bernot's tender affectionate care she had been spared the feeling of dependence which usually accompanies such bounty.

Now, however, strangers, or rather unfamiliar acquaintances flaunted it in her hearing, and she sickeningly realized that it was her poverty and dependence which made her a criminal in the eyes of fashionable society, which made the latter refuse to tender to her the sympathy that would have been lavishly given to a wealthy sister similarly placed.

"But do you think it possible," said the lady to whom Margaret was an object of such envy, "that Mr. Plowden will really marry her after all that has happened and that may still happen!"

"Oh, certainly," was the reply, "for, as Mrs Delmar says, persons of her stamp being so directly the opposite of the distinguished Mr. Plowden, have many artful ways by which to entrap gentlemen like him."

Goaded to the quick, Margaret Calvert involuntarily raised her veil; perchance the magnetism of her gaze compelled each of the fair slanderers to look directly at her. The interchange of looks lasted but an instant, for she dropped her veil as suddenly as she had raised it, but the libelous remarks ceased—something in her face had awed the affrontery of even these women of fashion.

Mrs. Delmar, whose name had occurred so frequently in their comments, was smiling, and bowing to them from an opposite part of the house; she had been careful not to obtain seats too near that "odious Margaret Calvert," as she now invariably termed Hubert's cousin, and they returned the salutations with smirks and smiles which they supposed to be graceful and becoming.

Margaret's eyes mechanically followed the direction of their glances, till they too rested on the interestingly pale features of Mrs. Delmar, who was still wielding her jewel-adorned fan.

She smiled faintly, as, for a moment, she remembered

that lady's former treatment—the almost motherly affection with which she was wont to receive her—and now to learn that this same estimable matron had been urging her friends to close the portals of society to the defenseless girl.

"For what?" Margaret asked herself, for, with all her sorrow and anxiety for Hubert, with all her dislike of the fashionable world, this coldness, and uncharitableness stabbed her to the quick.

The prisoner appeared, and immediately Margaret's thoughts and emotions became centered in him.

He was paler, and more attenuated looking than he had been even on the previous trial-day, but his mien and gait were as firm, as free from awkwardness, or embarrassment, as they had been on the former occasion. His eyes rested on Margaret, only turning from her as if to study Plowden's face. He seemed quite regardless of the multitude of stares bent upon him—of the buzz of whispered remarks which his appearance caused.

If the ordeal through which Bertoni had passed during the previous week had produced any strange, or untoward effect on the great lawyer, that effect was successfully concealed. He was the same grand eloquent counsel, sweeping obstacles before him with one stroke of his masterly precision, and bringing to the surface substances, that another and less able pleader could not have distinguished from the shadows lying on the stream.

Grand and triumphant, he made even less effort to conceal his triumph than he had done on the former occasion. If on that former occasion he had seemed confident of his power, on this, he seemed to breathe certainty of success with every word he uttered. There was a strange defiance in his very manner—a peculiar concentration on self, that told more than the magnificent sentences he uttered, how he knew and felt the power which was within him—how he defied even "Requelare." And Plowden's brow darkened, and Plowden's hand which he had thrust into his breast, clinched till the nails sunk through the flesh; for Plowden knew that, though Bertoni was now an expelled member of "Roquelare," yet that body, in order that no stain might be cast upon itself, would afford every assistance to the counsel for the success of the prosecution.

Perhaps that which exerted on uninitiated spectators an effect as peculiar as Bertoni's thrilling words, was the strange manner with which the latter gesticulated with his left arm—slow, methodical motions, as if each one had been carefully studied and had as deep and important a meaning attached to it, as the very sentences he declaimed. Frequently a certain gesture disclosed the red bandage about his wrist, and Plowden, giving to those motions a closer attention even than he paid to the eloquent speech, grew ghastly when the crimson bandage came in sight.

The servants were the first witnesses examined— not lengthy, minute examinations such as they had anticipated, and for which they fancied they were prepared—but a few, subtle questions that brought out the evidence in a clear, unmistakable manner. Their preparatory caution was not proof against the lawyer's cunning—their very zeal to serve Hubert's cause was but a foil to his wary attacks. He puzzled them with his adroit turns; he worked on their honest consciences till, in sheer desperation, they said more damaging things than, in their simplicity, they would have dreamed it possible to have spoken, and not all Plowden's careful-cross examination, conducted at first solely to calm their agitation, could restore their self-possession.

Perhaps the most self-possessed was Hannah Moore; she stepped up when her name was called with an assumption of fearlessness which she was far from feeling, and which would have been ludicrous had not her genuine woman's heart shone so plainly through it all

She stood before the prosecuting counsel with a manner that indicated as plainly as if she had spoken:
"You'll get nothing out of me."

But alas! for even Hannah Moore's staunch determination; the able lawyer shook even that; however, though he compelled her to fully corroborate the testimony already given by her fellow-servants, he did not draw from her what Margaret had told her of Hubert's crime, nor her knowledge of Hubert's presence in his own home on the night of the murder.

Perchance her straightforward, brusque manner disarmed the counsel of any suspicion which honest McNamee's somewhat confused evidence had roused, or that he deemed her corroboration of the preceding testimony all that was necessary, for the chief stress of his examination seemed to be applied to that particular point.

When on the close of her examination, she stepped from the witness-stand, her broad, full face as red as a peony, and her hands holding her shawl in a most awkward and uncomfortable fashion, she was too confused and too agitated to remember correctly all that she had said, and though, having a dim idea that she had not disclosed certain facts which would have done much to criminate more deeply her young master, she was still dissatisfied and provoked with herself at being so "flustered" as she afterward expressed it; and under the influence of these same feelings, when "Samuel Lewis" was called, she pulled back the little man to whisper excitedly in tones audible to every one in their vicinity.

"Mind now, and don't be a fool—have your wits about you."

But the little man's wits played him a very shabby and malicious trick. They would settle to nothing, but flew off in a most ungallant fashion, leaving his mind in a condition neither to understand a question, nor to answer it properly when he did dimly comprehend its import. He went off into the most lugubrious explanations of his intimacy with Liverspin, as if he was there and then begging pardon of Margaret; he whined out doleful apologies for what he had told the comedian, and he burst into involuntary eulogiums on the goodness of Mr. Bernot and Miss Calvert, but to obtain a straightforward answer to any one of his questions, Bertoni utterly failed.

Plowden, for the first time that morning, smiled as he saw the growing ire of the prosecuting counsel—the great pleader baffled by a man who had scarcely the common modicum of mind. At length, yielding to his impatience and annoyance, Bertoni thundered out a last question to the witness; but the poor little underwaiter terrified by the tone and mien of the counsel, broke down into a childish blubber of tears.

There was a general titter, for poor little Sam's childishness was so ludicrous, and Plowden smiled again, and he permitted the little man to retire without cross-examining him, for he knew *that* evidence at least had not helped the prosecution.

Order was restored, and heads were again thrust forward, and ears were once more strained to catch every word of the next testimony.

Bertoni seemed to have recovered from his annoyance, and his eyes met Plowden's with an expression of triumph as "Mrs. Murburd," was summoned to the stand.

Plowden started—an unequivocal, and plainly uncontrolable start that attracted the surprised attention of those in his immediate vicinity—and he bent forward with an excited eagerness which he made no attempt to conceal. Margaret Calvert also started, and bent forward with bated breath, and a sudden icy pressure about her heart. Well indeed must "Roquelare" have worked to ferret out this witness.

The prisoner did not start, but he smiled as if in triumph. He had felt that "Roquelare" so powerful, so vigilant, would not fail to discover this witness so important and alas! so fatal to him; but he had not spoken of his impression even to Margaret.

The witness—it was with difficulty that she could be induced, or forced to the stand, and people turned, and rose in their seats at the commotion made by her resistance. At length, she yielded to some one who seemed rather a grim guard than a kindly protector, and there appeared at last in full sight of the curious crowd, an old, excited, and apparently very much frightened lady. Her bonnet had become awry; her rich, old fashioned brocaded shawl had lost its fastening and hung awkwardly suspended from one shoulder, while her shriveled hands visible through very thin lace mitts, kept nervously opening and closing on a little leather bag.

That she was a gentlewoman of no mean pretensions to refinement and even wealth, was evident, despite the awkwardness rising from her strange position and the disarrangement of her dress, and that she possessed the natural modesty and kindly feeling which mark the true woman, was evident from the expression of her face, now covered with a blush as bright as if she had been sixteen instead of sixty.

She seemed to be very much frightened, and a feeling of pity mingled with the involuntary respect for her which surged up in even some of the callous hearts of the jurors.

Bertoni at first framed his questions more with a desire to calm her agitation and to soothe her into forgetfulness of her strange position, than to bring out her direct testimony, and he succeeded so far that when he returned to his usual mode of examination she was able to give with tolerable unembarrassment the evidence that made Plowden grow ghastlier than he had done at the sight of Bertoni's bandaged wrist; that made Margaret Calvert grow faint, but which had no other effect upon the prisoner than to bring into his face a more animated almost a joyous look, for that evidence was a gigantic stride toward the justice he coveted.

"My name is Murburd, "Amelia Murburd," she said with a painful tremulousness, and speaking hastily as if her evidence had been prepared beforehand, but having been banished from her mind by subsequent agitation, was only now returning.

"I am a widow and reside in C—— on the Hudson; I have one son, Hugh Murburd; my son and Mr. Bernot were at college together—" her voice suddenly sank, and her nervous hands spasmodically closed on the little leather bag, as if by that gesture she was quelling some emotion.

"Go on, " said Bertoni in a significant tone, and as if she were impelled by some fear, she resumed, her voice trembling more painfully than before.

"When their time at college expired they arranged to travel together, and Mr. Bernot came to my house on the third of September, twenty three months ago; my son was from home, in attendance on a dying friend, but I looked for his return every day, and Mr. Bernot remained with me; but Hugh was detained longer than he had expected and when Mr. Bernot had been in my house a week I received a despatch from a lawyer in this city requiring the immediate presence of my son or myself, or some trusty person, to arrange about some property which was mine by right of law. I disliked to summon Hugh from his friend of whom he had written on that same day that he could not last but a few hours, and I was too unwell to obey the summons myself. Mr. Bernot, on hearing the circumstances, kindly offered his services, and I accepted.

"He went on the afternoon of the tenth of September he returned early on the morning of the twelfth, bearing some papers that the lawyer had given him for me. He had transacted my business on that same evening of the day he had left me and he brought me such good news about my property that it put me in very good spirits and I thanked him warmly. I was a little surprised at the way he replied to my thanks; he seized my hands and asked me if *my* son did something very, very wrong, and looked into my face afterward and received my blessing as if he was still innocent, would I forgive him—would I love him as I did before if ever I should come to know of what he did? And I answered of course I would, if he was sorry; and then I asked him if such was *his* case, but he shook his head and laughed in his gay way, and replied that he had only been playing on my mother's fears; that we mothers were all alike, and he was just then thinking of the parting words of his own mother.

"Hugh had not yet returned, and all that day I could not refrain from watching Mr. Bernot; I was afraid he had got into some trouble as young men sometimes do, and knowing that his mother was a confirmed invalid, I was anxious if I could to help him, but everytime I approached the subject he turned it with some bit of pleasantry. Hugh came back the next day, and insisted, as so much time had been lost, that they should start that evening.

"I had intended to mention my suspicions, regarding Mr. Bernot, to my son, but in the bustle of such hurried preparations I had no opportunity. While they were partaking of a hasty repast, I was tying some parcels in the same apartment, I asked Hugh for a knife to cut a cord, and Mr. Bernot offered his, showing me how to open it by a spring in the handle. It was different from any knife I had ever seen before, having such peculiar shaped blades, and I continued to look at it after I had used it, till Mr. Bernot took it hastily and I thought somewhat rudely, from my grasp, at which my son said, laughingly:

"'Why, you usen't to be so chary of letting others see that wonderful knife—what is the matter with it now? Have you been committing a murder with it?'

"My son had bent his head to his plate again, but I

was looking at Mr. Bernot, and I saw him grow so pale that I thought he was going to faint. I was too much surprised to speak, and before I could recover myself he was tendering me the knife again, with an apology for his rudeness, and he added that there *was* an interesting memory about it which made it a very valuable object in his eyes. My son looked up and asked:

"'Since when? You did not speak of any memory being connected with it when we college fellows used to admire its construction.'

"Mr. Bernot made some laughing reply—I can't distinctly remember what; and having finished their repast both started up to hasten preparations for their departure. I remember distinctly events just as they happened at that particular time because my mind was uneasy about Mr. Bernot. I kept thinking about his poor, helpless mother, and worrying about what I ought to do, for her sake, for the young man if he was in trouble.

"I wanted to speak to my son more than ever but there was not a single opportunity, and the two seemed so happy and so full of spirits, that I thought perhaps it was as well to have no chance of dampening Hugh with my suspicions.

"They were gone eight months, and Hugh's letters always said that they were both enjoying everything to the utmost.

"I knew nothing of this murder, for in my quiet home, when my son is not there, very little of the outside world ever enters. And when Hugh came home and told me of the pleasant time he had, and how much good the tour had seemed to do Mr. Bernot, and how gay Mr. Bernot had been, I was glad that I had not spoken to my son.

"One day, in looking over Hugh's things I found some old newspapers carefully stored away—it was not his habit to save anything of the kind, and I wondered what important news they could contain, especially as they were the city papers dated about eight months before. I opened them and found accounts of the investigation of Cecil Clare's murder. I had never seen Miss Calvert, but I had heard Mr. Bernot frequently speak of her as his cousin, and when I read about her visit to the *morgue*, her identification of the murdered man as one who had been known to the family, her trial, and when I saw Mr. Bernot's name, my heart seemed to stand still; and Mr. Bernot's paleness when Hugh remarked about the knife, and Mr. Bernot's own strange observation to me when he returned from the city after executing my commission, all rushed to my mind. I tried to think but I could not, I was so numb with horror; and then my son hoarding those papers, it seemed to me that he must know if his friend was guilty.

"I put the papers back, and that night I told Hugh how I had read them, and I told him then for the first time, all my former suspicions and anxiety regarding the young man,

"But Hugh became angry. He said it was unlike me to have suspicions of any one, and least of all, of one of his friends; that he could vouch for Hubert Bernot being an honorable, noble young fellow, and little likely to get into any such trouble as I feared; that his mysterious connection with the murder case arose from the fact that in former years the murdered man had been intimately known to the Bernot family, and that he (Hugh) had simply preserved the papers, because the whole was such a peculiar and uncommon affair.

"And when I asked my son if Mr. Bernot had not been very much annoyed at having his name brought in such a way before the public; and concerned that his cousin should have been subjected to such a painful ordeal as that legal examination, he answered 'yes,' and 'no,' and 'I don't know,' all in the same breath, and in such a queer, hurried manner, that I was very much perplexed and troubled.

"Hugh saw that, and he asked me for his sake to banish the whole matter from my mind—that in any event it was no business of mine. But though I did not speak of it again I could not help thinking about it.

"When Hugh was home about two months, it became necessary for us to go abroad, in order to have a final decision about my property, and we were gone a little over eight months. Shortly after our return"——

She stopped abruptly, as if that part of her well-conned lesson had suddenly escaped her memory.

"Well, after your return," said Bertoni, soothingly, and as if his voice had the required effect, she resumed:

"We learned of Mr. Bernot's confession and arrest, and my son left me to visit him.

"He telegraphed to me that he would be obliged to stay in order to give his evidence in the case, and then I was brought somewhere here"—she put her hand to her forehead, as if trying to remember—"and I fell sick with worrying about Hugh.

"After that somebody instructed me what to do, and I was brought here to testify against this poor young man. I didn't want to do it—I hope he won't take it unkindly of me, but I had to—I had to."

She broke down into piteous sobbing, and even the ladies who had employed the early part of the morning in slandering Margaret, applied their gossamer handkerchiefs to their eyes in apparent sympathy.

Bertoni seemed to regard that evidence as sufficient, for he smiled slightly, and leaned back with a self-satisfied air, while Plowden waited for the old lady's emotion to subside.

Plowden's countenance wore no hopeful look, nor did his manner evince even the usual energy with which he was wont to begin his cross-examination.

He knew that he could gain nothing for the defense from that witness; that he could not weaken her testimony at any point, a testimony which ere long would tell fearfully against the accused. He could only verify his suspicions of the subtle, underhand way in which Bertoni must have worked to obtain this evidence.

When the old lady had dried her tears with a substantial handkerchief which she took from the bag, and when she had been made to comprehend that she was not yet free to descend from the witness stand, Plowden began his apparently useless questions. He gave them a drift which set the witness talking of herself and her feelings upon the present trying occasion, and after one or two adroit turns, he drew from her the whole story of how she came to be in her present position. She told it in her simple, natural way, becoming so absorbed in the recital as to appear to be conscious alone of Plowden's presence.

"While my son was home after his tour with Mr. Bernot, a strange, elderly gentleman came to our house one afternoon, inquiring for Hugh, and when Hugh saw him they were a long time talking together. I wondered what the conversation was about, but my son did not want to tell me, but he said to me, that if the strange gentleman, who had given his name as Mr. Walter Conyer, should speak to me about Hubert Bernot I was not to tell him that Mr. Bernot had executed any commission for me in the city. I was to say nothing more than Mr. Bernot was a very good young man.

"But Mr. Conyer, often as he called, never alluded to Mr. Bernot in my presence. When we had taken passage for England, almost the first person we met on board the steamer, the morning that we sailed, was Mr. Conyer, and I was surprised to find that he was going abroad also.

"My son did not seem to like it, and he said to me impatiently that I did wrong to tell Mr. Conyer the particulars about the time of our sailing; but I had only mentioned it in conversation a week or two before, and he told us when we met on board that it was a sudden case of pressing business which was taking him to England.

"I asked my son what was the matter—what cause of dislike had he to Mr. Conyer? but he only answered: 'Oh! nothing in particular; and it's a parcel of lies anyway.'

"I begged him to tell me what he meant, but he grew angry at my persistency, saying it was no matter for a woman any how, and I desisted, seeing his reluctance to tell me.

"He kept aloof from Mr. Conyer, but Mr. Conyer did not appear to mind that. He used to come up in his pleasant, gentlemanly way, and say such kind things about my son, that my heart warmed to him."

"When we arrived in England we found there would be a great deal of trouble and expense that we had not calculated on, and Hugh was almost in despair; but Mr. Conyer behaved very cleverly. Somehow, he seemed to know almost before he asked me, where our difficulties lay, and he seemed to have a great many friends. He introduced Hugh to some of them, and straightway my son's anxiety appeared to lessen, and his cheerful spirits to return.

"I heard him answer one day, when Mr. Conyer had been trying to impress on him the advantages which would be gained if he, my son, would follow a certain course."

"'I am afraid by my coldness in the past, I have wronged you, Mr. Conyer; if so, my friendship in the future shall atone.'

"And they shook hands and went out together. I was very glad, for I thought Mr. Conyer was a good friend; and when Mr. Conyer dropped in upon me the next day, and found me alone, I could not refrain from opening my heart to him, and telling him how grateful I was for his kindness, and how I wished I could do him some service."

"He put his hand to his breast and bowed his head in such a way that for an instant I thought he was crying, and when he looked up he seemed so sad my heart ached for him."

"'Mrs. Murburd,' he said, 'if it was in your power to help me save the son of a dearly loved friend of mine from a doom that is surely approaching him, you would make me the happiest man in existence. This son was a college mate of your own noble boy, and you know him also—Hubert Bernot. He is secretly charged with the crime of murder, and I have reason to fear that detectives are on his track. But let him be guilty or not I shall do all in my power to save him for his mother's sake—his mother who was once the cherished object of my affections, but who refused to return my regard; she said I bore her malice because of my rejection, but if I can save her son, that act will show her that I not only bear no malice, but that the love which I one proffered her has burned as brightly through those years as when I first laid it at her feet.'

"Those were his very words, I cannot help remembering them distinctly, for I was so struck I couldn't answer him, but he went on without seeming to mind.

"'This is why I called upon your son in the first instance. I learned that he had been at college with Hubert, and that they been intimate companions. I have not seen any of the family for many years, owing to my absence in distant lands, and on my return the first news which accidentally, and in secret greeted me, was Hubert's name coupled with the epithet murderer! The party who thus spoke was not aware of my acquaintance with the family and when I pressed for particulars, gave them freely—showed me the papers in which his name was connected with a murder case, and told me the suspicion regarding him which had been roused at that time had rapidly gained credence. He told me also, of Madame Bernot's helpless, invalid state. She was in perfect health when I went abroad, and I determined not to call at the house according to my first intention for I thought that by pretending to be a total stranger and, in that character, using all my vigilance, I could help them more than by visiting, and perhaps startling them with my own wild fears.

"'I called at the college from which Hubert had graduated, and learned that his conduct there had been exemplary. He was in the company of your son directly that he left college, and to your son I came for information. I did not disguise myself with him. I told my story frankly. But your son was incredulous, and being Hubert's friend, he would listen to nothing which implied a stain on Hubert's character. The utmost that I could obtain from him was a promise that he would not write to Hubert, nor in any way acquaint him of anything he had heard from me—I feared if he did so, it might startle the young man—if he was guilty—into betraying himself.

"'A few days before we sailed, I received private information that a certain person who had left for England the day previous had boasted in a drunken carouse of being in company at the very time of the murder, with the man whom Hubert is suspected of having murdered, and further information gave me clews that I thought would enable me to find this person if I also came to England; but I have failed to discover anything more, and nothing is left for me but to return with you and your son to America.'

"'If Hubert did commit this crime it was in the recklessness of youth, and he deserves more pity than censure; but, still, if I could only learn how the detectives managed to get the clews they seem to hold—whether they obtained them by Hubert's own want of prudence—I should know better how to save him from the consequences.'

"And then his head sunk on his breast, and he looked so dejected, that my heart ached more and more for him. I began to think that Mr. Bernot might have roused other people's suspicions as he had awakened mine, and it seemed to me that I ought to tell Mr.

Conyer of my own old perplexing thoughts of the young man—that perhaps by so doing I might help to save him if he was guilty; and Mr. Conyer was such a devoted friend of poor Madame Bernot, there surely could be no harm in telling him. I felt confident Hugh would not mind my telling at that time, however angry he might have been had I told before.

"So I opened my heart to Mr. Conyer, and I let him know everything I knew about the poor young man; how he kindly returned to the city to transact my business with the lawyer; and I showed the papers in which he could see by the date the precise day that Mr. Bernot had attended to my commission. I told him about Mr. Bernot's paleness when my son passed the remark on his knife, and he inquired if I would know the knife if I saw it again, and I answered that I could not help knowing it, it was so peculiar; then he asked me how I thought my son regarded these signs, or if he had noticed them, and I told him Hugh would not hear of such a thing, even when I spoke to him about the papers containing the investigation of the murder which he had so carefully put away, and how hurriedly and strangely he answered me when I remarked on Mr. Bernot's feelings at having his name before the public.

"Mr. Conyer thanked me for telling him all that, and he shook hands with me, and on his way out, when he reached the door he turned back and shook hands with me again, saying I had done him such a service; and I felt very glad, for I thought I had helped poor Mr. Bernot.

"I told Hugh when he came in, but he did not take it as I did. He became angry and said I had broken my promise to him; and when he saw me feeling so badly and crying to myself that I should be reproached so bitterly, he put his arm around me like he used to do when he was a boy growing up, and said:

"'I didn't mean to hurt you so, mother, and its all my fault. Perhaps if I had told you at first when you wanted to know, it would have been better. But I knew you already suspected poor Hubert of something; and I feared if I told you what Mr. Conyer had told me, you would only wonder and suspect the more, and perhaps betray your suspicions. So I thought it sufficient when I instructed you what to say of Hubert, should the gentleman ask you any questions.'

"And my son then further said to me:

"'I gave Mr. Conyer my promise not to write to Hubert, nor communicate to him in any way what he had told me, because I thought such a course was the better one for the time being; and Hubert's own letters to me were so calm and cheerful that I could not bear to startle him with my suspicions of this Mr. Conyer, whoever he may be.

"'I know Mr. Conyer has been exceedingly kind to us; that but for him we should have been disappointed in our hopes, and should be obliged to return to New York much poorer than we came, but for all that I distrust him. I distrust the very people to whom he has introduced me; there seems to be some secret bond between them that I don't like—something that savors strongly of what I have heard of that mysterous society 'Roquelare.'

"'He may be Hubert's devoted friend as he pretends to be, but for all that I distrust him, and I am sorry you told him what you did.'

"Then seeing me begin to cry, he said cheerly:

"'Well, never mind, mother, perhaps there's no great harm done after all.'

"I wasn't as warm after that to Mr. Conyer, but he didn't seem to mind it a bit; and to my surprise Hugh appeared to become warmly attached to him, even inviting him to spend some weeks with us when we returned home. I asked Hugh what was the meaning of his sudden friendship, and he said it was a feint, in order to watch Conyer; to learn when the latter would make the first attempt to make any use of what I had told him, But Mr. Conyer didn't seem to have the slightest idea of such a thing. He was continually deploring Madame Bernot's illness, and constantly asserting that he was afraid to meet her lest his anxiety should betray itself in some unpleasant way. He used to go to the hotel at the landing, every day, and Hugh discovered that these daily errands were for a letter directed there for him, and which never failed to arrive. And Hugh came home to me very angry.

"'He's a sneaking spy,' he said, 'and I'll unmask him before many hours,' but just at that moment Mr. Conyer entered, looking so distressed, and so much as if he was going to faint that I hurried to him with a scream.

"He held a city newspaper in his hand, and as he sank into the chair to which I helped him, he motioned Hugh to read something in the paper—it was the account of Mr. Bernot's strange arrest. Hugh looked blank, and I could do nothing but wring my hands and cry, while Mr. Conyer rocked himself to and fro, and said:

"'Oh,' and, 'I feared it would come to this,' and, it is too late to save him,' and such like expressions, and then he pulled a bundle of letters out of his pocket and holding them up said:

"'You were suspicious and angry, my dear fellow that I did not have those directed here. They are from a lawyer who has been making secret discoveries of the clews daily gained by the detectives—for Hubert has been sharply and hotly driven to the confession he has made; and I feared if the letters came here their regular and punctual arrival would make it necessary for me to say something of their contents; and the latter were so hopeless, so sad, as regarded the poor fellow's approaching doom, that I could not bear to sadden you by my sorrow and anxiety.

"And he threw the letters on the table in a careless manner, and buried his face in his hands.

"I could see by Hugh's countenance that he was doubting and distrustful yet; but when I saw Mr. Conyer so broken down, all *my* doubts vanished, and I tried to comfort him. He only shook his head and smiled sadly, and replied, when I had said all the hopeful things I could think of:

"'There is nothing for me to do now, but to go to see him, and after that to see his poor afflicted mother.'

"And the way he went on then brought the tears to my eyes, though Hugh didn't seem to be a bit moved.

"'I'll start this very afternoon,' he said, 'I can't delay longer,' and then he got up slowly, put the letters back in his pocket, and went to his room.

"Hugh remained a good while in thought; at last he said:

"'Mother, I'll accompany Mr. Conyer to the city; I must watch his movements, and I want to see Hubert.'

"I did not oppose him, and when Hugh announced his purpose to Mr. Conyer at dinner, Mr. Conyer jumped up, and shook Hugh's hand, and said he was *so* delighted, and that his own visit to Hubert would not be so painful since he should be accompanied by Hubert's warm friend.

"Immediately after dinner he went out, and I saw him go slowly in the direction of the landing. When he returned I was alone, Hugh having gone out on a brief errand, and I asked him if he had been to the hotel? I thought he looked surprised, but he answered:

"'Yes,' that he had been sending a telegram to the lawyer who wrote to him daily, to have permits secured in order that there might be no delay in seeing Hubert when he and my son should reach the city.

"So they went, and I bade Hugh good-by, little thinking it would be so long before I should see him again."

Her tears appeared again about to flow, but she pressed them back with her handkerchief, and resumed:

"My son telegraphed to me the next day, that he was well, but that he would have to remain and testify against Hubert Bernot.

"I could not believe the evidence of my eyes when I read that—Hugh, who was always Mr. Bernot's warm defender, going to testify against him. I thought it must be because he was sure of Mr. Bernot's guilt and deemed it his duty to do so; but even then it wasn't like him to drag a friend to punishment.

"He did not say in the telegram when I should hear from him again, nor did he mention any place where I could write to, and in the midst of my worriment Mr. Conyer came in. His presence without Hugh, even though I knew the reason of my son's absence, frightened me, and I wildly implored him to tell me where Hugh was, and why he didn't return with him Mr. Conyer seemed very much distressed; he told me how the lawyer had been false to him, that all the time he had been pretending to inform Mr. Conyer of the movements of the detectives, he had been in the secret pay of the detectives themselves, and instead of securing the permits for which Mr. Conyer had telegraphed, he had availed himself of his knowledge of the hour at which Mr. Conyer and my son should arrive in the city, in order to have them both seized by the detectives, and forcibly detained, in order to give evidence when the case should come to trial, letting Mr. Conyer go, however, when they found that he had not seen Hubert for such a length of time, but keeping my son because he knew Hubert so well; and making him swear that he would tell everything that had caused him at any time to suspect Mr. Bernot of any crime. And I did not doubt Mr. Conyer's statement, but a sudden thought came to me in the midst of my grief, and I asked him what in the first place had led the lawyer to think of giving him—Mr. Conyer—and my son, into the hands of the detectives, and he answered that he had indiscreetly mentioned in some of his letters to the lawyer, the warm friendship which existed between Hugh and Hubert, and how they had traveled together; then he told me that he could take me to my son, and that I must not be frightened if I found him a prisoner, for the detectives would keep him as such, till his evidence could be taken; so I got ready and came with him. He was very kind to me, treating me almost as Hugh would have done, but when I got here I didn't see my son."

Again she stopped suddenly, and looked for the first time at the grim, dark countenances of the jurors as if she feared to say more.

"Go on," said Plowden softly, "you shall suffer no harm."

"Fear not to speak," said Bertoni, bending slightly forward, "you have served the end for which you were brought here, and all that you may say now can make little difference."

Thus exhorted her sudden fear seemed to vanish, and fixing her eyes with a confident look on Plowden's face, she resumed:

"Mr. Conyer took me to the house of some friend of his, and I tried to wait patiently until he could arrange for me to see my son. He said they had removed Hugh to another place, making it difficult to find him, and at last he told me that I would not be permitted to see him unless I too would tell everything I knew about Mr. Bernot, and that from Hugh himself the detectives were already aware of much of what I had in the past months told to Mr. Conyer. I became sick then from excitement, and anxiety, and grief, at being obliged to testify, and I was sick a good many weeks, but I was cared for very kindly. When I recovered enough to sit up, I did not see Mr. Conyer, but I received a note from him which stated that he was still searching for Hugh, that he would not come to me till he had found him, and it assured me that I should be well cared for. It also said that the detectives had discovered my present abode, and it exhorted me in the event of any visit from them to consent, for Hugh's sake—for Hugh's safety—to tell in court all that I had told him.

"While I was trying to think what I ought to do, some one did come, who announced himself as a detective; he talked to me a long time, and he frightened me so with threats of injury to Hugh if I did not tell everything I knew about Mr. Bernot, that at last I consented; but I was so flurried I could not properly connect the things I wanted to remember and the gentleman came every day and wrote down all I told him and put everything in its right place and I studied it all. But when he brought me here this morning, aud I saw poor Mr. Bernot looking so pale and thought if it was my son was in his place, and Mr. Bernot's mother was going to testify as I was, my heart failed me; and when my name was called I would not have answered, but my escort remonstrated, and whispered that I might never see Hugh again if I failed to keep my promise, and that made me come up here. Now I shall see my son, shall I not?"

She looked about her as if in search of the gentleman who had brought her thither, and having caught sight of him down amid the crowd, she extended her hands to him imploringly, and said with touching pathos:

"He is all I have, you know; no one in the wide, wide world but Hugh."

Plowden signified that he had finished with the witness, and at a sign from the Judge, the clerk led her down to the gentleman who had escorted her that morning, and who now hastened to conduct her out of the court-room; but even as she went, she repeated in tones that brought the moisture to many eyes:

"Shall I see my son, now? he is all I have, you know."

The interest with which everybody had listened to that evidence, had been so intense, that many drew a long breath of relief when the old lady at last vanished from sight, and there was a general straightening of forms, and an effort to recover from the surprise and bewilderment caused by her singular testimony.

Plowden was talking to the Judge—apparently urging the adoption of some proposition—and Bertoni smiled, when Walter Conyer was called. No one answered the summons and Plowden with a bow to Bertoni, said, with covert sarcasm in his tones:

"Another evidence of the unflagging invention of my honorable opponent—as I surmised, Mr. Walter Conyer does not exist."

Bertoni rose with that slow, heavy motion which seemed so well suited to his massive form, and returning Plowden's bow, he burst at once into an account of the secret means by which he had hunted Hubert Bernot to his fate.

It was "Roquelare" no more—it was *he*, the one man, the work of but one mind; and all the power of that massive mind was put forth then. Men who were cast in common moulds caught a glimpse of such might as made them bend in involuntary worship before a creature so gifted. And the creature, in the triumph of beholding the effects of his power on each individual of that breathless throng, imagined his mind—that wonderful, grasping mind which had not been dismayed by dishonor—to be all sufficient for him. He seemed to recognize no dependence on a Creator—he appeared rather, to use the powers with which he had been gifted as if they emanated from himself. Men shuddered while they heard him, and yet shuddering, also wondered and admired. He had seized the opportunity apparently, not to show what he had lost by having the secret influence of "Roquelare" no longer at his command, but to reveal what that mysterious society had itself lost in having him no longer to wield its wonderful power.

Grand in the very attitude he assumed, grand in the expression of his face—which was lit up as men had never seen it before even in his most impassioned speech,—he seemed the impersonation of some heroism defiant and triumphant in the midst of the very arrows which sought to pin it to the ground.

As he designed that it I should be, every thought of "Roquelare" was absorbed in this picture of himself, and the very members of that mysterious body who had sat in inquisition upon him a few nights before—who shuddered to think of his after fate when "Roquelarian" influence should be directed against him—now paid involuntary homage to Bertoni of the master mind.

His eyes lit more brightly, his fiery words came forth with more thrilling force. What to him were dishonor, disgrace, since he could compel from his very judges such deference as they had never paid before, since he could prove that *he* had never failed in "Roquelarian" work, and now, expelled member though he was, he possessed that which was capable of arraying itself against the whole united body of "Roquelare" and defying its sternest menaces—his intellect.

Certainly, if the great lawyer wanted to produce an effect on the society from which he had been expelled,—an effect that should cause his dishonor to be somewhat forgotten in the brilliancy of his talents and power as a man—he was eminently successful, and he was satisfied of that success. He gradually let his listeners down from the hights to which he had raised them, and dropped his voice to its wonted tone:

"My honorable opponent," he said, "would have Mr. Walter Conyer, or the person who represented that mythical individual, upon the stand; he would interrogate him in order to discover with whom originated the plan of playing upon poor old Mrs. Murburd's garrulity; he would ask him the reason of such an iugenious acting, of a part only to wean from the old lady her suspicions, and why there should be so long a delay in prosecuting this case when such a witness was at hand. It is in my power to enlighten him."

He raised himself to his full height and stood for a moment as if he would awe by his mere presence those about him; then he resumed, his tones becoming more impassioned, his voice filling the place as no voice had ever filled it before.

"Bertoni never sleeps upon a thought. Bertoni's mind never relaxes its grasp upon an idea until that idea has served his purpose. When other men buried their cares in the joys of domestic affections. Bertoni worked at the problem of bringing a criminal to justice Had the latter been some waif in the dregs of humanity whose whole neglected, miserable life pleaded in extenuation of his crime, there would be little need of so much secret and disguised work to track him to his doom; if, perhaps, sheltered by that honor which is sometimes found amongst the worst of criminals, such an one eludes the law for a time, still there are not wanting the indignation and merciless vengeance of an unreasoning populace to urge on the pursuit of the unhappy wretch; and when he is found, a whole community shudders and recoils from his bloated face and matted hair, and self-righteousness asserts that, 'death is too good for him.'

"In this case, however, there were neither poverty, nor ignorance, nor ill-training. The prisoner who to-day stands self-accused of a dire crime, was born in wealth, reared with every aid of culture, and trained in the most perfect code of morality. Why should justice have slept upon *his* track—why, when it was so unmistakable from Miss Calvert's manner on her first examination, that she knew more than she wished to communicate, were not strenuous efforts exerted to learn that which she concealed—the details of her cousin's traveling tour, *where* he went directly after leaving home, and if his sojourn at that place was uninterrupted until his tour with Hugh Murburd began. Why did every one, on the conclusion of that first investigation seem to be thoroughly satisfied that no member of the Bernot family knew anything of the murder. Even 'Roquelare', his voice took an accent of intense scorn, "failed to discover the clews which were at that time so plain. It was left for me to gather them up, to give the warning, and then to wait—to wait for Hubert Bernot's return, to watch him when he did return, to institute careful inquiries which won the information, *with* whom Bernot had traveled, and *where* he had gone directly on leaving his home.

"While reading in Bernot's face and manner, sufficient to tell me that his remorse of conscience together with his fear of 'Roquelare', would eventually compel him to court his doom, I still resolved to weave about him such a web of circumstantial evidence as should prove at least the thoroughness of *my* work."

Then briefly, but so clearly that the least intelligent mind must have comprehended, he detailed the successive means by which *he* had planned all that had been done by the gentleman represented as Mr. Walter Conyer. The mode of proceeding adopted by Conyer, the very excuses given by that gentleman to render his actions less suspicious, were due to Bertoni's orders— orders issued almost before they were evolved out of existing circumstances—and yet, though his statements were so brief he omitted nothing, even to an explanation about the daily letters which Mrs. Murburd had said Conyer received. They were his replies to Conyer's epistles, and they were directed to the hotel rather than to the home of Hugh, lest their punctual and regular arrival should excite the young man's suspicions.

"But lest their regular arrival should in any case be commented upon," continued Bertoni, "I had prepared an explanation for Mr. Conyer, that explanation was set forth in Mrs. Murburd's evidence, or rather in the apology for her evidence"—with a bow to Plowden.

Then he told triumphantly how *he* had made "Roquelarian" influence, even in distant England, render to the Murburds an important service, in order that *his* one object might be gained. He showed how the very possession by "Roquelare," of the persons of Hugh Murburd and his mother, was due to his foresight and care—the separation of the old lady from her son was owing to his thought, that there might be afforded a better opportunity for imposing upon the old lady's fears.

"And this," he said, bowing again to Plowden, "probably accounts for the absence of both mother and son, when my honorable opponent himself made a journey to C—— for the purpose of interviewing the Murburds."

Plowden savagely bit his lip, and glared for an instant at the opposing counsel while the latter continued, that, but for Mrs. Murburd's illness the trial would have taken place at a much earlier period.

He paused for a second, and when he resumed, his voice contained all the sarcasm which no one else save Plowden could use with such withering effect.

"Perhaps my honorable opponent would ask why I waited to ply my enquiries until the return of Bernot from his tour; why I waited until that time to learn from Mrs. Murburd what I might have learned before, and perhaps with much less trouble. I answer, that I waited to see and to watch Hubert Bernot—to read in him the signs that never fail to betray a man on whose conscience rests the burden of a secret crime.

"Perhaps also, the honorable gentleman would further ask, what course I should have pursued if my plans had failed—if the orders I gave to my agent"—with a haughty emphasis on the word *my*—"had failed of their effect.

"I answer, that regarding Hugh Murburd, if his

friendship for Hubert Bernot had been found by Mr. Conyer to be a sordid thing—if he would build up his own fame or fortune on the ruins of his friend's honor —then would his evidence have been very easy to obtain, and if I had utterly failed to get Mrs. Murburd's testimony, other evidences of the prisoner's guilt which are yet to be shown, would be produced, and those evidences would almost set aside the necessity for examining the last witness.

"I inflicted on myself the care and labor which were necessary to obtain this peculiarly-given testimony"—his voice quivering with sarcasm—"that the reputation which 'Roquelare' bears for vigilance and expert tracing of clews, however slight, might be maintained. I have detailed the successive means which I have taken to gain this evidence, to manifest, as I said before, the thoroughness of my work.

"Whether the counsel for the defence will endeavor to show that the crime of the accused was committed in the rash impulses of youth, or possibly in self defense, though it was shown on the coroner's inquest that malice alone could have struck the blow which sent the unfortunate man into eternity, I know not—I only say"—again he drew himself up and looked scathingly about him—" if, when there is completed every link in the evidence which is still to be adduced, and no doubt as to the guilt of the prisoner remains on a single rational mind; when it is proven that he did not give himself up until he felt upon him the very grasp of the law; when it is remembered that he is one of the elegant young men of society about whom wealth and social standing often form a defense for every crime; when it is shown that if it was some poor, illiterate wretch who occupied the place of the prisoner, justice would speedily have its course; when reflection summons the number and frequency of the red-handed murders which disgrace our city, and how necessary are salutary examples to deter immorality from cor rupting the very laws themselves; when all these things have been carefully weighed, and yonder prisoner pays not the penalty of his crime, then is 'Roquelare' an empty title which means neither truth nor justice, and I shall be glad to fling its very memory amid the contemned things of the past."

For an instant Bertoni raised his bandaged wrist in full sight of the gaping, startled throng, then slowly lowered it, and took his seat amid the most profound silence, and not until it was announced that the court had adjourned for that day, did the awe-stricken people seem to recover their startled faculties.

Hannah Moore, having at last recovered from her own especial flurry, was so indignant that " Roquelare " should have produced such damaging evidence, and so angry with Bertoni as being the prime and successful mover in the case, that it was with difficulty she prevented her ire from launching forth an exceedingly discourteous epithet at the great pleader, and delivering it in such a manner that it must be heard by the gentleman himself; but she contented herself with saying, in a voice so loud that her words were distinctly audible to every one in her vicinity.

"It's the divil's own work, so it is—that ' Roll-your-care '—to be entrapping any decent body as it does. And faith, the divil will give that great lawyer beyond there, that flustered me so, his wages yet; mind that now!" glaring fiercely on the strangers about her, who were beginning to show their appreciation of her amusing anger by various grins, and whispered pleasantries, which the honest-hearted woman was very much inclined to regard as insults to herself.

John McNamee, fearing the result, should her indignation become too hot, as it very easily did, took her hurriedly on his arm and escorted her to the street, while the other servants of the Bernot household closely followed.

" Where's Sam Lewis?" said Hannah, when John,

quite sure that she was beyond the reach of any stray spark being applied to her inflammable temper, released her from his somewhat overtight grasp.

The little man was not certain but that the manner in which he had given his evidence, after Miss Moore's caution to keep his wits about him, was such as to incur that formidable lady's anger, and much in doubt as to whether her tongue, or her hands, if indeed, not both, would be applied first, he thrust his person timidly forward.

"Come here, Samuel Lewis," she said, "and let me shake hands with you,"—extending her own stout fist —"you're a credit to everybody this day."

The little man pricked up his astonished ears, and stepped with alacrity to her side.

"I say you're a credit. You gave your evidence beautifully. You bamboozled the great man till he couldn't make nothing out of you; and that's what none of the rest of us done"— looking back scornfully at her fellow-help—"you're a credit to the house you live in, Samuel Lewis, and I'm proud of you," with another grip of the little man's hand that almost brought the water to his eyes.

The little under-waiter never stepped so lightly; he never held his head so high; he never made so much of his little thin form in walking; holding himself so erect that he felt as if he had grown two inches in as many minutes; and he offered his arm to Miss Moore, and Miss Moore accepted it, and he looked at everybody they met, and he wondered what they would think if they only knew that he was Samuel Lewis who had given his evidence "so beautifully." And when they arrived at the Bernot mansion, and found a poor itinerant musician droning some most doleful ditty beneath the parlor windows, the quick, brave manner in which the little man darted at the poor Italian, and the sudden way in which the latter retreated with his hurdy-gurdy, were very creditable evidences of Mr.

Samuel Lewis's desire to perform the most gallant acts of duty.

"We've had music enough," bawled Sam, after the poor old musician, "music's near been the ruin of this ere family, and we don't want no more of it."

"You're a jewel, Sam," said Hannah, delightedly patting him on the back when he returned after his exploit, "and when all this trouble is over, as God grant it will be soon, and that poor, dear Mr. Hubert will be home safe and well, we'll have one night of it, and you shall be honored for this day's work."

CHAPTER XVIII.

THE prisoner's countenance looked serene, and even happy on the conclusion of Bertoni's speech; so happy that Mrs. Delmar adjusted her glass a second and third time to be sure she saw aright—a man almost smiling in the very shadow of the gibbet—for in her mind, as in nearly every other mind in the court-room, the last speech had left little hope for the prisoner, but she would not despair, however; the trial was not yet finished, and something would, something *must* happen if not to effect an acquittal, at least to cause a comparatively light sentence.

She desired her daughter to look at Hubert in order to be convinced that her own eyes had not deceived her. But Louise was already looking—looking with such a hopeless, heart-sick look in her eyes, and such a pitiful quivering of pain about her mouth, that any one save her vain, fashionable mother would have been moved to compassion and sympathy.

"It is very strange that he can look so pleasantly," said Mrs. Delmar, "in the face of all that evidence against him. I can't understand it, unless indeed," her face suddenly brightened, "that he is aware of something yet to be shown, which will alter the effect of all previous testimony," and quite reassured by that thought she put down her glass, and disposed herself comfortably while she made disparaging remarks about that "odious Margaret Calvert."

Her daughter made no reply; she scarcely heard, being so absorbed in watching Hubert, and when he had gone—having departed with the same fearless erect gait with which he had entered, she turned her gaze on motionless, veiled Margaret, wondering what were her feelings ; if her heart was just such a quivering, aching thing, as she, poor spoiled child of fashion, was bearing for the first time in her whole life: but she thought that could not be.

Margaret Calvert engaged to another, must be unable to grieve over her cousin's doom, as one would do, who loved that cousin, and when Eugene, having escorted her and his mother to their carriage, was about to leave them that he might tender, as on former occasions, his sympathy to Margaret, Louise detained him to whisper:

"Come home soon—I want to know what you think—how much hope there is for—for Hubert."

To any eyes than those of her unsuspecting, honest-hearted brother, the sudden color that swept into her face, and the strange trembling hesitation with which she spoke would have betrayed her unhappy attachment, but he, little dreaming of the real facts in the case, gave his opinion as he would have given it to one of his club-companions had the latter asked it.

"I am afraid there is very little hope for him, and I think that Plowden begins to entertain the same fear."

He closed the carriage door, and turned away.

Mrs. Delmar leaned back, still plying her fan, and asked languidly:

"What did he say, my dear?"

Louise trembling responded.

"Pshaw!" said her mother pettishly. "An elegant young fellow like Hubert Bernot will never be hung; it would be an outrage—a sin crying for vengeance from society if they should treat him as they do those poor, low common wretches one shudders to look at."

Louise buried her face in her hands and said she had a headache in the hope that her mother would cease her tiresome twaddle, and the carriage rolled on, and tired, heated pedestrians envied the occupants of the costly equipage, and many of them perhaps would have smiled incredulously if told of the anxiety and discontent which reigned in the heart of one of those occupants, the utter misery which filled the other.

Sad, hopeless Margaret; she could not answer Delmar when he murmured his low, gentle-toned expressions of sympathy, but she pressed his hand in grateful acknowledgment, and quietly took her way between him and Plowden to the hack in waiting. Bertoni stood in conversation with a gentleman near the entrance of a private corridor which led from the courtroom. He looked up on the approach of Margaret and her escorts and bowed profoundly to the former—in the same instant, from without, they heard a coarse, bass voice saying in a high, excited key.

"I tell you it's *Mind*, and *Mind* only that makes or mars the man—and such a mind as yonder great lawyer has, will succumb to nothing that time or circumstances may produce."

Bertoni's eyes flashed with triumph, but he turned with an apparently careless air to resume his suddenly interrupted conversation, and the party passed out, confronting in the passage the man who had just given utterance to that singular comment on the lawyer. He was still talking in that same high key—a heavy-whiskered, black-eyed man, having the swarthy complexion of a Spaniard, and very much of the ferocious look which novels ascribe to the bandits of that country—evidently disputing with a mild-faced individual at his side, who was meekly endeavoring to show the disastrous results of intellect when untempered by religion. But the fierce-looking man was not to be convinced that anything save Mind itself was necessary in the world, or that a great mind required to be dependent on a higher power than itself.

Plowden, whispering to his companions to proceed and wait for him, laid his hand on the dark-looking in dividual's arm, and said, quietly, though with the appearance of one who was holding a severe struggle with himself ;

"Wait until you have witnessed the end of this trial, and then, if Bertoni's mind appears as great under bitter defeat as it has done to-day in fancied triumph, speak, as you have spoken, if not, return to the allegiance you owe to your Creator."

He turned quickly and followed Margaret and Delmar.

"Who is he?" asked the astounded, dark-looking man of his companion, the latter answered:

"Why, you ought to know him—Mr. Plowden, the counsel for the defense—a very good man, with a great mind also, but a mind that is not too proud to acknowledge its Maker. They say he is a Catholic."

"And what is Bertoni?" asked a stranger who had been listening with great interest to the dispute.

"What modern *little* men would term an infidel—what *I* call a freeman; free from all your abject, slavish worships, relying, dwelling alone upon that which elevates man above his fellows—*Mind*," said Bertoni himself, who in the act of passing out, had heard the last question and, as he answered it, drew himself up with a haughty gesture of defiance and went quickly on.

The mild-faced man blessed himself, and the dark-looking individual gazed after the lawyer with an expression of passionate admiration.

"To have a mind like his," he said, "to be one of the most talented men of a century, who would not be willing to resign the trammels of religion?"

"Nay," replied his companion with a shudder, "but to avoid being like him, who would not grovel all his days a poor, simple, hooted fool, with no knowledge but that which had told and taught him to worship his Creator."

Margaret and Delmar, waiting in an outer passage for Plowden, did not hear his remark to the stranger, nor did the lawyer refer to it—he seemed absorbed in very troubled thought, too absorbed to do more than press slightly, Delmar's hand, when the latter having assisted to escort Margaret to the hack, took his leave.

In the vehicle, Plowden threw himself back, and shaded his face with his hand as if to prevent its expression being seen by his companion. She waited the withdrawal of his hand to ask the question which trembled on her lips—she could scarcely explain to herself why her question should be stayed by that trifling circumstance, unless for the reason that often actuates troubled minds—the desire for any pretext, however slight in order to delay that which they are eager to hear and yet which they dread to know.

But Plowden retained his hand in its position, and not until the hack had almost reached her own door did Margaret find courage to speak; then she said, suddenly, and with such anguish in her voice, that he dropped his hand and looked up with a start:

"Is Hubert's case as hopeless as it seems? Will Bertoni, cause the sentence to be death?"

Plowden looked away for a moment, as if something in the street through which they were rapidly passing had attracted his attention, but it was to conceal from her the expression which her words had called to his face. The lawyer was becoming less able to mask his feelings in presence of this girl whom he loved as only strong, passionate natures can love.

"I cannot quite answer you yet," he said, when at length he turned to her. "I must think a little longer—till to-morrow. Perhaps—perhaps"—his voice grew strangely tremulous—" all will be well."

They were at Madame Bernot's door, and he paused on the stoop to ask at what hour he should return to escort her to Hubert. He bowed at her reply, and with a brief adieu hurried back to the vehicle, while she, entering the house, rushed to her room and poured out in a wild burst of tears the grief that seemed stifling her.

Hubert Bernot was as calm and self-possessed when Margaret visited him in his cell, as he had appeared to be, in the court-room, three hours previous.

Ordinary spectators looking at the two, and listening to the young man's quiet, and even cheerful conversation, would have thought him the comforter, and Margaret the only grieving one. On this occasion such appeared to be the fact, for Margaret was saying in a voice choked with sobs:

" Why, oh, why, Hubert, did you carry that knife with you after—after that dreadful night ? You assured me when we parted that you would be careful and guarded ; you repeated, when you returned, that you had been, and yet see how much you revealed to Mrs. Murburd. Oh, Hubert !"

" Ah, Margaret ! I fancied that the carrying about me of that knife from which you had cleaned the bloody stain, would inure me to the thought of what I did— would give me a certain bravado ; but on the occasion of my handing it to Mrs. Murburd her close examination of it unnerved me. I feared there might be still a stain upon it, that perhaps you had not taken all off, but I would not allow myself to think that she attached such importance to the manner in which I treated Hugh's remark about it. Never after, though I continued to carry the knife did I allow it to betray me. I *was* careful."

" Think," said Margaret anxiously, " think, if, while you were away, you let any word or action betray your secret to Mrs. Murburd's son—probably, they will examine him to-morrow."

" If I did," he answered, " it was unconsciously to myself—but even in that case what does it matter ? it will but aid everybody to arrive quicker at the truth, and procure speedier justice for me. I hope I *have* betrayed myself to him, and that ' Roquelare ' will leave nothing undone to prove my guilt. Would you have it otherwise, Margaret ?"

"Yes," she answered piteously, "I would not have such evidence given as must make your life the penalty of your crime, and I would be released from my pledge to give in my testimony the confidence with which you entrusted me, for that will supply the last link, and, together with Mrs. Murburd's evidence will be sufficient to—hang you."

She gasped the last words.

Hubert only smiled, and reiterated what had been frequently on his lips during the interview

"I feel that the salvation of my soul demands this: a life for a life.' Nothing less can obtain pardon for my crime."

She besought him at least, to permit her to tell certain circumstances which might extenuate his guilt in the eyes of the law, but he immediately became stern and angry.

"If you would recall all the pledges you have given me of your affection, if you would leave me *now* when you have been faithful *so* long"—his voice dropped suddenly into an accent of touching mournfulness— "do then as you desire—but, if you would be true to the last, if you would have your image enshrined in my heart as that of her who brought peace to my soul, and helped to win for me God's pardon, tell, to-morrow, or whenever they summon you to the witness-stand, how when, and where, I murdered Cecil Clare."

Margaret wrung her hands, saying:

"If only your mother knew—if she could only be told, she would release us both from our promise."

Hubert's face brightened.

"Margaret," he said, softly," do you not see how even Providence seems to accept the atonement I am trying to make. I have offered my life to Him; I have prayed Him to accept it; and I am confident that He will, else why, when my mother's permission to tell what might possibly lighten the penalty of my crime, is so much desired, does He render her state such that she cannot even be made acquainted with what I have done?"

Margaret summoned her strength for a last effort.

"And when they have brought in a verdict of guilty —when they ask if you have anything to say why sentence of death"—her voice faltered despite her endeavor to keep it firm—"should not be pronounced upon you, will you even then say nothing? Will you not then tell the circumstances of the past?"

He put his hand on her head and stroked softly the curls which escaped from her bonnet as if he would soothe her into calmness before he spoke.

"Even then I would only acknowledge the justice of the verdict, and pray in my heart that no earthly mercy might be shown me."

Margaret shrank from him to the other end of the pallet on which they sat. Alas! for woman's fancied strength when there bursts upon her the full consciousness that a passionately beloved object is about to be removed—her stanchest virtues are subjected to the merciless attacks of the tempter. So it was with Margaret. There leaped up suddenly within her a wild burning desire not to do as Hubert wished—not to tell the confidence which would help so materially to criminate him; and then a fierce war between Right and Wrong began in her heart; a war during which she half savagely wondered why God made some people suffer so much while others apparently careless of His very existence seemed so happy. And then she became frightened at herself and she looked up at Hubert who was sadly watching her, and visions of a rope encircling his slender neck and his visage bloated and purple, rose before her. Her overcharged feelings could endure no more. She threw herself at his feet and sobbed out:

"If I could but die too—but to have to live when it is *all* over."

"You forget my mother," he whispered, and just tnen the cell door opened and Margaret hastily rose. It was Delmar, who, feeling that he had disturbed the cousins, would have immediately retired, but Hubert beckoned him forward. "I should not have intruded," apologized the young man, "but the time is almost up, and if I had waited longer I could not have seen you to-day," grasping Bernot's extended hand with the pressure of sincere, manly friendship.

Margaret would have retired, feeling utterly unable to assume a composed demeanor, and wanting to take her poor, distracted, struggling heart, where she invariably took it in its disturbed moments—to the foot of the altar; but Plowden, who had escorted her to the prison—without entering however, on the plea of business connected with Hubert's case which demanded his presence elsewhere—had promised to return for her; so there was no alternative after her trembling response to Delmar's greeting, but to avert her face, and try as best she might to repress every outward sign of her grief.

Hubert put his arm through Delmar's and drawing him to an opposite corner of the cell began a whispered conference. He need hardly have taken such precautions to guard his communication from Margaret's ears, for every faculty of hers was so absorbed in contemplating that fearful probability—his death—that she had almost lost consciousness of her present position.

Delmar's face as he listened to Hubert, grew graver and sadder, and at length as if he would hear no more he interrupted with an eagerly whispered:

"Why speak of such things yet? Your sentence may be much lighter than you anticipate; there will be sufficient time when you know what the end is to be."

Hubert shook his head.

"When I know what the end is to be the time will be too brief to attend to other matters, and I must know now if you are willing to assume this responsibility. I cannot speak of this matter to Margaret—she would not listen to money affairs now—to what will come into her possession at my death. I broached the subject twice to Plowden, but neither would he listen."

"I don't wonder." burst out Delmar with his usual

frankness, "being Miss Calvert's accepted suitor he would have been less than a man to be willing to listen to what your execution would bring his promised wife."

"*Promised wife!*" echoed Hubert, almost aloud in his surprise, and then he smiled bitterly, and continued, half savagely, though he lowered his voice to its first whisper. "Report has made a long, long stride in advance of the truth, and has duped you too."

Without seeming to notice Delmar's start, or the wondering, incredulous expression which came into his face, he poured forth the story of his own and Margaret's love, but in so passionate a manner that it seemed more like the incoherent ravings of a demented mind than the tale of a devoted and mutual attachment.

"Now," he concluded more calmly, "you understand why I am anxious to provide for her comfort—since I cannot for her happiness—to place her beyond the possibility of want in the event of my mother's death which would leave her alone and unprotected. This is the only return I can make for her long and true devotion—to give her the fortune which, as my wife, she should possess. And you, Eugene, who have so nobly proved your friendship for me, will, for my sake, not withhold the same from her. I want it all settled now, while I have time and opportunity to think and speak about it. Promise me, Eugene, that you will assume this trust, as I desire."

Delmar bowed his head. His astonishment at what he had heard kept him silent. But Hubert was satisfied, and he turned away to Margaret. She was still absorbed in that bitter reverie, and it required a third repetition of her name to make her raise her eyes.

Delmar was taking his leave; he wanted to be out somewhere—that he might have space in which to reflect upon the strange, sad story of those two unhappy hearts. The kindly-feeling young fellow had pitied Hubert and Margaret before; but now his heart had all the tender sorrow of a woman's nature, and when he murmured his adieu, his eyes glistened with something very like a woman's tears.

At the prison entrance a man dashed by him with such strangely excited manner, that it was only after a second look he recognized Plowden—Plowden, who had excused himself from entering with Margaret, because he wanted time to wrestle with thoughts which he could keep no longer at bay. He had shut himself into a private room in the immediate vicinity of the prison, and never had man a fiercer, or more desperate struggle. Once, when the contest was at its height, he raised his head and caught the reflection of his face in the small mirror opposite—the veins in his forehead were frightfully swollen, his whole countenance of a purple hue, and overspread with heavy drops of perspiration—he shuddered, and covered it again with his hands, till the minutes wore on, and a knock at the door in obedience to his previous order, lest in his excited thoughts he should forget the lapse of time, made him start to his feet.

"For *her* sake," he muttered fiercely, and pouring out the brandy which he had ordered, but until that moment had left untouched, he drank it quickly, and hastily departed.

He saw Delmar as he dashed by him at the prison door; he had no desire to speak, and in the excitement of his own fierce thoughts he cared little what the young man might think; and simple, ingeneous Delmar passed his hand across his forehead, and said to himself as he walked slowly on:

"Plowden is a strange man, a very strange man—I can't understand him."

Wiser heads than Delmars could scarcely have understood, even could they have known the antagonistic feelings which struggled for the mastery in the proud, passionate heart of the lawyer.

CHAPTER XIX.

"You promise, Margaret," said Hubert, as he held her hand in a farewell grasp, "if they call for your evidence to-morrow to give it according to my desire. Remember, my whole peace of mind depends upon it, and I shall watch you, and linger upon your words as I have never listened to a voice before."

"I promise," she said huskily, and then she turned to the cell door, while Plowden still anxious-looking, and somewhat agitated, murmured his leave-taking.

"If to-morrow would but end it," said Hubert wistfully.

"The day after may," answered the lawyer gloomily breaking from Hubert's grasp as if fearful of being questioned.

"Forego your visit to the church to-day," said Plowden, laying his hand somewhat heavily on Margaret's arm, when they reached the street at which she usually left him.

She looked up in surprise.

He continued:

"I have something to say to you which can only be said in your own home—something that must be said soon."

She bowed assent, and continued in the direction of her residence. She could not have answered him because of the sudden faintness which his words had caused. What could be the something, that had to be told in her own home, and told soon, but an announcement to prepare her for Hubert's approaching execution? She was obliged to take his arm to support her trembling limbs, to lean heavily upon it when the mist came before her vision; and Plowden's blood leaped wildly in his veins, and the struggle in his heart grew fiercer, for how could he, as he was about to do, sever himself from the friendship, from the sight of this being whom he so madly loved?

He did not suffer his excitement to betray itself, and when she ushered him into an ante-room that opened from one of the parlors, though his face was as white as her own, and his lips compressed with mental agony his manner seemed free from the agitation which had marked it in the prison. He motioned her to a seat, and for a moment each looked silently into the other's countenance—he, as if to divine from her face how she would receive his communication, she to read in his very lineaments an answer to the question she could not ask.

"Do you trust me, Miss Calvert?" he said at last, "trust me entirely? I have fancied that you did not —that you accepted my services solely because you had no other alternative. I seek not to know the motive of such distrust. I do not desire to learn if anything in my conduct has given rise to suspicion—I only ask, do you trust me *now* as Hubert's true friend?"

His eyes had in them something so mournful, his whole face was so strangely expressive of some secret suffering, that the girl's tender heart even in her own sorrow, had compassion for him—she was even stricken with a pang of remorse that she had ever entertained a doubt of his sincerity—under the influence of that feeling, she extended her hand and answered frankly.

"Whatever suspicion—whatever distrust I have entertained, has quite gone. Believe me when I say I trust you entirely."

He pressed her hand slightly, and bowed his head as if in gratitude for the assurance.

"If," he resumed, with that mournful, haunting look

still in his eyes, "your cousin's sentence should be comparatively light, the happiness of both of you would be eventually ensured, would it not?—that is, after the lapse of a proper time your marriage would take place?"

Margaret answered:

"You heard the resolution he announced in his cell a few days since; and in very gratitude to God for a light sentence, both Hubert and I should consider it little to make the sacrifice he spoke of."

"If an acquittal were possible," said Plowden, "surely in that case you would marry."

She shook her head.

"You heard him also upon that point, and his desire is, in every instance, mine."

The lawyer's manner became agitated and eager.

"Miss Calvert, if it were possible—" bending toward her—"remember, I only say if it were possible to make your cousin believe that he had been laboring under a mental delusion—that there was no murder upon his soul—if he came forth with no stain upon his character, would you two, who love each other so well, *then* be united?"

Oh, the sudden light that broke over her face; her whole countenance shone as if it had been transfigured, but it was only for a second; for a second that her fancy had caught his words and made them a delightful reality; sober, sorrowful truth however, rent the fabric, and left her more desolate, more heart-broken than before.

The hot tears fell fast upon her cheeks as she answered:

"Could that happen, there might, indeed, be no obstacle to the event you mention—but why torture me with such an impossibility? I know he committed the murder—I who listened to his story, and washed his knife; then, all the world could not make him believe himself guiltless."

"Bear with me, Miss Calvert, even if I do give utterance to impossibilities; it is necessary to do so in order to satisfy myself of one thing; and prove your trust in me by listening, and answering, even though you cannot understand the motives of my questions. Was such a happy ending of this trial possible, and was it accomplished by the effort of *one* man, what would be your regard for this man?"

"What could it be?" she answered, "but a gratitude so deep and tender that he should hold the next place to Hubert in my heart."

Plowden grew more strangely excited; the veins in his forehead began again to swell, and his face to flush so suddenly and deeply, that the livid color seemed to merge into a purple hue.

"But, suppose this man's own life had been a guilty one; suppose dark heavy crimes rested on his soul, what would it be then, Margaret—Miss Calvert—what would be your regard for him then?"

She would fain have looked away from him; his countenance, his manner, so strangely unlike its calm dignified wont, frightened her; but the very intensity of his gaze riveted her eyes and compelled her to answer:

"No matter what his past had been I should remember alone the happiness he had given me."

Plowden grasped her hands.

"No matter what he was, Miss Calvert—no matter what he had done, you would still give him a place in your heart?—you would not loathe him, you would think of him when a just fate had separated him from you forever, and when society mentioned his name only to heap obloquy upon it, you would repeat it in your prayers, and pity its miserable owner? Would you do all this, Miss Calvert?"

Frightened Margaret felt more like screaming for help, than answering him. His grasp had tightened upon her hands till she could feel them throb from the pressure; his eyes had grown wilder and wilder, until to her heated fancy they resembled those of some infuriated animal. She felt sure that his mind had become unsettled, perhaps from his close application to Hubert's case, and perchance also because he was certain of the failure of his efforts; but either case showed the sincerity with which he had labored, and she tried to put the frightened look out of her countenance and the alarm out of her voice, as she answered, softly:

"I should pray for, and pity, and regard him always. No matter what the world might say, he would have proved himself mine, and Hubert's friend."

He released her hands as suddenly as he had seized them, and he leaned back in his chair still looking at her, but no longer with wild eyes and an excited manner—his manner had recovered its wonted calm, and his eyes wore only their mournful expression.

"God bless you, Margaret!" he said slowly, and without apologizing for his unwonted use of her Christian name. He rose, continuing:

"Forgive me if I have talked strangely to you this evening, if I have pressed upon your wounds only to open them afresh and not to heal them; forgive me, because I, too, am suffering, Margaret—the memory of a broken heart, which blessed me in its last throbs, has haunted me all day—the thought of a wrong which blasted that young heart has pursued me everywhere; it seemed to connect itself with the ghastly wrong which stands between you and Hubert, and if it has led me to speak a little incoherently, to betray the haunting regrets which to-day have been fiercer than usual, forgive me—extend to me a little of the sympathy with which you sweeten Hubert's life. For the rest, I have only to say that all hope has not yet gone; only trust me, and whatever happens, remember your promise to pity and pray for him who should restore happiness to you and Hubert."

He wrung her hand and hurried forth.

Margaret remained where he had left her, too bewildered, too wildly troubled to do anything else than stand as it were, while a whole multitude of thoughts rushed in a confused and distracted manner upon her mind. Was she to fear or hope from Plowden's words, or, as she had already done, to regard them as the ravings of a suddenly unsettled mind; if the latter, who would take his place as Hubert's counsel—who would, or could work for Hubert as he had done? Then she remembered what Hannah Moore had said about the lawyer, and she found herself wondering in a vague way if there was any connection between the cook's mysterious knowledge of him, and the strange things he himself had spoken.

She would have hurried to Father Germain with her doubts and fears, but she had been so little with the invalid that day, that it seemed like neglect to defer attendance upon her aunt simply to have her own trouble allayed or calmed.

Her temples throbbed with pain from the intense excitement and grief of the past few hours; her form was weak and trembling from the little sustenance she had taken, and her eyes ached from want of sleep and the long and passionate bursts of weeping to which she had become only too well inured. Truly, Margaret, even when she had changed her out-door costume, and bathed her face, as she went totteringly down to her aunt's room, was a pitiable object.

Madame Bernot's physical condition still remained weak and precarious, though her appearance—save that her face was oftener convulsed by spasms of pain—gave no indication of the alarming increase of her disease. She smiled faintly when Margaret, taking Kreble's place began to bathe her hands; and when the fiery darts of pain, which sometimes shot through her fingers, subsided, she said, softly: "You have been out oftener than usual to-day, Margaret, have you not? Every time I asked for you they said you were out. I only wish it did you more good, my darling, for you look very pale."

Her neice did not reply; she knew not what excuse to frame, so she bent closer to the vessel in which she was saturating the bathing-cloth.

Madame Bernot continued:

"I wonder if Hubert could leave his friends just a little while to come to me; sometimes I think my end is not very far away, and I should like to bless him before I go. And yet it would be selfish to take him from those poor people now. He says in his last letter that poor young man may be hung, and if so, I would not deprive him of a minute of my son's companionship —nor that poor mother who is soon perhaps to be childless. No; his place is with them since he affords them comfort, and perhaps God will spare my life till he can come to me—my own noble boy; but Thy will be done."

She looked at the picture, and for a few moments was oblivious of everything save that blood-stained face; then, as if with an effort she turned her eyes to Margaret, and resumed:

"I have been thinking my dear child, what your future will be when I am gone; so far as means of support are concerned, my own private portion shall revert to you, and Hubert also will make ample provision for you."

"Don't—don't!" pleaded Margaret piteously, and lifting her hands in deprecating entreaty, "don't talk of your death—I cannot bear it."

And, indeed, it looked as if it would take little more to make her frail strength wholly depart.

The invalid faintly smiled.

"I know your affectionate heart, my dear girl, and how you have repaid my little care with more than a daughter's tenderness; it is for that reason I would say something now—something that flashed on my mind to-day very suddenly, and for the first time. Will you answer me very frankly, and will you promise not to feel hurt even though I should be very far from the truth?"

Margaret bowed assent, and Madame resumed:

"Long ago, when you came to me a little, sacred trust, and grew up so fair and sweet, twining yourself about all our hearts, I used to think that one day he who is dead"—she stopped suddenly as if threatened by one of her occasional spasms, but the symptoms, if such they were, passed away—"might hold a near and dear place to you. He was much older, it is true; but the difference in your ages would be amply compensated by his love. Do you remember, Margaret, his affection for you, how frequently he spoke of the future when you would be old enough to marry, and I fondly hoped it would be so, until that sin blighted us all? To-day when I reflected on the lonely position in which my death would leave you, there came suddenly into my mind the possibility of your union with Hubert. Perhaps you are already attached to each other, only I, in my blindness have not perceived it—I have been so accustomed to regard your affection for each other such alone as exists between brother and sister; but perhaps it is different, Margaret. Tell me, has Hubert ever said that he loved you, and, if so, what has been your answer?"

Margaret could not speak; she could only lift her face for an instant while the hot, sudden color dyed every feature, and then bury it in her hands; but it was enough for Madame Bernot.

"I shall not embarrass you further, my darling," she said, "I think I understand it all now, and I shall wait until Hubert comes home. Perhaps the dear God will spare me so long, and if He should not, you can transmit to my son, my wishes on this subject. Why have you been so silent, my dear girl? Was it that you feared my displeasure? Ah! Margaret, you hold too dear a place in my heart for me to wish to withhold my son from you."

If she could only have looked into the heart of the girl kneeling beside her, how, inured to suffering though she was, would she not have started back appalled from the anguish burning there ; how would she not have yearned in pity and tenderness over poor Margaret's wild desire to throw herself on that loving breast, and sob out *that* union could never be—that cup of happiness had turned to gall and wormwood months ago.

But the invalid saw nothing only the bowed, motionless head of her neice, and she suspected nothing save that Margaret's heart was in Hubert's keeping, and then her eyes wandered to the beloved picture. But the effort which it had cost her to say so much, and to revert to that past which had been hitherto as a sealed book, even to her own thoughts, brought on one of her severe spasms. They were wont to come suddenly and without warning, but they rarely left her so white and corpse like as did this one, and Margaret knelt in terror, while Kreble raised the cushions and laid the still, white face softly back.

The same lone night hours that witnessed Margaret's vigil in the sick room, looked upon an unusual scene in the Delmar homestead. Louise, immediately on the return of her mother 'and herself from the court, had shut herself in her room on the plea of a headache, and she had given way unrestrainedly to the strange and painful thoughts which agitated her mind.

Too vain and shallow, too superficially educated to know how to reason with her passionate desires, and lacking the one infallible guide, true religion, she could only shrink and writhe under her strange mental torture without even attempting to combat it. In all her previous trouble her usual course was to flee at once to some one of her confidants—as what girl of fashion has not one or more of such?—and talk herself out of her real, or imaginary sorrow ; but this troubled state of feeling was something so different from anything she had yet experienced, that she turned impatiently from describing that pain to any of her frivolous companions.

She thought of her mother, but it was only to turn with the same impatience from the idea of giving *her* such a confidence, divining instinctively that the latter would not understand it, and, if she did, would not be capable of sympathizing with it.

The hours wore on. Mrs. Delmar had sent to know how she was, and on learning that she was no better and had even refused to partake of the repast sent to her room, came herself with affected maternal solicitude to advise that the family physician be summoned. But Louise was in no mood for questions or endearments, and to both returned such churlish answers, and gave such other unmistakable evidence of being in a very ill temper, that the fashionable lady was glad to return to the visitor she had left.

And the unhappy girl flung herself on the lounge again, and tossed and moaned until she heard her brother ascend to his room.

Her thoughts were becoming unendurable. Poor, pampered child of fashion! she could not bear pain, and she sought to fling it from her at any cost. She must tell her trouble to some one; she must obtain sympathy, if not relief, somewhere, and to her brother, who, she fancied—because he was Hubert's friend—would be the most likely to compassionate, and perhaps to help her, she determined to pour out the unhappy passion of her foolish heart.

Hitherto, there had been few confidences between the brother and sister, partly owing to their different dispositions, and partly owing to the training which Louise had received—a training that taught her to look abroad for confidantes, that made her regard other young men as more fitting objects upon whom to lavish attentions than an old-fashioned brother whose ideas of right and wrong were rather too strict.

Eugene's sex had saved him from the pernicious training of his sister; it had removed him during his boyhood, and a good portion of his early manhood from his mother's soul-destroying care, and with impulses naturally good, and parts though not brilliant, yet steady and sure, he had escaped scathless from the temptations which beset most youths. Seeing but little even of his mother and sister until he had left college, he considered women as something beyond his understanding—creatures to be wondered at, and to be venerated, but on no account to be made familiar with manly affairs, or the recipients of manly confidences. His feelings, so far as veneration was concerned, underwent a considerable change before he was many weeks within sight and hearing of his fashionable mother's foibles; and at last he burst into very unsparing reproofs of the same, but the reproofs had no other effect than to make Mrs. Delmar declare herself the worst treated mother in the world, and dub Eugene in his absence, "A hateful, old mentor."

For Louise, he had all the proud affection which a young man naturally entertains for an only sister; he was proud of her showy style, and because of her youth he could overlook the faults she had so accurately copied from her elegant parent; he basked in the sunshine her presence made in the house; he was restless and lonesome at any protracted absence of hers from home, but to bestow upon her any of the little endearments with which brothers sometimes petted sisters, he would have thought as soon of embracing Miss Calvert. When, through any chance inadvertence she requested him to button her glove, or adjust her shawl, he would evince such trembling awkwardness, and such evident dislike of the task, that she invariably broke from him in impatience.

To have told her any of his own affairs, or to have expected from her a similar confidence, would have been to him a preposterous idea, and had a sudden chasm disclosed itself in the floor at his feet, he could not have been more astonished than when she stood on the threshold of his room asking:

"May I come in? I have something to say to you."

Louise, who never by any chance entered his apartment—he could not understand it; and he stood with the portion of a cigar yet in his hand, and a thin wreath of smoke still curling about his head.

She repeated her request, and he, as if not yet comprehending, answered:

"Yes; I shall be down in a minute," and he turned away as if to prepare to descend, but she sprang after him, saying:

"I mean here—to speak to you here; mamma would interrupt us below."

He looked ruefully about him, as if his bachelor apartment would suffer some terrible innovation if he permitted this visit; but Louise had already pushed her way to his own easy chair, and nestling down into it began to cry as if her heart would break.

This was a new phase of that peculiar creature—woman—and slightly alarmed, Eugene closed the door, threw his cigar into the cuspidore, drew a chair in front of his sister, and waited quietly for her emotion to subside.

It was harder than she had imagined it would be to impart this new and strange confidence—to open her heart at once to one to whom even its most casual workings had never been laid bare, and she made a feint of still continuing to weep, even after her actual tears had ceased, that he might be the first to speak. But the simple fellow, not knowing what to say, kept an equal silence, and which he would have protracted for an indefinite length of time, had she not, provoked at his apparent want of tact, burst out impatiently at last:

"I want to speak to you about Hubert Bernot."

Eugene gravely nodded; he understood no more

than her words implied, and if he wondered what connection her tears had with that gentleman, certainly no glimmer of the truth entered his mind.

"Did you visit him to-day?" shading her face with her hand; and looking down, that not meeting his eyes, she might have more courage to speak.

"I did," was the reply.

"And "—in a faltering voice—" Does he think that —that he will have to die?"

"He seems fully to expect it."

"Do you,"—in a *very* faltering voice—" Really think so, too?"

"I am afraid it will be so—yes," with a sigh.

"And he will die and never know that I loved him,"—burying her face in her hands with sudden shame.

Eugene looked at her in dumb-stricken wonder. Feeling how useless it would be to wait for him to draw forth all she would tell, she flung her hands from her face, as if defiant of the very shame which had caused her to put them there, and told it all—the beginning of her attachment to Hubert—when the first spark was applied by her mother—the rapid growth of that attachment, and now its sad uselessness if he was to die without even knowing of its existence.

The young man comprehended at last. Perchance he more easily understood his sister's suffering from the fact of a like pain having been once in his own heart when he had dared to dream—he ventured nothing more—of a village belle about whom half the college students had raved betimes. He answered very sadly, but with almost a woman's tenderness.

"Hubert is already engaged to his cousin. This afternoon he extorted my promise to be one of the executors of the wealth which he will leave her in the event of his death."

If the more womanly and better part of Louise Delmar's nature had asserted itself up to this point, though in a weak and unmaidenly manner, the hard, warped part of her nature came uppermost now—jealousy, as bitter as it was sudden, swept over her soul, and transformed her from the tremulous, love-sick girl into the rigid, vindictive woman.

Her brother continued to speak as if to one who was suffering from the generous impulses of an over kind-heart. He repeated the tale that Hubert had told him, but repeated it in a more touching and affective manner. He described Margaret Calvert's faithful devotion—such a description as his own noble feelings could alone give, and he affected what men of more powerful intellect but less innate goodness must have failed utterly to do—he touched the heart, the passionate, jealous heart of his sister. Never perhaps had all the woman been so roused in her nature; never had springs of goodness in her soul—long, long sealed—been so widely opened; and the tears that dropped so hotly on her cheeks were shed, not for herself now, but for unhappy Margaret Calvert.

She murmured, between passionate sobs, the base part she had taken in the calumnies which were first spoken of the unoffending girl, and how it was due to her mother and herself that society contemned Miss Calvert.

Simple Eugene had never before beheld the interior of a woman's heart, and it disclosed to him such appalling depths of malice that fain would he have turned away, and closed his ears to the wretched story. His own heart was so pure, so upright in its dealings with all men, that to find women—women whom he had so revered—only filthy dross, was a shock from which he would not soon, nor easily recover.

But it was difficult not to pity the poor, sobbing creature beside him; her distress was so unfeigned, her penitence so real.

"Tell me how to undo it all, Eugene," she said; "how to let her know that I am so sorry."

But he was as helpless as herself to advise her what course to pursue in that respect, and he only sighed, and looked at her in a tender, reproachful way which made her tears come afresh.

Perhaps it was because in sorrow the heart is ready to cling to any sympathizer, that her brother had never seemed so dear to Louise as he did at that moment that she felt the value—now an inestimable one to her—of the goodness it had been her wont to term "old-fashioned," and "straight laced," and that made her feel it was that goodness which enabled him to bestow the sympathy she would have sought vainly from others. To obtain his pardon, to merit his approbation, was now her sole desire.

"I shall try to think what I ought to do," she said, rising, "and when I have done all I can, will *you* forgive me?"

She stood shyly beside his chair, the tears yet undried on her flushed cheeks—a pretty and touching picture of timidity and embarrassment—and Eugene's heart beat with new tenderness and new joy as he reflected that it was not yet too late to undo the work which the world, aided so efficiently by his mother, had done; his would be the task of raising his sister's character to the standard he would have it.

He rose, and for the first time since his return from college, kissed her, then he led her to the door and bade her a good night.

Slumber well, Eugene Delmar; let not, as there sometimes do, regrets because of thy lack of mental gifts, mingle with thy dreams. Thou hast done what those with more brilliant parts would have been powerless to effect—thou hast turned a heart from its evil ways.

In her room, the young girl was inditing a letter to Margaret Calvert, blistered with tears, Without betraying her own unhappy attachment to Hubert, she poured forth the penitence and remorse her brother had roused.

She hinted at, without naming the calumnies that had been spoken of Margaret, frankly confessing her own part in them, and humbly begging forgiveness.

"And now, Maggie," the letter concluded, "perhaps if I had known you long ago as I know you now, I should have been a much better girl; but I did not understand you in time and I yielded to the counsels of my own evil nature. I shall not go to the court any more for I could not look into your face after all I have done; but I shall pray for the best—for the very best—for you and Hubert.

"Good bye, and forgive me, for I am very miserable.
LOUISE."

One hour after midnight, when Margaret had resigned her place by the invalid chair to Kreble, and was creeping to her room, Louise Delmar, having directed and sealed her letter that it might be ready to give her brother in the morning, had thrown herself on the bed, and pressed her hands over her eyes to shut out the image of Hubert Bernot.

CHAPTER XX.

NEVER, in the records of the great metropolis, had a case excited more interest than this trial of Hubert Bernot. Men, whose feet rarely passed the threshold of a court-room, sought early for places; merchants, who could hardly be spared from their business, dropped in to listen for a brief while to Bertoni's wonderful voice; brokers left their counting rooms to catch a glimpse of the great lawyer; and politicians forgot, for the time being, their party interests in the excitement attendant upon the peculiar trial.

But all was due to " Roquelare "—that secret and mysterious body of whom there were few who had not heard, but many who had known nothing beyond its name. This was the first instance in which it had come so prominently before the public, and that secret awe of, and attraction for the mysterious which exists among all classes had done more than anything else to draw together the motley crowd which filled the court-room.

That anything which reminded one so strongly of the secret practices of a past age as this society seemed to do, could exist in an enlightened nineteenth century, and in a country where independence had begotten universal knowledge, was a subject of marvel even to the illiterate, and in the poorest, as well as in the wealthiest homes, the one much-discussed topic was that singular institution, " Roquelare."

Reporters sharpened their pencils and arranged their books with delighted haste, for on this third day of the trial they looked for more sensational *denouements* than had yet been given to the public; and the anticipation of the people was whetted to its utmost, so that on every face shone the same expression of deep and eager interest.

The prisoner's demeanor was the same, outwardly— as it had been from the beginning—calm, and free from the slightest trace of embarrassment.

Margaret sat in her old place, veiled as usual, and as usual, she was unaccompanied by any friends of her own sex.

Mrs. Delmar, unattended by her daughter, who had feigned illness in order to be permitted to remain at home, had beckoned a lady friend from another part of the room, and was deep in whispered comments on the prisoner's appearance, while Eugene, occupying a seat at his mother's side, was engrossed with thoughts of the confidence imparted to him by his sister on the previous night; and occasionally he felt for the little missive, directed to Miss Calvert, lying in his vest pocket.

The silent, anxious people seemed to be prepared for strange, untoward occurrences; to look for proceedings different from those of other similar trials, so that when the first witness summoned was again poor old Mrs. Murburd, with her trembling gait, and her strange, old-fashioned costume, and Bertoni held a knife to her view, and asked her if she had ever seen it before, and having received an answer in the affirmative, something was taken out of a paper wrapping, and a plaster cast of a face exposed, the people did not manifest any greater degree of wonder or interest than they had already done.

But Margaret flung aside her veil and gazed horror-stricken, while Hubert started and bent forward, suddenly and uncontrolably excited.

That cast was a *fac-simile* of the murdered man's face as it had appeared after he had met his miserable end, and with the nicest, but to Margaret the most horrible, precision, the peculiar knife with its golden-lettered name, was opened, and its blade adjusted to the gash that extended the whole length of the left cheek. It fitted perfectly, and for an instant Bertoni's eyes wandered with their almost habitual expression of triumph to Plowden, who returned the look with one of glaring hate. Margaret looked at Hubert, but he, beyond the flush which still dyed his cheeks, appeared to have recovered his wonted composure, and she made desperate efforts to regain her's; but her heart continued to beat as if it would burst its bonds, and her breath came in short labored gasps.

The trembling old lady was permitted to descend, and her escort led her out of the court-room as on the previous day, but those near whom she passed heard her half-audible whisper:

" How soon now shall I see Hugh ? "

The next witness summoned was Hugh Murburd, and in a few moments a door opened, and there advanced—apparently from some private apartment—a stout low-sized, sturdy looking young man, and fearlessness never had a truer personification than in his whole bearing and expression. Indignation also seemed to have powerful sway in him, for the very color that burned in his cheeks, added to the lightning-like flash of his blue eyes, as he turned them from Judge to jury, told, as plainly as words, the passion working in his soul. With true national obstinacy he parried every thrust of Bertoni to obtain his evidence; and before they could stop him, he had given in brief, but contemptuous terms, *his* opinion of the manner in which they had worked to obtain his testimony.

"I presume you have worked on my poor old mother's fears," he said, "and have obtained her evidence before this, but from me you will learn nothing, save that Hubert Bernot, once my class-mate, and from the first day of our acquaintance my friend, is the purest and most honorable man I know."

And true to his word, he would not testify to, nor even admit anything else; in vain Bertoni confronted him with the portion of his mother's testimony which went far to show that he must have had at least suspicions regarding the prisoner, the witness only presented the same sturdy, unflinching mien, and refused to answer. The cross examination, disclosed only the depths of his noble friendship—it made public, traits of such unselfish goodness in the character of Hubert Bernot, that many tender and admiring looks were turned upon the prisoner.

Margaret raised her veil and darted upon young Murburd a glance of heartfelt gratitude—how she blessed him in her heart for his testimony; and Hannah Moore on the opposite side, was wiping the tears from her eyes, and whispering to John McNamee.

"God bless him—it's the good heart he has for Mr. Hubert."

Murburd descended from the stand, his cheeks still flushed and his eyes still sparkling from recent anger, and he was immediately conducted out of the court-room.

Jorolamon Jumley was next summoned, and a little dapper man with an exceedingly light, agile gait stepped quickly to the stand. His evidence, which was given in a very brisk, decisive manner showed that he was the lawyer who had been engaged by the Murburds to conduct the suit for their contested property, and consequently the one with whom Hubert had executed the commission entrusted to him by Mrs. Murburd.

He identified the prisoner as the young man who had called upon him once, in relation to some matter connected with the Murburd property.

"I have a full account of it here," he said, producing a small, thick-leaved, red-covered note-book.

"Always keep full account of everything—even

most trivial circumstances—find it's the best way—best way," rapidly turning the leaves as he spoke, and then reading in the same brisk, emphatic manner in which he talked:

"September tenth, eighteen hundred——. Young man called this evening on Mrs. Murburd's business; smart, gentlemanly, intellectual. Gave him the papers, together with some written instructions—did not inquire his name; left me at a quarter to seven," and he closed the book with a snap as decisive as his tone was, and looked at the jury with an expression that seemed to say:

"Gainsay that testimony if you dare."

Plowden signified no desire to cross-examine that witness, and the little, dapper lawyer descended from the stand with the high-stepping air which was evidently the most, and perhaps the only, important part of " Jorolamon Jumley, Esq., practicing attorney."

People were beginning to relax a little from the strain so severely imposed on their mental faculties. Ladies straightened in their seats and assured themselves that their toilets retained all the bewitching arrangement of the morning; and brothers and fathers stirred themselves to remove the stiffness caused by their rigid position; but suddenly, every one resumed his, or her attitude of intense interest, for "Margaret Calvert," was called.

She had expected the summons—she had fancied she was prepared for it; but, at the first sound of the voice that pronounced her name, it seemed to her as if her heart ceased to beat. She felt herself growing cold, as if she had been suddenly exposed to a mid-winter blast, though fans had been plying in all directions a minute before, and when she strove to rise, her limbs seemed to have lost all power of motion; but, in a moment the blood came surging back through every vein with a frightful velocity, and her heart resumed its agonized beating. She rose and throwing aside her veil, looked at Hubert.

It was as a last appeal, and the earnestness, the passion, with which she would have spoken, had opportunity presented, was expressed in her imploring countenance. But his face gave back no answering sign; pale and rigid, he leaned slightly forward and looked at her—that was all.

She ascended the stand, feeling the multitude of stares which were directed at her, though she saw none of them, not even the gaze of those directly in front of her, for her head was slightly bent, and her eyes cast down.

Standing there to supply the last link in the evidence which would criminate him whom she loved dearer than her own life—that was the only thought in her mind, and once more, even after Bertoni had put the preliminary question and was waiting for her answer, and while the people waited also in breathless expectation, she turned and looked at Hubert.

He had folded his arms and stood erect, not even a faint color in his cheeks to betray his inward excitement, and he met her look with one as rigid and impassable as though he were but returning the glance of some curious stranger.

Her promise to him, his own importunate pleadings, returned to her with new force—her heart beat wilder, the blood surged hotter through her veins, and her face before like marble, was now as red as the bandage which still bound Bertoni's wrist.

She had withdrawn her eyes from Hubert, and by a desperate effort lifted them to the great lawyer's face. Her voice, that indescribable, and peculiar voice, which on the very first occasion of its being heard, produced such an effect, was not without a similar effect now. Sad and low, as it was until requested to speak louder, it thrilled the hearts of her hearers, and more than one. even feminine, head was twisted and thrust forward to catch a glimpse of the face which belonged to such a voice.

She told of her cousin's departure from home in order to visit the Murburds at C——; of his sudden and unexpected return a week after; of his ring startling her from her lonely midnight watch in his mother's apartment, but there her courage and her voice utterly failed.

She stopped abruptly, looking at Bertoni, with the expression of one suffering from intense alarm, and before the lawyer had quite decided what course to pursue, the prisoner, in defiance of every rule of the court, and reckless of his pledged obedience to Plowden, said loudly and distinctly :

" Remember your promise, Margaret, to tell what I at that time told you of Cecil Clare ; of the bloody knife I gave you to clean; of——"

He was interrupted suddenly, for men had recovered their startled faculties and the order of the court was restored.

Bertoni's face flushed with triumph ; it required but an instant—now that he understood the motive of her evident effort to tell what she knew, however damaging as evidence, that knowledge might be—to frame his questions in such a manner that they elicited enough of the wretched story to form the most important link in that superabundant chain of testimony.

She was scarcely aware how much she was telling. In her confused alarm she fancied that her monosyllabic answers were of much less importance than she ought to have given, as Hubert had requested full responses to the skilfully put questions.

She did not say that he had told her he had murdered Cecil Clare ; and she told nothing about the knife; but Bertoni had gradually wormed out the whole tale ; and he knew that just as soon as his ingenuity should place the desultory portions of the testimony in their proper places, people all would understand how, on the evening of the tenth of September, having executed Mrs. Murburd's commission, Hubert had taken a train to return to C——. That an accident, productive of no personal injuries, but occasioning much loss of time, had occurred, when the train had proceeded but a few miles, and that Hubert, tormented by self-reproach at not having seen his mother again when opportunity presented, took passage on the train to the city which happened to be due at a station in the vicinity of the accident, and arrived in the city a few minutes past eleven o'clock that same night. That owing to the night being fine, and the distance not far, he had determined to walk home—that he met on his way an old enemy of his family—how hot, taunting words passed between them, and finally the fatal blow which rendered Hubert a murderer. That the deed had occurred in a very retired street, and that immediately after, Hubert fled, pursued only by his own terror and remorse. That he walked the streets until he remembered that generally after midnight his cousin took the attendant's place in his mother's sick room, and hoping, and trusting only to meet her, he hurried home. How he gave her his confidence only after importunate appeals, and how he remained concealed in his own room all that day while she searched the papers for any account of the murdered man—how she saw none until the afternoon issue; and then, at Hubert's request she paid that fatal visit to the *morgue*.

But, though she had not given the evidence as Hubert had requested, misgivings filled her mind—perchance from the triumph which flashed so unmistakably in Bertoni's eyes—that her testimony was after all as damaging as she could possibly have made it; and, influenced by that fear she burst suddenly into an appeal for mercy for Hubert, as though in atonement for the very evidence she had given, her simple heart trusting that her account of his penitence and remorse must have weight with the stern men of law. Alas! that very appeal but strengthened her preceding testimony. and for that reason she was not interrupted, and Plowden, knowing any objection he could urge would be instantly overruled, sat grimly listening, and biting his lips to suppress the rage that rose at Bertoni's triumph to which the simplicity of the witness was unconsciously administering.

"I have given my evidence," she concluded in a voice of such mournful pathos that more than one masculine heart was stirred to rare depths of feeling, " because I was bound by a sacred promise to the prisoner to do so ; but I would deem it little to give my life if it could purchase mercy for him."

Never, at least to those who looked upon it that day, had a face been so expressive of utter sorrow; it was the saddest countenance they had ever beheld, and men, so inured to sad and painful scenes that the latter seldom caused a throb of compassion, sympathized with the situation of this broken-hearted girl compelled to give evidence against so near and dear a relative.

A strange expression came suddenly into Bertoni's face—almost a tender look ; that heavy countenance that was never known to relax into any of the soft or genial expressions which mark the faces of men who are much attached to domestic joys.

He was believed never to have married, and it was said that for sake of study and power, he had so completely alienated himself from his kin, that none of his blood dared to claim relationship with him.

Perchance, something in that touching sorrow penetrated the callous heart of the great lawyer—woke into sudden being some impulse of the *man* which so long had been stifled—for, with that unusual expression in his face, he bent forward and said, slowly:

" Is the readiness to purchase with the life of the one, the safety of the other, always a part of cousinship? Are even sisters an example of love that would go to the length of bearing a wretched burden, and retaining a secret, when the secret was such as to wear out the life of the confidante? Is it the fact of your relationship alone which is the motive of your affection, and of your desire to save the prisoner from the penalty of his crime?"

Plowden started, and flushed angrily, as if he would resent Bertoni's right to thus probe the heart of the witness. But the simple, guileless girl, reckless of time, place, or circumstances, answered out of the uncontrolable feelings of her heart.

"Every tie that gratitude can claim binds me to use my efforts to save him; his mother became mine when death robbed me of my own—his mother gave me a home and friends when there was but one shelter open to me—a pauper asylum. I am not Madame Bernot's niece—I am only Margaret Calvert, the child of poor, obscure, deceased parents; in obedience to her express desire, the pretence of being her niece has been retained from the first; but, now that I have repaid her love and care by giving testimony against her only child, it is but just to pretend no longer relationship to which I have no claim."

An electric shock seemed to have gone through every listener. Men started, and women gave vent to half suppressed exclamations, while the pity excited a brief while before by her sorrowful demeanor, and the evident struggle it cost her to testify, gave place in some feminine hearts to a feeling of supreme contempt. Margaret Calvert, now known through her own avowal to be poor in her own right, and of humble parentage, was an object fit alone for scorn and loathing, and the fair lady, to whom she long had been an occasion of sore envy, looked relieved, and darted a glance of exquisite tenderness at Plowden. Surely the elegant lawyer had not been aware of *that* fact pertaining to Miss Calvert, or his attentions never would have been bestowed on so unworthy an object; and indeed, Plowden's face expressed all the astonishment which well might make one believe that the announcement had fallen upon him, too, like a thunderbolt; but there were also deeper feeling than astonishment expressed in the lawyer's face, only the fair Miss W—— was unable to read them.

Mrs. Delmar was exultant, and when surprise permitted her to speak, she whispered to her companion:

"All that I conjectured about that brazen girl is actually coming true. I am sure our circle must be forever indebted to me for putting it upon its guard against such a creature."

And her eyes wandered to other parts of the house, in search of glances which would show that her fashionable friends remembered the service she had rendered them, continuing to wonder even while every eye was turned upon the prisoner.

He had started from his seat, and raised his arm as if about to burst into expostulation or denouncement; but the order of the court was not again to be disturbed, and he was forced into his seat. He covered his face with his hands, while his form shook as if with sudden palsy. Margaret saw that—saw him trembling from where she stood, even to the shaking of the attenuated fingers that covered his countenance.

What could such sudden emotion, such an attitude mean, but fear which had come upon him—fear of what his sentence must be, since, despite all her caution, her testimony had supplied the only link which seemed wanting.

She did not remember that he had, as it were, extorted her evidence, she thought only that *she* had given the testimony which would bring upon him the extreme penalty of the law, and that he now regretted it, when too late.

Her feelings, already strained to their utmost, could endure no more—there was a moment of blind groping for a support she would have been unable to hold, an instant of dizziness in which the faces of judge and jury multiplied themselves to an infinite number—and she fell fainting from the witness chair. Some one caught her before she quite reached the floor, and she was gently carried to an ante-room, and female attendance summoned.

Order was immediately restored, and the business of the court resumed as if there had been no interruption.

Hubert had looked up as they were bearing her out, his face assuming a ghastly hue, and Plowden had flushed and paled alternately, as if under the influence of feelings entirely beyond his control, while Mrs. Delmar had whispered to her lady friend:

"A very fine piece of acting; but these low, obscure creatures always play their parts well."

Bertoni gave the summing up briefly and clearly.

"There were but few more proofs to adduce," he said, having shown how completely Margaret Calvert's testimony established the guilt of the prisoner.

"And, in order,"—raising his voice slightly, and glancing at Plowden,—"that no one who may be suspected of knowing anything of this case, may be left unexamined, I would suggest that the testimony of Madame Bernot's special attendant be taken, for, though, as we have been made to believe the prisoner's mother knows nothing of her son's crime, such ignorance may not extend to her attendant; and though Madame Bernot's precarious state of health precludes the possibility of *her* examination, her attendant is not included in such an exemption.

"And soon," his powerful voice swelled to its full magnitude, "there will be welded the very last link of the chain of circumstantial evidence which binds the prisoner; justice will mete to him the fate which he merits for having imbrued his hands in a fellow-creature's blood."

Plowden had already determined upon *his* line of action,—the last battle with himself had been fought; the last effort to continue in his path of duplicity over come—he was ready for the consequences be they what they might; and strong emotions thrilled the hearts of the people when he lifted his tall, lithe form to its erect height, and swept about him an unshrinking, defiant glance of his piercing eyes. His voice had not the sonorous ring of Bertoni's, but it had all the exquisite modulations, the clearness and the distinctness which make a perfect delivery; and, when having paid a sarcastic compliment to the learned skill of his honorable opponent, he begged to show that instances still remained in which that skill had failed to assert itself—that there were doubts regarding parts of the evidence which it had left uncleared—people suddenly began to wonder whether Bertoni was so much the superior of Plowden after all.

"Does the honorable counsel," he said, "ignore the fact that on the inquest held twenty-two months ago, eminent physicians gave as their opinion that the cause of the death of Cecil Clare was a blow, or blows on the breast?—that it was only casually asserted the murdered man had died from the cut supposed to have been produced by a knife in the hand of the prisoner? Nothing in the evidence thus far has tended to prove that the prisoner dealt this murderous blow on the breast; further, the testimony has elicited that there were hot, taunting words between the supposed murderer and his victim. These words, on the one side, might have embodied threats which justified the drawing forth and the use of that knife. Is it because the prisoner labors under a species of hallucination with regard to something done perhaps in self defense, that we are to believe on supposition, because it is proved he gave the cut, that he must also have dealt the blow?

"According to the evidence of the last witness, the supposed murderer left his bleeding, dying victim in H—— street, a very retired side street; but the records of that date distinctly state that the murdered man was picked up in a prominent thoroughfare five blocks distant from H—— street. My honorable opponent will account for this by citing the disturbed state of the prisoner's mind; he will say that remorse and terror and his subsequent wandering through various streets made the murderer forget the locality of his deed. But I require only time to show how far from the actual truth even a great lawyer, like my distinguished opponent, may be.

"Step by step he has shown *his* work for the sake of justice—" speaking the last words with an accent of intense scorn—" and step by step *I* shall show how this member of 'Roquelare'—who worked for the attainment of his own ends and not for the common good as the rules of that society require—has been pursuing the wrong track. To-morrow, the witnesses who will testify to the truth of my assertion, who will prove directly the guilt, or innocence of the prisoner at the bar, will take the stand."

Plowden sank into his seat amid an awed silence.

Bertoni veiled the surprise caused by the latter part of his opponent's speech, under a sneering expression that gave to his face a sinister look, and caused to come out more plainly in his countenance a resemblance to the Jewish race to which, some said, he originally belonged.

People could scarcely define the feelings with which on that day they emerged from the court-room—some had it that it was but a feint of Plowden in order to begin another line of defence; others said, that there was a "wheel within a wheel," and that Plowden never would have made such a startling assertion if he did not have powerful evidence to support it.

Mrs. Delmar was in a tremor of delight.

"I knew that dear Mr. Plowden would accomplish all he set out to do, and any one can see now that he is sure of success. Do hurry, Eugene, for I am impatient to tell Louise," seizing her son's arm, and bidding a smiling adieu to her lady friend.

Eugene, anxious himself for haste in order to ascertain Miss Calvert's condition, was only too obedient to the injunction; he half led, half pulled his mother through the crowd, regardless of the rude treatment to which he was subjecting her elegant attire, and wholly deaf to her expostulations. When at last, she found herself seated in the carriage, with leisure to survey her crumpled, and torn lace shawl, her anger was raised to a white heat; but her dutiful son, without waiting for the maternal reproaches, closed the carriage door, and hurried to see Miss Calvert.

She had gone home, some employé told him, had gone immediately that she recovered from her swoon—and his search for Plowden was equally unsuccessful. That gentleman, had also, contrary to his wont, hurried off, so there was no alternative for Delmar but to return home, where his sister anxiously met him to know if he had found an opportunity to deliver her note. She had already learned from her mother much of the days proceedings, but when Eugene told her in *his* truthful, kindly way, she sighed and repeated sadly:

"Poor, poor Margaret!"

Sorrow for another was helping to assuage her own woes.

Mrs. Delmar barely waited to partake of an immoderately hurried lunch, so eager was she to call on Hubert, in order to congratulate him on the sudden bright aspect his case had assumed. Louise still pleading illness, was excused from accompanying her.

"But I shall convey to him your congratulations also, shall I not?" said the mother, "and tell him how anxious you are for his acquittal."

"Certainly; tell him all that," was the reply, with a significance in her tones which Eugene understood.

And Mrs. Delmar swept out to the carriage still in waiting, charitably hoping that Miss Calvert's swoon would keep her from paying her visit *that* day to the prison.

Margaret had gone home directly on her recovery. Physical and mental powers were so utterly prostrated, that she had but one desire, to shut herself away from everybody; to meet no face, to hear no voice, only to be let *alone* in her agony. An employé had kindly summoned a hack for her, and had as kindly promised to tell Mr. Plowden that she had felt too ill to remain.

When she arrived at home, she did not, as on every other occasion, go to her aunt's apartment, but she hurried to her own room, locked the door, and waiting only to remove her hat, threw herself upon the bed.

Hours passed; the servants were all at home, and at their various duties, snatching opportunities however, in which to interchange comments and opinions on the testimony of the day. Some were surprised at, and inclined to censure Miss Calvert's evidence, insisting that she might have refused, as Hugh Murburd had done, to return any answers when Bertoni pressed her so hardly, but Hannah Moore was loud and obstinate in her defence.

"He flustered her, the sneaking, deceitful villain, as he flustered me, and the whole of us, saving 'Little Sam' there."—"Little Sam" on hearing himself thus honorably mentioned, strode with an air of great importance for the napkins on the laundry table—"that's what he did," continued the cook, working herself into a state of righteous indignation, "and it wasn't enough for him, the heartless blackguard, when she fainted, but he must make everything she said plainer to the people; and isn't it the effect of all that, that's kept her in her room all this time without answering the luncheon bell, or letting Annie Corbin in, only telling her she was better, and didn't want anything. Oh! he'll suffer for it yet—the heretic.

There was a sudden and sharp tinkle of the parlor bell.

"That must be Miss Calvert," said one, to which Hannah Moore responded:

"I hope so, for it's an awful thing to think of her staying all alone, and she in such trouble."

But it was Father Germain, and he requested Annie Corbin who answered his ring to summon Miss Calvert, "I *must* see her," he said; "if she is unable to leave her room, I shall go to her."

The little maid delivered the message to Miss Calvert through the keyhole, the latter, having asked, without rising from the bed, who knocked.

Margaret forced herself to get up, and so unconscious of outward things as to be heedless even of the somewhat disorder of her attire, she descended to meet the priest.

He was waiting in the hall as if his anxiety would not permit him to remain in the parlor and while she was yet descending the last steps of the stair, he broke forth:

"Thank God, my child, your prayers are at last answered—Madame Bernot knows all about her son."

What a wonderful effect his words produced—that form, late so bowed and trembling, so reluctant to make the least physical effort, was suddenly erect, and endowed, as it were, with supernatural strength.

"How did she learn it?—how does she bear it?" she eagerly asked.

"Providence Himself seemed to bring it about; and she bears it with singular calmness—but she is waiting for you; go to her."

She turned to obey the injunction, then suddenly paused—the thought of her evidence was upon her with crushing weight—how, having furnished such damaging testimony against Madame Bernot's only child, could she look into the face of that soon-to-be bereaved mother.

"You do not yet know," she began hurriedly to the priest, "my evidence to-day"——

"I do know, my child," he interrupted, rightly divining the agony into which the giving of that evidence had thrown her, and which he felt she was now about to describe to him, "I heard it all; I was present in the court all the time you were on the stand, though obliged to leave immediately after, and you said nothing for which to reproach yourself. As I told you when you consulted me before upon this point, your evidence cannot make any great material difference, for even if you had refused to testify, Bertoni would still find means to compass his end. From random remarks which I heard on my way here, there is still reason to hope that the worst will not occur. Now, go to that breaking heart up stairs."

The breaking heart upstairs—even a disinterested spectator would have affirmed the same on one look at Madame Bernot's countenance—and the most singular, and not the least striking thing about it was the resemblance in its expression to the agony depicted in the pictured face opposite; as if her long and perpetual survey of the suffering lineaments in the painting, had suddenly imprinted a likeness of them in her own features.

"Margaret, Margaret!"—the cry was so like Hubert's wail of agony months before—and Margaret knelt, bursting into passionate sobs, and the invalid dropped the first tears she had shed for nearly nine long years.

"My own boy! Margaret, my only one! Oh my God! it is hard to say now Thy will be done! But what am I saying?" and her eyes turned to the pictured face.

"Bring me his letters—his last letters—and read them to me again. Father Germain says I am the desolate mother mentioned there—that my son is the poor young man who may be hanged. Oh, my God! Thou hast not accepted my sacrifice after all—Thou hast not pardoned that first sin, or this would not have followed.

Margaret brought the letters and read them all, though with frequent pauses, because of the tears which choked her voice; and then she asked what message she should bear to Hubert—would it be one of forgiveness and love.

"It is not for a poor, frail mortal like me to give or withhold pardon"—was her response.

"That is God's right; but tell him that my love for him is deeper, more tender now in his affliction and and penitence than it has ever been—Oh! that he could have doubted it."

And her mother's tears fell fast and hot on the helpless hands in her lap.

She *would* know everything that had happened since the commission of the murder; in vain Margaret begged her to think of the injury it might do her; in vain she besought her to wait until the hour for Doctor Durant's arrival, that they might be guided by his advice; she only answered:

"There are some things which are the occasion of supernatural strength, and this is one of them; so do not fear for me."

Margaret told it all—the torture of the months before Hubert's arrest; his penitence, his remorse, his passionate desire to atone; the proceedings of the trial, down even to her own fatal testimony.

She half feared and expected that the latter would obliterate whatever kindly feelings Madame Bernot might entertain toward her for her efforts to comfort Hubert. But far from it. The invalid, from very suffering, rendered keen in penetrating hearts, understood all that the sorrowful creature beside her had undergone, and never, perhaps, was riven heart more sweetly comforted, than was Margaret's by that saint-like mother.

"Now, that you know it all," said the weeping girl, "you will release Hubert and me from that promise we both gave you beside Maurice's coffin—you will let the past be told—it may influence those who are trying Hubert's case."

"Certainly—my poor boy; to fear to confide in his mother— as if a mother could be harsh or unforgiving; but there is much to be done—I must see this Mr. Plowden; send for him immediately, Margaret—nay, don't look at me, but *obey* for *my* peace of mind is at stake now."

A messenger was hastily despatched for the lawyer, and Madame Bernot insisted that Margaret should go below and take some refreshment, as it was now evening, and she had tasted nothing save a draught of ice water in the early morning. Kreble was summoned to attend the invalid.

Plowden, on learning that Margaret had gone home ill, also hurried from the court, without speaking to any one, or even replying to the salutations which greeted him as he passed out, and having arrived at home he shut himself in his room to write unintermittingly for hours, crossing, erasing, and adding to the legal papers that lay before him; here connecting clews, and there inventing questions which must elicit unmistakable statements from the witnesses, who, on the next day, were to be examined, until his work was completed, when evening shades had fallen over the city. He ordered a cup of strong coffee, and drinking it quickly, put on his hat and hurried forth.

A grim, dark building raised its gloomy front in an obscure, side street—a building where the windows were constantly draped with curtains as dark as the stone walls themselves; where little feet never pattered, and little voices never sounded, and about which the only signs of life were the dark-robed, austere-looking forms that sometimes passed to and from the massive portals. From its position the very sun only shone on it at rare intervals, and its peculiar style of architecture caused it to stand out in lonely grimness, a very monument, as it were, of the victory that was there gained over rebellious flesh.

Before this edifice Plowden paused, and rang the

bell with an impatient hand. He was admitted, the person giving admission keeping himself hidden from view until the lawyer had wholly entered the bare, dimly lighted hall. Then the spare, serge-clothed form, having closed and barred the door, inquired the business of the visitor.

"To see Lorguette," was the reply.

The form bowed, and conducted the lawyer to an apartment that opened from the hall. Like the hall it also was but dimly lighted and destitute of carpet, or other covering, and for furniture had only a few rush-bottomed chairs, a common table, and a picture of the Crucifixion.

Plowden seated himself to await the coming of the person summoned.

In a few minutes there entered a man not clad in serge, not wearing the trailing, loosely cut robe of the residents of that grim building, but having a short heavy cloak over his common citizen's dress, and which was swung round to one shoulder so that his form was well displayed.

That form was a painfully tottering thing—with every step the head shook, as if the very tread was too feeble to maintain a proper balance; while in singular and startling contrast to this apparent weakness, was the impression of strength and beauty given by the appearance of the form itself,—every limb was in magnificent proportion; the head set grandly on the shoulders; the superb eyes flashing with the lustre of vigorous manhood. His age was probably fifty, though the unmixed gray of his long, abundant hair made him seem older.

Plowden sprang to his feet, and stood with flushed face and folded arms, while the tottering form, having carefully closed the door, slowly advanced.

He looked in silence as if to be sure of the identity of his visitor before he spoke; then he said in a whisper:

"You have come at last—Heaven has answered my prayer."

"Yes, at last," Plowden replied with gloomy earnestness, and in a louder tone than he had spoken, who had been summoned as Lorguette.

"Hush!" said the latter putting his finger on his lips, and glancing uneasy about him, "no one here must know anything, yet."

"I have provided for that," answered the lawyer, taking a paper from his pocket.

"Read this; it contains all that you would know."

Lorguette repaired with the paper to the low pendant lamp, turned the latter so that its rays fell full upon the written contents, and hurridly read. His face flushed, and his eyes, when he had finished the perusal, seemed to have become more brilliant. He hastened back to Plowden.

"You are prepared for *all* the consequences?"

"All," was the hoarse reply.

"Your motive for doing this thing *now*, when you have spared yourself so long?"

"To rend a wrong which separates two young lives to restore happiness to a broken heart."

"And what do you expect to sustain you in the last dread ordeal."

"A woman's prayers."

The tottering form grasped Plowden's hands.

"My boy, by the old, old love which cemented us so closely; by *her* memory which we both love and revere, I conjure you to answer me truly—are the feelings in your breast now that were there when you answered no to all *her* pleadings—that you had when *we* parted?"

The lawyer bent his head and answered softly:

"They are not."

"Neither unforgiveness, nor hatred, nor desire for revenge?"

"All have gone."

"Through whose or what agency have they disappeared?"

"Through the silent, unconscious influence of a

woman who was brave enough to do her duty in suffering, defiant enough of the world's opinion to proclaim in public that she had no claim beyond that of charity, to her position; and from whose teachings to another, I have learned of the peace which true penitence brings."

"God bless her, whoever she may be; she hath wrought a wonderful work."

And the white, trembling hands which belonged to that tottering form were clasped earnestly together.

"You will not fail me to-morrow;" said Plowden, preparing to take his departure.

"A thousand times no!" was the response. And when the massive door had closed upon the lawyer, the tottering form ascending to an oratory, muttered:

"Free at last! free! free!"

When midnight was chiming over the city, and a chorus of voices ascended from the cowled forms assembled in the chapel of that grim building, there was one wearing no cowl, and having the upper part of his dress hidden by a short cloak, who knelt in their rear, and said his beads for Margaret Calvert.

The messenger despatched for Plowden had been obliged to wait for that gentleman, so that the evening was far advanced when the lawyer arrived at Madame Bernot's residence. He fain would not have met Margaret, at least until the next morning; but the summons was too imperative for him to refuse, and he nerved himself to conceal the excitement under which he labored.

Dr. Durant had arrived a few minutes before, and was astounded to learn that Madame Bernot had been told the dread tidings, and as yet had betrayed no symptoms of any injury caused by the communication.

"It is most unaccountable," he said, hurrying to the sick-room, while Margaret herself answered Plowden's ring.

The lawyer also was surprised to learn that Madame knew everything about Hubert; but he bit his lip with sudden vexation, when told that a subpœna had been served that evening upon Kreble.

"So," she continued, "It seemed to be providential that Hubert's mother—" she carefully refrained from saying "aunt" any more—"should have known all before the subpœna came; for Kreble, when enlightened by the 'server' as to what was required of her, could obtain no sort of command over her feelings. Divided between her fear that harm may be meant to herself, and her sorrow for Hubert she is giving away continually to fits of crying."

Just then a knock sounded at the door, and Kreble's German face bearing the traces of very recent tear stains, looked in to say in very broken English that Madame wanted to know if the gentleman had come.

The object of the invalid's conference with Plowden, and during which the doctor and Margaret were present, was for the purpose of announcing her intention to be present in the court, on the morrow, in order to give *her* testimony.

All three of her auditors stared aghast, and Dr. Durant searched for symptoms of the attack with which he was confident she would be immediately seized. Madame smiled slightly, even while submitting to his examination saying:

"I am stronger, doctor, and my mental faculties are clearer than they have been for some time."

The puzzled physician had to assent to the truth of her assertion.

"But how will you get there, my dear Madame?" asked Plowden, on whom her remarkable appearance—it was the first time he had seen her—had produced a strange and indescribable effect.

"Go in my chair as I was borne to this house," was the calm reply.

"It will kill you," said Margaret weeping, "to go through such an ordeal."

"Nay, my dear girl; I have gone through an ordeal

as severe in the past, as you know, and it did not kill me."

"But," said Plowden, "there is no necessity for your appearance in court; it is fully understood that you have been kept in ignorance of all that has happened. And what testimony have you to give."

"The story of the past, which, as it falls from a mother's lips, will act as the plea for her only child, and as such, may win leniency for my boy."

A wonderfully softened look came into the lawyer's face as he answered:

"There is no necessity even for that, for it is in my power to bring forward evidence which will put a new and different aspect on the case—which will make your plea only superfluous."

"Nay," said Madame Bernot, " he has taken, according to his own confession, the life of a fellow-creature— I would not have that fact denied, but I would tell publicly of the past, so that people may not judge too hardly of my poor boy ; and it will be in some measure an atonement for the selfish manner in which I have shut myself from his pursuits and his interests these nine long years."

It was vain to attempt to dissuade her; Dr. Durant insisted on permission to accompany her, knowing, he said, that she would need his services before she should leave the court-room ; and Plowden having promised to call for them in the morning took his departure in company with the physician.

Then began Kreble's lamentations; she was obliged to search her mistress' wardrobe for a suitable dress, in which to array her, and having learned the purport of such an unwonted proceeding, she lifted up her hands and cried:

"Mein Gott! dot I come to dis country where dyin' peoples goes out of dere bed to de court!"

Plowden had parted with the physician, and impelled by some strange, wild fancy, had taken the direction of

Herbert's prison. He wandered round the gloomy pile; at length, reclining under an arch formed by one of the projections;

"To-morrow," he murmured, raising his eyes to the clear, starlit sky, "to-morrow, and where shall I be?"

A sad, pale, coffined face stole before his mental vision, and another as sad and pale, but with young life in its features, came beside it.

"Aye," he murmured, addressing the imaginary countenances, "you shall both be avenged; and the one in her grave shall be at peace, and the living one—oh, Margaret, Margaret!" he broke forth aloud, "will you keep your promise? will you think kindly of me when you know me as I am?"

He rushed from the spot and dashed homeward.

Within those prison walls, Hubert was thinking sadly of Margaret; he had not for one moment supposed, nor wished, that she should have proclaimed the truth about her position in his family, and, in order to counteract, as it were, her statement, he would have told there in open court, had he been permitted, that she held as dear a place in his own, and his mother's heart, as the closest relationship could have given; and all the afternoon he had waited and longed for her, that he might tell her what perhaps he had never said in so many words before—how he fain would shield her with his love from the coldness and scorn with which the world would be sure to treat her now. He wanted to tell her, that, though dissatisfied because she had not given her evidence in the manner which he had desired, yet how dear to him she had been made by the struggle which it had cost her to give that evidence; and he wanted to be assured that her fainting fit, of which he accused himself as the cause, was nothing more.

But she did not come; no one came save Mrs. Delmar, and glad of any diversion from his painful fears and anxieties, he was rather more civil than usual to that lady, who accordingly returned home in a very elated state, to describe Hubert's delightful courtesy to her daughter; but the latter had gone with Eugene for a drive.

Louise, anxious to escape from *her* thoughts had made the proposition to her brother, and the goodnatured fellow, in order to gratify her, gave up, though not without much secret reluctance, his intended visit to the prison.

CHAPTER XXI.

EARLY the next morning Margaret despatched a messenger to Father Germain to acquaint him of Madame Bernot's determination to appear in court, and also to request him, if it were possible, to see Hubert and prepare him for his mother's presence in court.

As the prisoner's spiritual adviser the clergyman had access to the jail when he would, and the messenger returned with the reply that all should be done as Miss Calvert desired.

Great was the astonishment and consternation among the Bernot servants when they witnessed the preparations for conveying Madame Bernot to court—muffled in a large cloak, and closely veiled, she was borne in her invalid chair, which was so constructed that it could be readily used upon this occasion.

The bearers were the head-waiter and the hostler who assisted McNamee in the care of the horses, and Dr. Durant, who in company with Plowden, walked beside, had given particular instructions to go slowly and steadily, that no inadvertent jar might increase the pain which he felt she was suffering; if he could have looked beneath her veil he would have beheld her face covered with clammy perspiration produced by physical agony; her lips white, and her mouth drawn from the same cause; but she gave no sign. Was she not going to plead for the life of her son—her only child? What then could be any physical pain compared with the thought of what was likely to happen to him.

She had requested Margaret to use the carriage; so, for the first time since the trial began, the young girl entered the handsome equipage, accompanied by Annie Corbin, and Kreble, and it was driven slowly in order to keep the chair in sight. Windows were flung open, and heads stretched far out to view the curious procession. Fashionable ladies in unfashionable morning costumes, ventured even to the stoop, to obtain a closer sight of the strange cortege, and gentlemen who had just risen after late debauches, rushed from their breakfasts at the risk of having only cold mocha to drink, to catch a glimpse of this mother going to a legal court.

The court-room was more densely crowded than it yet had been, but the party were admitted through a private entrance.

Plowden had been early astir that morning, and he had made such arrangements, that no one of the judicial gentlemen seemed surprised at Madame Bernot's appearance. A passage was respectfully made for the invalid chair, and she was borne close to the judge's seat whither chairs were courteously placed for Margaret and Dr. Durant.

Some one in the crowd who had obtained his information from a court official, voluntarily enlightened those about him, and in a few minutes the identity of the large muffled person in the peculiar chair, was whispered all about the court. People stood on tiptoe to get a closer look, but the thick veil baffled every effort.

Mrs. Delmar adjusted her glass a third time in a very perplexed state of mind. She had not even Louise to whom to communicate her conjectures, for that young lady, despite the drive from which she had returned with unmistakable roses of health upon her cheeks, still pleaded illness, and was, though with every symptom of irate dissatisfaction on the part of her mother, permitted to remain at home.

Eugene, the provoking fellow, would only return monosyllabic replies to his mother's remarks. Truth was, the young man was as much puzzled as Mrs. Delmar herself, to decide upon the identity of that strange muffled form.

"It must be Madame Bernot," she said, re-arranging the position of her glass, "for Margaret Calvert is so attentive to her."

Margaret was unfastening the invalid's cloak, in order to throw it slightly back, the atmosphere of the room was so warm.

The prisoner entered. Before he quite reached his place, he paused and swept a hurried anxious look about him, till his eyes encountered the large form in the invalid chair. Margaret whispered to Madame Bernot, and in another moment the young girl, in obedience to a request had lifted the veil which shrouded the invalid's face, and mother and son's eyes met.

It was an interchange of looks, on the part of the one so full of tender love that it made many eyes humid; on the other so expressive of intense relief, and at length of sudden joy, that there fell from Margaret glad tears because of her very sympathy with the full heart of the prisoner.

He passed to his place with an elastic step. Margaret dropped the veil again over the invalid's face; and people awoke from the strange spell in which a sight of that rare and saint-like countenance had seemed to bind them. Even Mrs. Delmar was pettishly wondering what it was that gave to the sick woman's features such great and peculiar beauty. She did not remember even the color of Madame Bernot's eyes.

On conclusion of the customary legal preliminaries, Kreble Karldat was called for examination. On reaching the court, Annie Corbin had been conducted to the place, assigned the Bernot servants, who had already arrived; and Hannah Moore had undertaken to reason the poor, trembling German woman into something like a state of "decent behavior," as she herself termed it.

Sam Lewis had also with an air of great importance proffered his advice.

"Bamboozle him like I did, when he's asking you the questions; that's all you've to do; there's nothing like bamboozling."

But poor Kreble would only shake her head and reiterate.

" Mein Gott ! "

On the stand she was little better.

" I know notings," she said; " I comes to dis country six years ago. I goes South and gets von place to nurse Madame Bernot; den for vat you ask me such tings about Mr Hubert ? " with a sudden burst of indignation directed full at Bertoni which almost provoked even the risible faculties of the Judge.

Kreble was permitted to descend without being cross-examined, and Bertoni made a few brief remarks, the purport of which was to show, that the last witness had been examined, not because her testimony was an actual necessity, but that his honorable opponent might be quite satisfied of his desire to examine every witness, in order that anything favorable to the prisoner which could be produced might be shown, to which remarks Plowden bowed, and smiled scornfully well knowing that the opposing counsel had proceeded to such lengths only because they were so many opportunities of displaying his own triumph.

Margaret lifted Madame Bernot's veil, and there was a breathless silence for her testimony was the next in order. Dr. Durrant hurriedly felt her pulse; the beats were more regular than they had been for days.

"I can't account for it at all," said the puzzled physician. His own appearance presented greater evidence of mental excitement than did Madame Bernot's, for she was as calm, apparently, as though quietly resting at home.

People expected the low, tremulous, indistinct tones which are usually accredited to invalids; they were not prepared for the exquisitely sweet voice which floated out clear, distinct, and perfect in its articulation.

When she had answered the preliminary questions she was allowed to proceed with her tale, uninterrupted as she evidently wished to do.

"I have requested to be heard to-day in behalf of my only child who has been charged with the crime of murder. I do not seek to avert the penalty which Justice would inflict upon him. I have no hope of influencing the hearts of his Judges to lighten the rigor of the law in his case, but I desire to state facts which may cause his memory to be less dishonored—which may win for the remainder of his existence less opprobrium than that with which he is now visited.

"Thirteen years ago our home was one of the happiest in Louisiana, my elder son, Maurice, was at college. Cecil Clare whose home was also in our state, was his class mate and warm friend.

"One morning there was a duel on the outskirts of the college grounds, and my son fell with a ball through his heart.

Over his coffin we learned from some of his college mates more definite, but sadder particulars. Cecil Clare who had frequently partaken of our hospitality, jealous of Maurice's superior scholarship, of his popularity—formed a pretext for rousing my boy's hot southern blood, and a duel was the result. Maurice fired in the air—fired in the air, though his antagonist took aim so sure that it was proof of his intention to take a life, and over my son's dead body Clare paused a moment to exult even while his friends were urging him to flee. My husband speedily followed his murdered boy, and my present state of suffering came upon me. Where peace and happiness had reigned ten days before, grief and desolation now made their abode.

"We forgave Cecil Clare—my husband with his dying lips had pronounced his pardon,—and over Maurice's coffin, for *my* sake, Hubert had retracted the boyish vengeance he had sworn, and for the execution of which he sighed for manhood, I also obtained from him and Margaret Calvert, a solemn promise never, upon any occasion to mention the sad circumstances of Maurice's death.

"My illness compelled the utmost seclusion; but I had other reasons for severing myself as completely as my poor weak nature would allow, from all worldly affairs. It were better I had not done so, for then my son would not have feared to give me his confidence, and it would not have been for another to tell me that my only child was charged with murder.

"It were better also that we had never come North —though we did so only to be near Hubert during his college term—for then he would not have met so unhappily his brother's murderer. I have heard that hot words passed between them; I know not—I know only, that, from my son's unfailing tenderness to me, from his disposition in boyhood, from the tenor of his whole life up to that one unhappy deed, he never would have committed an intentional, a deliberate murder; and I ask of the gentlemen who may have my boy's life in their hands, to remember, before they unite in a final and fatal decision, that he is the sole remaining child of a widowed, broken-down mother, that his life before this unfortunate affair has been blameless, and that the man he is said to have killed, was himself a murderer. I have done, gentlemen."

Margaret Calvert dropped the veil over the pale, beautiful countenance, Dr. Durant felt her pulse again, and then the people began to move in their seats, and to whisper their admiration, and wonder, and sympathy, till "order" was called.

The prisoner had kept his face bowed in his hands while his mother was speaking, and he did not remove them when she had ceased. The various emotions caused by the sound of her voice, and the memories which she was awakening, were almost beyond his control, as might be perceived by the trembling of his fingers, and the deep flush visible on the side of his face and neck.

The doctor urged Madame Bernot to permit herself to be borne out, now that she had performed her part, but she refused, whispering:

"I have not seen my son for so long; do not ask me to leave him now."

She was suffering acutely; but no pain would have induced her to leave the court-room while Hubert remained.

Every witness for the persecution had been examined, and Bertoni waited with a look of supercilious contempt, for Plowden's promised proceedings. That gentleman, from the very moment of his entrance, had seemed to watch a certain part of the room; turning his keen glance frequently in that direction, and wearing at such times a look of anxious expectation; with that exception, he seemed to be singularly preoccupied; as if he was more intent upon some determination of his own, than upon the testimony then under way, and it was with that same strangely preoccupied manner that he rose, and leaning forward, spoke a moment to the judge.

Directly after, Hannah Moore was called.

Great was the consternation among the Bernot servants who some time before, had arrived at the pleasant conclusion that no more testimony would be required from them; and the puzzled, frightened cook turned to John McNamee and whispered:

"Is it me, he means?"

"Yes, to be sure: go on——they're waiting for you."

She gathered her shawl about her with no very definite idea of what she was doing, and took her way to the stand, while her broad, good-natured face bloomed like a very peony from sudden color.

When she had taken the oath and stood trembling

as if she was herself a culprit, Plowden leaned slightly forward, and looked at her long and earnestly, and almost tenderly; it was a look designed to recall other times, to awake in her heart all the kind feelings which *he* knew slumbered there. She read his expression, and her eyes dropped, for her Irish heart was full.

"You once held the position of nurse to a certain Mrs. Clare, did you not?" he asked in a peculiar softened tone as if he would coax forth her reply.

Her surprise permitted no answer for a moment, and then it was given with reluctance.

"I did."

"Mrs. Clare had a son, Frederick, whom you knew well?"

"She had," her astonishment growing visibly greater.

"You had ample opportunity of knowing Frederick Clare's disposition to be turbulent and untractable, did you not?"

"I did," falteringly.

"You knew him to be passionate, with a firmness in his passion which would yield to no power under heaven, did you not?"

"Yes," with a half gasp.

"What relation was this Frederick Clare to the murdered man, Cecil Clare?"

The witness refused to answer. Pale as she was before red, she stood with resolutely closed lips.

"Speak, woman!" thundered a voice from the crowd —"your promise is no longer binding, for a human life is at stake."

People looked in vain for the owner of that voice; no one could point him out to the officer whose duty it was to preserve order in the court.

"Yes, speak!" said Plowden, softly, to the startled witness, "answer every question I shall put, if you would not hear the sentence of death passed upon your young master, Hubert Bernot."

A desperate struggle was evidently going on in the domestic's heart—the perspiration came out thickly upon her face, and her hands fidgeted nervously with her shawl.

"Speak!" reiterated Plowden, "in mercy to the living, and in justice to the dead, speak!"

Still struggling with her conflicting feelings, she answered with much hesitation:

"He was the brother of Cecil Clare."

"Sons of the same father, but of different mothers, were they not!" asked the lawyer.

"Yes."

"You were in the confidence of Mrs. Clare; you knew that she had been deceived by a mock marriage with her child's father; that she had only learned that fact when she found herself deserted, and was told that her deceiver had gone to England, where he had already a wife and child?"

"Yes; she told me that."

"You learned further from her confidence, that, when in the course of years she heard of the death of the legitimate Mrs. Clare, which event took place in Louisiana, she, accompanied by her son, journeyed to that state for the purpose of appealing for her rights to the man who had deceived her?"

"Yes."

"That the result of that journey was a stern refusal from the elder Clare to acknowledge either mother or son, and insulting scoffs from his legitimate son, then a young man of twenty; that the youth, who had accompanied his mother, only to find himself further than ever from a father, swore boyish vengeance on Cecil Clare; that desire for revenge grew to be part of the lad's very being, so that when he returned with his mother to their northern home, he talked and thought of nothing else. You knew all this, did you not?"

"I did."

"What member of that household was there beside mother and son?"

"An only brother of Mrs. Clare."

"How long did you remain with the family?" speaking more rapidly.

"Until Mrs. Clare died."

"That will do for the present."

And, as the witness stepped down, so trembling and confused, as to be proceeding in a wrong direction, till some one kindly set her right, Plowden, in a rapid, impassioned manner, requested that the gentlemen of the jury would be careful to follow, and connect the clews as he would now present them.

"It has been shown conclusively in a previous testimony," he said, "that the prisoner, even though he did not act upon it, had a motive to incite him to the murder of Cecil Clare, and in the testimony just adduced, we learn that there was another being who had treasured vengeance in his heart for this same Cecil Clare. It has not been proved yet, either by the prisoner's own confession, or by any evidence so far obtained, that the prisoner struck the fatal blow in the breast. Improbable as it may seem, it is not impossible that Frederick Clare, the half-brother of the murdered man, may have given the fatal stroke."

He stopped suddenly, inclined himself again toward the Judge, and in a moment the latter called:

"Nicholas Neville."

A tall, grand form made its way from the densest part of the crowd—a form, the first sight of which conveyed the impression of uncommon beauty and strength; but a longer look made one recoil with a feeling akin to pain, the whole frame was such a tottering thing. He wore no cloak, as he had done on the previous evening, during his interview with the lawyer, but his dress was entirely black, and his vest was buttoned up close to his collar.

On arriving at the witness-stand he looked searchingly, for a moment, as if seeking to recognize the faces of the Judge and jurors—those faces—they seemed to be transfixed with mingled astonishment and alarm; Bertoni's was bleached with horror, and his strong form visibly trembled.

The strange, tottering form raised its left arm and made a single sign. In an instant Judge and some of of the jury had risen to their feet, stood in perfect silence for a moment, and then slowly resumed their seats.

People stared at each other with wide, wondering eyes. Never had such proceedings been in any court of justice before; but, reading no explanation of the mysterious doings in the countenances of their neighbors, they were fain to turn their glances back, and wait for time to solve their yet unspoken questions.

At the first sound of Nicholas Neville's tones everybody recognized the voice which, so strangely, from the crowd, had issued the command to Hannah Moore.

"I am the uncle of Frederick Clare; his mother was my only sister. When she learned that her marriage was legally invalid, I brought her away from her native New England hills, that the breath of censure and scorn might not touch her. We came to this city, and it was in direct opposition to me that she sought her deceiver when she learned of the death of his legitimate wife. That journey only seared a desire for vengeance into my nephew's heart. On his return; at his studies, in his sleep, in conversation, he would break forth on one topic—to hurl vengeance on his half-brother, Cecil Clare.

"He fostered ambition, he sought for power, only that it might help to accomplish his end. On the death of his mother, he begun his search for Cecil Clare. I accompanied him through love for him, and because of the promise I had given his mother on her death-bed, to watch her son, and if possible save him from the effect of any rash deed he might commit.

"We traveled South in search of the Clares; but father and son had gone to Europe some years before, in consequence of a duel in which Cecil had killed his antagonist. We followed to Europe—from city to city, wherever the slightest clue led us. At last in Germany we came accidentally upon the bankers who transacted the business of the Clares; from them we learned that the father was dead, the son a constant attendant on the *salons* of Paris. To Paris we hurried, and one night we met the object of our search, but, well as my nephew fancied he remembered the features of him whom he so hated, he failed to recognize them until the fragment of a conversation which we overheard, revealed the identity of Cecil Clare. We learned further that he was an accomplished *roue*; but something must have alarmed him, for that same night he hurriedly left Paris. We pursued our search for months, but without success, and we at length determined to return home.

"My nephew applied himself to his profession, but his hate and desire for revenge were as deep and unconquerable as ever.

"On the night of the tenth of September, or rather on the early morning of the eleventh—for it was past midnight when we were returning from a visit—a man whose face was partially covered with dry, encrusted blood, staggered toward us; we feared he might be severely hurt, and we hastened to offer assistance. He was somewhat maudlin from intoxication, and yet he had all the anger and obstinacy of a drunken man. We urged him to accompany us, that something might be done for the wound in his face; but he broke into cursing Hubert Bernot, saying that the latter had inflicted the wound, and had left him for dead on the street, but that he,—Cecil Clare—would yet have vengeance.

"Up to that time we had not recognized him, for we had not seen his features closely; but when he mentioned his own name, my nephew sprang back. I whispered to spare him because of his intoxicated, helpless state, and my nephew came close to me, and put his hand through my arm. Cecil Clare continued in his maudlin way to speak of himself, of his flight from some one whom he said pursued him to kill him, and then suddenly with a burst of drunken passion he referred to the mother and son who had called upon his father years before, stigmatizing the mother by some foul name.

"I felt the arm within mine suddenly withdrawn, I saw a form rush past, I heard a heavy thud, and Cecil Clare was lying on the sidewalk drawing his last breath. Vengeance had been dealt at last, and Frederic Clare was the murderer of his half brother."

There was not a motion among the spell-bound crowd; there was scarcely a breath drawn by the prisoner, who in his intense excitement had risen from his seat and now stood pale and motionless; there was scarcely a breath drawn by Madame Bernot, or Margaret Calvert; the latter had thrown aside her own veil, and was leaning forward with clasped hands and parted lips; and there was scarcely a breath drawn by any of the Bernot servants, who grasped each other in their wonder, and looked with eyes that seemed to have become strangely extended.

Even the impassible face of the judge betrayed something of the strange emotions under which he labored; and Bertoni's visage was purple—swollen and purple—like that of a man suffering from some fell disease.

Plowden drew himself slightly up, and looked for an instant toward Margaret Calvert; then with a rapid glance at the motley crowd of upturned faces, he said, slowly:

"Since the testimony just given, the veracity of which even 'Roquelare' will hardly question, has fixed the murder on another than Hubert Bernot, there remains only to ask of the witness to point out this Frederick Clare who gave the blow which sent Cecil Clare into eternity."

The answer came from the witness in tones as slow, as loud, and as thrillingly distinct:

"Frederick Clare and Charles Plowden are one and the same person."

Plowden stretched forth his right hand.

"And I here acknowledge myself to be the murderer of Cecil Clare. My honorable opponent was on the wrong track when he pursued Hubert Bernot."

There was a sound from Bertoni, who had sprung to his feet, as if an effort to speak had ended in a hoarse, half-stifled scream, and then he sank helpless into his chair—so helpless that his head dropped to one side and his hands sought vainly for some support. Two gentlemen near caught him, but even their faces turned white at the swollen, disfigured visage which rested on the arm of one.

Madame Bernot had risen from her chair—Madame Bernot who, for nearly nine long years, had been unable to lift even her hands; yet there she stood, her veil flung aside, the large cloak slipping from her shoulders, and disclosing her soft white robe; there she stood, with her hands extended to her son, and her face shining with such an expression as a saint might wear on a first glimpse of Heaven.

Margaret Calvert was standing beside her, winding her arms around her and trying to force her into her seat.

The first gush of the girl's own sudden and intense joy was absorbed in fear for Madame Bernot when she saw the invalid rise without any help, and in her wild alarm she almost expected instant death to follow.

Dr. Durant's wits appeared to have entirely deserted him, for he could only murmur while he looked from Madame Bernot to Margaret:

"I think we are all going mad together."

The Bernot servants were all on their feet, Hannah

Moore crying, and saying loud enough to be heard by all in her vicinity, if everybody had not been too excited, and too intent upon his or her own comments:

"His poor mother in her grave always feared it would come to that. Och, I'm glad for Mr. Hubert, but I can't help being sorry for Mr. Frederick."

For some minutes it was impossible to restore order in the court; the wildest excitement reigned, but amid it all the prisoner never once turned his eyes from his mother's face. As yet he but dimly comprehended that the crime of *murder* was no longer upon his soul; as yet he only partially realized that something wonderful had happened to his mother, and he continued to look until at least the tumult was somewhat quelled.

Bertoni was borne out, and the case was indefinitely adjourned.

The prisoner was taken out; the people began to go slowly forth, and then Plowden wrote on a scrap of paper:

"MISS CALVERT,
 Remember your promise to think kindly of him who should restore happiness to you, and if we should never meet again, still pray for the wretched
FREDERICK PLOWDEN CLARE.

"N. B.—Hubert is safe now from every penalty; 'Roquelare' will resign his case to attend to mine, and a day or two at most will see him free from prison walls. F. P. C."

He gave the paper to a gentleman to pass to Margaret, and by the time she had read it, the writer, together with his uncle, Nicholas Neville, was disappearing through a private passage. And while Margaret looked, too bewildered between the sudden, unaccountable change in Madame Bernot's physical condition, and her own sudden transition from sorrow to joy, to know exactly how she ought to regard Plowden, a dark-faced, heavy-bearded man rushed in a state of wild excitement after the lawyer. Overtaking the latter on the threshold of the passage he plucked frantically at his coat. Plowden paused and turned, recognizing in the Spanish-looking countenance one of the disputants on the greatness of Bertoni's mind, and to whom he had spoken a day or two previous.

"Well," he asked curtly, "what would you say to me?"

"You told me," was the reply in husky tones, "to wait and see if the other great lawyer's mind would be so great under defeat, I went to see him when they carried him out, but they told me he was a raving maniac—that his *mind* was gone."

A softened, kindly look broke over Plowden's face.

"And you, my friend," he said, "what effect will this have upon you?"

"I shall turn to my God and my Faith again, knowing that *Religion* alone survives all shocks."

He bowed his head and spoke in a solemn, and reverential tone, as if he was suddenly inspired with some deep, religious feeling.

Plowden clasped his hand.

"I know not who you are, my good fellow, nor whence you come, but you have given me courage for *my* fate; my right-doing has already gained a soul from infidelity; it seems like an omen of my own pardon."

And while the stranger, having wrung the lawyer's hand hard, departed, Plowden looked back at the court-room to where Margaret stood, and murmured, in tones audible alone to his uncle:

"Oh, Margaret Calvert! to you I owe having done what I did to day."

"God bless her!" responded his uncle, and both turned and pursued their way, not to the sunny streets, but to the rigorous guardianship of "Roquelare."

Margaret had witnessed, though of course without being able to hear, the colloquy between Plowden and the strange man, and she had seen the lawyer's lingering look toward herself. In her intense happiness she could well afford to have no feeling but the most tender kindness for every one, and after the first few moments of perplexed feeling, she wanted to rush to the lawyer, and to assure him not only of her present kind feelings, and of the prayers which she should constantly offer for him, but that the most tender gratitude and sisterly affection should ever linger round his very memory.

Before, however, she could summon courage sufficient to cross the space between them, he had disappeared, and some of the court officers, including the Judge, were pressing about Madame Bernot to tender their congratulations, and she was courteously informed that Hubert would be permitted to see her, and that he now waited for that purpose, in a private room.

She rose on the reception of that news.

Those about her stood in respectful and marvelous silence, for the change in her physical condition so miraculously wrought had produced a singular impression.

Dr. Durant was in such a state of tremor that his very voice shook as he said:

"My dear madame, be careful; do not presume on your suddenly-acquired strength."

She answered with a smile:

"Nay, Doctor; since Heaven has vouchsafed me two blessings in one day, surely I may testify my joy by using and showing the wonderful goodness of God," and she went on leaning slightly on Margaret's arm.

She trembled, and walked unsteadily at first, but her step continued to become firmer, until at length she could withdraw from her support, and walk alone to the apartment in which Hubert waited.

A court officer opened the door for the party, and mother and son met as they had not met in nine long years—her arms around him, his form strained to hers in a long, tender embrace. Then Margaret gave way to the feelings of her own overcharged heart—averting her head, she cried for very joy. She was so happy that she was almost unhappy with a vague feeling that such extraordinary happiness must be followed by some equally great calamity. Even the eyes of the court-officer were moist, and Dr. Durant saying to that official in an undertone:

"Madame Bernot's state is a very unnatural one; a reaction is sure to follow, and it may cause her death," was wiping his own eyes.

Without, in the court-room, Mrs. Delmar still lingered, uncertain whether to hasten home to communicate the good news to Louise, or to remain in order to gratify her curiosity about Madame Bernot; which curiosity had been raised to a white heat by the peculiar beauty of the invalid, as well as the wonderful change which had been effected so suddenly in her physical condition.

Eugene had learned that Hubert was permitted to receive a visit from his mother in the private room to which the latter had adjourned, and when he communicated that fact to his own maternal parent, she joyously responded:

"It will not be amiss to follow with *our* congratulations." Her curiosity to see more of Madame Bernot and her desire to make a favorable impression on Hubert by being among the first to testify her joy at the sudden, happy termination of his trial, made her defiant enough to meet even that "odious Margaret Calvert."

Eugene looked ruefully when he heard the proposition—his finer feelings revolted from intruding upon that sacred meeting between mother and son—but Mrs. Delmar seized his arm and with brazen effrontery pushed toward the door. It was half open, and the position of the parties within was disclosed.

Hubert had disengaged himself from his mother's arms to call Margaret, and when she came, to present her to his mother as the angel who had guided and assisted him through all the troubled, fiery time ; and when Mrs. Delmar and her son entered, he was still holding Margaret's hands, and pouring out what his full heart *would* prompt of her virtues, her devotion.

Eugene tremblingly introduced his mother, and Madame Bernot slightly smiled, and bowed to the fashionable lady, who immediately went forward to pour into Hubert's ear what she considered a graceful and appropriate little speech.

The young man drew Margaret forward.

"Together, Mrs. Delmar, we must accept and thank you for your congratulations; together, for Margaret has been so intimately connected with my sorrows, that it is but just she should participate in my joys; and, though not my cousin, she shall soon hold a far nearer and dearer relation to me."

He put his arm about her and drew her to him, and Margaret was fain to hide her blushing joyous face in her hands.

For the worldly woman who looked on the scene, through the false smile she forced to her lips, through the false expression she forced to her eyes, that their glitter of disappointment and rage might not be seen; through the false words she forced herself to speak, could be discerned and heard, the bitterness which struggled up from her heart.

The lovers were too happy to notice it, or had they done so, to care; and Madame Bernot was too recently from a purely spiritual atmosphere to understand the rage and malice which panted more than ever to crush that "odious Margaret Calvert."

But Eugene, owing to his sister's confidence, partly comprehended the feelings which raged in his mother's heart, and having slipped Louise's missive into Margaret's hand with a whispered :

"Read that when you have leisure," took Mrs. Delmar on his arm, and hardly waiting to have her finish her smirking adieus, through which her forced smile shone sickeningly false, hurried her out.

How different was the going home from the coming to the court. Madame was able to go in her own carriage, she was accompanied by Margaret and Dr. Durant, and what happy faces and light hearts the vehicle carried! Even the doctor had rallied from his nervousness, and though still declaring it unaccountable he was beginning to believe in the permanency of the wonderful cure.

The Bernot servants—the warm-hearted faithful domestics who had sympathized with their master's trouble, who had borne fears and anxieties on his account as if they had been their own—now rejoiced as if some wonderful good fortune had befallen themselves. Even Kreble's excitement, not unmixed with terror, when she beheld Madame Bernot rise, had caught the joyous infection of those about her, though she did not quite understand the cause of such sudden and boisterous joy, and she was exclaiming with a stronger Teutonic accent than ever.

"Mein Gott! das is all wonderful."

She was undecided whether to remain lest Madame Bernot might require her attendance, or to accompany the help, now that the court-room was being rapidly cleared, but Madame, herself, having at length disappeared, she decided on the latter course.

The streets through which the domestics passed on their homeward way, resounded with their voices, and in the very car which they entered, was heard above the rattling of the vehicle such fragments as:

"It's wonderful about Madame Bernot!"

"Something always told me Mr. Hubert would get off!"

"It was a judgment of God on the blackguard." The last remark from Hannah Moore, in reference to Bertoni's sudden illness. "I wonder what they'll do with Mr. Plowden now"——

"Sure I keep thinking all the time that I saw his uncle somewhere before,"—from Rosie the chambermaid.

The car stopped for them to alight, and when Samuel Lewis had gallantly assisted John McNamee to help the ladies out, Hannah Moore said in a very confidential manner:

"Rosie there's after saying that she thinks she saw Mr. Plowden's uncle before, and maybe she has—and now that everything's come out, I'll make a few explanations myself; but not till to-night, when we're having a sociable glass together."

At which the pompous head-waiter condescended to bring his fat hand down on Miss Moore's shoulder, in token of approval, and Mr. Samuel Lewis said, "good, good," after the manner in which they cry, "hear, hear," at political speeches.

At home, each hastened to his, or her respective duties, and never was work done so easily or so quickly.

They looked for a visit from Madame Bernot, but Miss Calvert alone came to them, shortly after the arrival of the carriage. She came to them looking radiant with happiness, and crying from very joy while she thanked them. The warm-hearted domestics wept also.

She announced to them that Madame Bernot would remain in her room, as she had always done, until Hubert's fate should be definitely decided, and she requested them to pray for his speedy release; then she lightly ascended to meet Father Germain, to whom a messenger had been despatched with the wonderful news, and the result of which was that the good priest came himself to see Madame, and to tender his congratulations.

The radiant expression of Margaret's face told him all, before she had uttered a word, and he extended his hand, saying with deep emotion:

"Thank God, my child, for He has been very, very good."

Madame Bernot received him standing; she whom he had never beheld out of her invalid chair, and whom he never expected to behold out of it until inclosed by her coffin. He broke forth involuntarily into a psalm, extolling the wonderful goodness of God; and Madame and Margaret bowed their heads and reverently joined him. Then he made particular inquiries about her physical state—she suffered no pain, she was free from all weakness and tremor, and as she sat in a chair similar to the one he occupied, save for the appearance which her white merino robe gave her, and the spiritualized expression of her face, one could scarcely imagine that she had been confined to her chair for nearly nine long years. Her eyes had not forgotten their old habit; occasionally they turned to the pictured head of the Saviour, and when Father Germain at length took his leave, it was with a feeling, priest as he was, akin to awe; for he knew that he had been in the presence of a saint—a saint on whom the Divine seal was already set, for he clearly foresaw that her Heavenly reward was not far distant. But he had not spoken of that to Margaret—he could not bear to cast a shadow on the girl's happiness.

The social glass over which Hannah Moore had promised to make her own particular explanations, was prepared, and sparkling in the hands of those for whom it was intended. Goodly slices of cake accompanied it, and every one was eating and sipping, and waiting with manifest interest for the promised tale.

"Mind you, it's not much," said Miss Moore, smoothing out her glossy apron fresh from the iron, and settling the stiff cuffs on her wrists, "it's only to let you all understand why I'm feeling so badly about poor Mr. Frederick, as I always used to call him, and how it was that I came to know so much about him.

"Once I was out of a place a good while, and stopping with a sister-in-law who didn't much care about having me on her floor, and when I heard accidentally of a delicate lady wanting a strong girl to wait on her I went to see about it. When I found she would take me on my own terms my heart danced for joy. That lady was Mrs. Clare; and delicate indeed she was, and fair and sweet as an angel. I wasn't there long before I knew she carried a breaking heart in her bosom; and it used to make my own heart weak to see the way she'd be cryin' to herself when her son and her brother would be away.

"I thought she was a widow, and so did the rest of the help, and we used to wonder among ourselves how long her husband was dead, and at what age she was married, for she looked so young to have a son, a young man. We used to call him Mr. Frederick, and though he was always kind and polite, and though we couldn't but admire his handsome looks, there was something about him that used to make us kind of frightened of him. We thought it might be because he was so much with his uncle—and he was dark and strange enough, Heaven knows.

"I used sometimes to overhear the mother and son, talking; she would ask him to give up something, and he'd get into a passion and swear that he never would; and then she'd fall to crying and he'd rush out.

"Things went on that way for a good while, and one day he came up to his mother in a great hurry. I was in a closet in the next room folding away clothes. I couldn't make out everything they were saying, and I thought it would be mean to try to listen, so I went on with my work; but I couldn't help hearing enough to know what it was about.

"He wanted to accept some place that had been offered to him—he said it would give him power, and place him just where he wanted to be. But his mother begged and entreated him not to take it, because if he did he would have to give up his religion. She might as well speak to the wall—he wouldn't listen to her —he wouldn't listen to anything but his own hot passion, and when he rushed out as he always did, I heard her fall. I went in to her, and picked her up, and brought her to, and after a little, seeing I suppose how my heart ached for her, she told me everything about herself, and how she feared that her son would yet murder either Cecil Clare, or his father, and that was the reason she was constantly praying him to give up his wishing for revenge. She asked me not to tell anybody what she had been saying to me, for she didn't want people to know the facts about her son's birth, and I promised to keep everything secret. After that she wanted me near her all the time, and Mr. Frederick and Mr. Neville knew that she had told me the secrets about herself, but seeing that she thought me so faithful-like, and was so fond of me, I suppose they didn't much mind. I said before that Mr. Neville, the brother, was a queer man; he was a ventoquist—"

"Ventriloquist!" interrupted the pompous headwaiter, but Miss Moore, heedless of the interruption, continued:

"And he used to be trying to teach his nephew the same bad trick. Sure it was him that bid me speak that time to-day when we were all startled by the strange voice from the crowd; myself was frightened as well as the rest for I couldn't think what would bring him there. Well, at last, the poor gentle creature was dying, and though I've seen Mr. Frederick at her bedside cry like a child, yet he wouldn't promise her even then that he'd give up wishing for the revenge. She made me swear with the prayer-book in my hands that I'd never tell what I knew about her son; and I took the oath with Mr. Frederick and Mr. Neville looking on.

"'Perhaps you will meet him sometime with another name, Hannah,' she said to me, 'and if you do, don't speak to him till he speaks to you first, for fear people might find out.'

"And I promised, though I think her son put her up to make me promise that, lest I'd be claiming acquaintance with him when he wouldn't want me to.

"Well, she died—that is nearly five years ago—and I was in and out of place till I engaged with Miss Calvert. Sure enough, I met Mr. Frederick with another name—wasn't he the Mr. Charles Plowden that examined us all on the first go off, and didn't my heart stand still, when I saw by his look that he knew me! I thought of all sorts of distracting things then—I was sure, somehow, that the murdered man, Cecil Clare, and the Cecil Clare the poor, dead woman used to speak of, were the same. I thought of the passions Mr. Frederick used to get in, and the way he used to swear that he'd have vengeance, and that nothing in the world should stand between him and it. And when I saw him going so hard on Mr. Hubert, I was almost tempted to tell all I knew, but my oath to his dead mother held me back. I think he was afraid of me, for, if you remember, he dropped the case kind of sudden.

"But the first thing that greatly puzzled me was the beggar that came here once—the beggar that Rosie wanted to tell you all about on the night that Miss Calvert came home ill from the ball. I wouldn't let her make much of it, if you recollect, but I had reasons for that. The beggar was Mr. Neville—I knew him at once, in spite of his old, ragged dress, and he knew by my look that I did, for he put his finger to his lips, unknown to Rosie. He asked questions about Madame Bernot and Mr. Hubert, and Miss Calvert; but he asked them in a careless way that one wouldn't be apt to think much about and Rosie answered them all. I thought maybe he'd make a sign, or say a secret word to me going out, and for that reason I went to the door with him myself; but he didn't even look, only hurried off. I didn't know what to think—I felt sure it was not poverty, for he was rich out and out; and I couldn't relieve myself by speaking about it to any one, without, in some way, breaking my word to the dead. That was before we were examined, and then, when we were examined, and I knew that Mr. Plowden was just Mr. Frederick Clare, and nobody else, I couldn't help but think that Mr. Neville visited this house so that he might help his nephew by finding out all he could about the Bernots; and I felt bitter toward them both to be trying to bring trouble into a noble family.

"I wouldn't let Rosie tell you about it, as she wanted to do, nor make much of it, because at that time Mr. Frederick used to come here so friendly-like, and I was afraid if you got talking about the circumstance it might make mischief in some way, so I just shut up everything in my own heart. But I had very queer thoughts, especially after Mr. Hubert's arrest, when Mr. Frederick was so attentive to Miss Calvert. I used to think sometimes, that if Mr. Hubert did murder Cecil Clare, Mr. Frederick would try to bring Mr. Hubert to justice for having taken the vengeance out of his own hands; and that perhaps all his friendliness was only on purpose to get all the clews he could. I knew he was sharp, and I always thought he was cruel from the way he used to repulse his mother's entreaties. But he has proved himself brave and noble for once; perhaps it is owing to his mother's prayers in Heaven for him—and, anyway, I'm sorry for him this night, for I'm afeared its round his own neck the halter will be at last."

She stopped suddenly, and threw her apron over her head; then, finding her emotion becoming too powerful, she begged the company to excuse her, and retiring to her room she indulged in a hearty fit of crying, after which she said her beads for the real murderer of Cecil Clare.

The remainder of the help, in deference to Miss Moore's sorrowful feelings, retired also, when they had exchanged a few brief comments on the tale, and offered some conjectures as to why "Mr. Frederick" had changed his name to Charles Plowden.

In Madame Bernot's room there was taking place, a sweet, happy communion of two pure hearts; the interchange of a confidence to which the angels might have listened. There was no hesitation now in pouring into Madame's ear the tale of her own, and Hubert's love—how the crime which he had supposed rested on his soul had prevented the utterance of a word of lover-like affection, and Madame bent to the kneeling girl, and wound her arms about her, and answered:

"In the past, when I fancied there would be a union between you and Maurice, because of his passionate affection for you, I little dreamed that it would be Hubert who should at last possess such a treasure."

And still holding the beautiful head close to her, she continued to speak, softly, of the past:

"When, over Maurice's coffin, I extorted from you and Hubert the promise never to speak of how my boy met his death, I did it because I thought it would help more surely to eradicate any rancor which might remain in Hubert's heart, and because I thought it would seem like a more complete forgiveness of Maurice's murderer; and when I shut myself from the outer world and sought to die to all, save spiritual things, I did it as a sacrifice to be offered for Maurice's soul. You know that he died unshriven, Margaret; that no priest administered to him the last rites, though I have reason to believe that his life, up to that unhappy time, was pure and blameless. It was that which made me freely forgive his murderer, and pray that God would send *me* sufferings, anguish, anything, only to pardon my murdered boy. *He* sent them, and he has taken them away as suddenly as he visited me with them. I think my sacrifice has been accepted, Margaret—that my son has been pardoned."

Her eyes turned to the picture, and her whole face

seemed to shine with an inspired, ecstatic expression.
It was as if she saw the realization of her desire, and
Margaret little doubted but that to the mental vision of
the dear saint was presented something of the scene which
is permitted alone to Heavenly dwellers, and when the
young girl bestowed her good-night kiss, it was with
much the same feeling of reverence as that with which
she was wont to pray in the church.

In her room, for the first time since she had hurriedly thrust it into her pocket, Margaret thought of
the missive which Delmar had given her, and she drew
it forth to read.

She was too happy to be affected by the knowledge
of the calumnies which society had heaped upon her,
and she was too generous not to pardon immediately,
and even, in some measure, to love the writer for the
frankness and penitence which were so simply, but so
touchingly expressed.

She answered in her own kind, gentle way—penning
words which must rivet the good influence that Eugene
had begun already to exert upon his wayward sister,
and which must assure her not only of Margaret's entire
forgiveness, but of her sincere affection; and, having
prepared it for the morning mail, she knelt to offer up
her happy, grateful prayers.

There was but one cloud on the dazzling brightness
of her joy—the thought of Plowden. If she could but
see him to pour forth her gratitude, and to assure him
that she remembered nothing for him save the one act
which had given to her so much bliss; but she must
wait, as she had waited before in Hubert's case, and as
she had done then, she would do now, pray for the unhappy murderer of Cecil Clare.

On that same day, in the home of the Delmars, a
painful scene had occurred, occasioned by a woman's
temper, and Eugene, appalled, listened to, and looked
at his mother, as if she had been suddenly transformed

into some totally unknown being. She tore through the parlors like one half-crazed, venting bitter reproaches equally on the Bernots, and on her son and daughter.

Louise having replied to the news which Mrs. Delmar so indignantly communicated on her return from the court, that she rejoiced at Hubert and Margaret's happiness, it flamed into fiercer fire, the rage which already burned so furiously in her mother's breast.

Like every other maniac she only darted her wrath on the very kindness that would have soothed her back to reason and calmness. Louise, in obedience to a sign from her brother, controling, by an effort, her desire to retort to the false accusations of her mother, forced herself to answer quietly, how just and nobly Hubert Bernot had acted, and how unnatural it was to suppose that his heart could be won at will. But the frantic woman was only made worse by the attempted justification; and, at last, Eugene, with such a look of pain in his face as perhaps had been there never before, drew his sister's arm within his own and led her from the room, while the irate woman, having continued to storm until her passion had somewhat spent itself, ordered the carriage, and driving to one of her numerous fashionable confidants, relieved herself by reviving all the calumnies about Margaret Calvert, and complaining of her son's and daughter's want of sympathy with her own unhappy feelings.

Hubert Bernot no longer occupied his old cell; and that first night on which he was free with a freedom no prince of earth could have given, one would scarcely have recognized in the changed expression of his face, the pale wan countenance he had worn in the court-room that morning.

Like Margaret, he had one anxiety; to know what Plowden's fate would be, and to see him; and like Margaret, he too prayed for the unhappy murderer of Cecil Clare.

Plowden, or rather Frederick Clare, around whom, despite his crime—despite the wrong that he had suffered for so long to separate two lives—there clustered the grateful, tender feelings of two happy hearts, sat alone in his grim prison, battling with the doubt, and fear, and despair of his strange unhappy position. He fancied that if he could receive some assurance of his pardon by Hubert and Margaret, that he could meet his fate as a brave man should; but the uncertainty of knowing whether he was hated and abhorred, rendered him restless and excited. For one smile of forgiveness from the face which rose so often before him, for one kind word from those lips, death in its most disgraceful form would have been little to bear.

Silent and grim as the grim walls which confined him, he sat viewing the pictures which memory conjured up—it conjured up one scene more frequently than any other; a pale, lovely face always lifted up in entreaty, and then always drooping in the bitterness of disappointment—it was the entreaty to which he would never listen, the entreaty which, coming from an overwhelming love returned, on its refusal, only to break at last the heart which loved "not wisely but too well."

When the long night hours yielded to the dawn, the prisoner bowed his face in his hands and murmured:

"Mother! mother!"

Perchance she was about him then with her angelic ministrations, perchance, her prayers before the Mercy Seat of Heaven had softened his heart to true penitence at last—that her influence there had completed the work which Margaret Calvert had so unconsciously begun here.

CHAPTER XXII.

"ROQUELARE" did resign Hubert Bernot's case; and men, whom fear of that society had deterred from offering their aid before, now volunteered their influence in the young man's behalf. There was not wanting even high judicial power to effect Hubert's speedy release, so that in a few days there was a brief trial on which it was shown that Hubert Bernot was in no way the cause of Cecil Clare's death; that the cut he had given was done in self-defence, the murdered man having recognized Hubert because of his strong resemblance to his deceased brother, Maurice, and the prisoner was acquitted, on which a storm of applause burst forth, and congratulations, and handshaking were administered to the young man in a very promiscuous and democratic fashion.

His mother and Margaret accompanied by Dr. Durant who would insist still that his services might be needed, waited for him in a private room, and fond and ardent were their embraces and congratulations.

At last Madame Bernot, leaning on her son's arm, and accompanied by Margaret, descended to visit the servants, and tears of joy were shed by those good souls as in turn they courtesied, and took her proffered hand, and offered their simple and heartfelt congratulations to Mr. Hubert. Then the three took their way to the dining-room, where it was so strange, and so happy to have Madame presiding at the table, and where the heart of each was so full, that but a pretence was made of eating.

Their ignorance of Plowden's fate was the only cloud upon their happiness. Father Germain had made constant and persistent inquiries, but he elicited only very vague and varying information.

The press, particularly the sensational press—which had devoted columns to the trial of Hubert Bernot, now pretended to inform the public that Frederick Clare, alias Charles Plowden, was in a certain prison awaiting his trial, but those who bore the insignia of "Roquelare," knew that it was no ordinary prison which confined the murderer of Cecil Clare.

Later in the day Eugene Delmar came to testify his honest joy, and to Margaret's inquiry, why his sister had not accompanied him, he gave some faltering and insufficient excuse, which Miss Calvert charitably construed into meaning that Louise still hesitated to meet one to whom she had made such a frank confession.

But Margaret was mistaken, Louise owing to the unmistakable assurance of welcome in Margaret's reply to her own penitent note, had no hesitation to meet Miss Calvert, but she dreaded to meet Hubert—she had not yet succeeded in quite dislodging his image from her heart; the mere mention of his name still had power to make her thrill, and when her brother had rather insisted that she should accompany him on his visit to the Bernot's, she put her hand in his and said coaxingly:

" You understand it all, Eugene ; make some excuse for me."

Eugene and Hubert together detailed every practical plan for the discovery and the aiding of Plowden, and when the young men separated it was with the mutually avowed determination to leave no means untried which should ensure their success.

Weeks passed, and the search was as fruitless as when it first began. The marriage of Hubert and Margaret was delayed until something definite could be learned of the lawyer, for the lovers thought it would be somewhat heartless to consummate their own happy union while his fate remained so uncertain, and apparently so dark.

But Hubert grew importunate at last, and Margaret urged:

"Only a few weeks longer."

The Bernot servants had their customary social evening assemblies, and they had celebrated Mr. Hubert's release with full Irish fervor; but Hannah Moore had neither taken part with her wonted spirit, nor, did she perform her daily tasks with her wonted cheerfulness. "Little Sam," as if by that means alone he could testify his gratitude for past kindness tried to imitate the melancholy of the cook; and he succeeded so well, that not even the complimentary allusions which the help still occasionally made to his last evidence in court, seemed to rouse him from his sad and somber mien.

Warm-hearted Hannah Moore was sorrowful with thoughts of "Mr. Frederick." She summoned courage to ask Miss Calvert about the lawyer, and emboldened by the kind, sympathetic manner in which Margaret replied, she poured forth the tale which already she had told her fellow-servants, adding:

"His mother was so fond of me that it seems as if I ought to be near him for her sake when he is in such trouble. Maybe he's sick and wants nursing, and has only the hand of the cold stranger about him."

"Maybe he is, Hannah," was the troubled reply, "and that is why we are all so anxious, and trying so hard to find out where he is; and just so soon as we learn anything about him, you shall know."

"God bless you, Miss;" was the grateful response.

But the weeks wore on; even the "few weeks more," for which Margaret had urged, without gaining any tidings, and even Madame Bernot, whose wonderfully-restored health still continued, advocated the uselessness of a longer delay of Hubert and Margaret's marriage.

"One more month," Margaret coaxed; "Strange as it may seem, I have a stronger feeling than ever, that we shall see him soon; and the postponement of our marriage until we shall have learned definite news of him, will seem as a proof of our regard."

The pleading girl won her way, though Hubert with a sort of tender sternness, stipulated that it should be the very last postponement.

The press had ceased to have even a desultory word concerning the lawyer, and morning after morning the lady who had so envied Margaret because of Plowden's attentions, threw down the paper in bitter disappointment. Why was there not something about the lawyer's impending trial, as there used to be about that of Hubert Bernot?

Now that Miss Calvert was known to be betrothed to Hubert—Mrs. Delmar had long since scornfully promulgated that fact in fashionable circles—this silly creature of uncertain age fain would storm the citadel of the handsome lawyer's heart with her own faded charms. Murderer though he was, Miss Lydia Lonnes felt that she could magnanimously lay her heart and fortune at his feet, providing that horrid "Roquelare," did not secretly assassinate him, or the laws of the country put a rope about his neck before the performance of the marriage ceremony.

On the last of the chill autumnal evenings, just four months after Hubert's acquittal, when the wind went sighing about the house in true, dismal fashion, and sudden and fierce gusts of rain poured down at intervals, a quick, sharp ring sounded at the street door. Margaret, who was crossing the hall, answered the summons, and admitted a tall, manly figure, so muffled up —either as protection from the weather, or to serve as a disguise—that but little of his features could be seen, and that little seemed quite unknown to her.

He spoke, and she recognized with a glad cry which brought both Hubert and his mother from the parlor, Plowden, or rather Frederick Clare.

They drew him further into the light of the hall,

Hubert and she, and they joyfully pulled the muffler from his face.

"Not hated then, after all," he said huskily, and for an answer Margaret pressed one of his hands, while Hubert warmly shook the other.

They drew him into the parlor, and when he had shaken hands with Madame Bernot—who immediately retired, ostensibly to order a repast, but really to give the young people an opportunity for any secret confidence they might desire to impart—and was seated, they noted more closely, and with new surprise, the sad changes which had been wrought in his appearance; he was pale and emaciated to a pitiful degree, with deep lines in his forehead and about his mouth, that never had been there before. Margaret could have wept at the too-apparent evidence of his suffering, and even Hubert's face wore a grave, sad look, and his voice took a tender tone, as he said:

"Answer one question first—have you escaped from prison?"

Clare faintly smiled.

"No; they have let me go," shuddering as if some terrible memory was connected with the words, and then he pulled out his watch and said he had not long to stay.

"Not long to stay;" echoed Margaret in dismay, while Hubert in surprise asked the reason; but Clare, without answering, turned to Margaret:

"*Your* happiness has been completed long before this, so that *my* congratulations come late; but still, accept them Mrs. Bernot."

Margaret drew back, blushing hotly, while Hubert rising, said hurriedly:

"We waited to know your fate—you who have been the cause of the happiness Margaret would not accept until we should learn something definite about you— she is not Mrs. Bernot yet."

"It is enough," he said, "I am strong now for the future since I know that not only am I not hated, but that I have been regarded by you both with something like affection.

"When I came to-night it was for the purpose of assuring myself that you had forgiven me the wrong which kept you two so long apart, to beg your prayers, and then without saying more, to bid you a long farewell. But I owe it now to your regard for me, to tell you, as much as I may, of a life which has only begun to pursue a right course; and I owe it to the kindness of one who has helped to place me on that course, to tell how her influence, unconsciously to herself, has performed a good work.

"You heard, in common with the charitable public," there was a little of the old sarcasm in his tones—"the tale of my birth, and the desire for revenge with which my boyish years were filled. My mother—" his voice changed suddenly to touching tenderness—" could only look on and weep that her influence was powerless to subdue that determination in my character which was to prove so fatal to myself and to others. From my first meeting with Cecil Clare, when he cast foul aspersions on my gentle mother, my desire for revenge —for vengeance for *her* wrongs—grew until it would yield to *no* power. From that time I dropped the name of Frederick Clare, and adopted that of Charles Plowden. Plowden had been once a much venerated name in my mother's family, and she had caused it to be added to Frederick in baptism, so that I was christened Frederick Plowden Clare. But I would have no name of my father's and neither my mother nor uncle made much opposition when I declared my determination to sign myself in future, Charles Plowden. Only my mother *would* call me Frederick Clare at home. Clare was *her* name she said, and I would not seem her son if she could not call me by my own name. I did not oppose her for it made little difference as I had no friends to come to the house.

"My uncle's constant companionship left me little

wish for other associates so that I was almost completely unknown, and at liberty to change my name without question or remark. Once I was offered a position that would help me to the pinnacle my ambition desired, but there were terms annexed to the voluntary gift which would require a renunciation of the practice of my Faith. I promised to accept in defiance of my mother's frantic entreaties. I did not deny that I was a Catholic, I even promptly avowed my religion when occasion required, but I went no more to Mass, and for the Sacraments, I had ceased to frequent those from the time of my first meeting with Cecil Clare.

"My uncle was a member of 'Roquelare.' His natural and acquired intellectual gifts, his superiority in his profession, his wise judgment, his keen penetration into human motives, all had conspired to raise him to the very highest degree of that society. Unmarried himself, my mother, several years his junior, was the only creature he loved, and for her sake his love for me became the one passionate, absorbing affection of his life. When she died, and he accompanied me on my search for the Clares, it was for the purpose of preventing any rash act of mine, not of permitting me to commit one; but when the deed was done, and under his own eye, and he knew that as a member of 'Roquelare' he was bound to surrender me to justice, he fell into a pitiable state of remorse and terror. His terror was augmented by the thought that if *he* failed to give me up, some other member of 'Roquelare' might discover my crime, set the society on my track, and because of his near relation to me, might even ferret him out, and compel him to bear witness against me.

"I was exultant—the revenge which had been my sole thought for years, was now accomplished, the man who had heaped such foul aspersions on my mother was lying dead by my hand. I thought of nothing else, and I felt neither terror nor remorse until we turned from the spot—then, the dead body seemed to pursue me. I drank brandy when we reached home, and I plied my uncle with the same, until we both fell into a heavy, drunken sleep.

"The next day I looked steadily at my position, and I had to acknowledge to myself, that, brave as I had been in the attainment of my revenge, I was not brave enough to face the consequences—I, who had taken a human life, shuddered at the thought of death for myself.

"We had assured ourselves that there were no earthly witness of my crime, and we watched for the comments of the press on the dastardly deed. I saw the account of Miss Calvert's visit to the *morgue*, how it was considered an important clue, and I at once formed *my* determination. I would announce myself as a friend of the murdered man—my knowledge of his antecedents would enable me easily to do so—and having been admitted previously to legal practice in the city, I would take up his case. I fancied that such a course must be a sure means of averting every shadow of suspicion from myself. I did not know then how Miss Calvert was connected with the Hubert Bernot about whom the murdered man had drunkenly raved; but from her manner during her examination, I concluded that she had some fear, some anxiety, as it were, to conceal, and, simply to test her, and to prove the truth or falsity of my own suspicion, I charged her with a knowledge of Cecil Clare's murder. The result proved the truth of my conjecture; but it also somewhat puzzled me. *I* was the murderer, then why her fear, her anxiety for some one whom she evidently believed to be guilty

"In order to ascertain as much as possible about her, my uncle, in the disguise of a beggar, called at this house, and was admitted, as he expected to be, for charity's sake. He recognized in one of the servants the attendant to whom my mother had been much attached, and she recognized him despite his disguise; but she understood the secret motion he made for silence as to his identity, and she obeyed him. He asked sundry, and apparently careless questions, which, however, drew from another of the servants many particulars about the family who occupied the house, and on his departure the domestic whom he had recognized, accompanied him to the door, probably for some explanation of his strange disguise. But he deemed it best to say nothing.

"When he detailed to me the particulars he had learned, and I heard the name Hubert Bernot, we knew then it was the same Hubert Bernot mentioned by the murdered man, and, connecting all the circumstances, I arrived at what eventually proved to be the truth: that you"—looking at Hubert—"imagined yourself to be the murderer of Clare, and that you had made a confident of Miss Calvert. I exulted at my discovery. I could now forever avert earthly suspicion from myself —I could work up the case on that knowledge, even though an innocent man should hang for *my* crime. Success would bring me honor in my profession and for any fear, for any remorse, save that of having *my* guilt discovered, I had none.

"I bared my plan to my uncle; though, like myself, a Catholic only in name, he was appalled at my proposition, and he endeavored to make me forego at least my determination to prosecute an innocent man. But I who had scorned a mother's entreaties, found little difficulty in contemning his. He shut himself in his room, feigning illness, lest going abroad an accidental word, or look might betray anything to 'Roquelare', and he remained thus secluded, until I told him I had dropped the case because of my recognition by Hannah Moore and her implied threat to tell something of other people which I alone understood. I feared that she might tell, notwithstanding her promise to my dead mother, all that she knew about me, and that my own fears might lead to the discovery of my crime.

"I became as anxious for the speedy termination of the case as I had been for its prosecution, and I described Madame Bernot's pitiable condition in order to foil Bertoni's efforts for *her* examination. The particulars which my uncle had learned during his visit in the guise of a beggar, enabled me to give that description, as well as other details which must have surprised Miss Calvert.

"I felt relieved when I found that no testimony of any value had been obtained from Madame Bernot, and that at last the case had been dropped. Then, my uncle told me of the resolution which he had formed; unable to endure longer his intense fear of 'Roquelare', since he had made himself amenable to its utmost rigor, and loving me too well to betray me, he had determined to shut himself forever from the world. He had already an interview with the Superior of a religious house, during which he solicited an asylum in order to elude the vengeance of a secret society which he intended to abjure; if permitted a home with the Religious without being required to join the Order, he promised to endow the house with a considerable portion of his wealth. When assured that he was a Catholic and in need of their spiritual aid, his request was granted.

"On the last night that we spent together before he went to his new home, he disclosed to me as much about 'Roquelare' as he dared to do, because that knowledge might help me should I ever be dogged by any member of the society. I would have become a member long before, but in that case I should have been obliged to forswear even the slightest intention of private revenge. My uncle gave me also certain details relating to one or two who occupied high place in the society, and who might, in the strange future sit in judgment on my crime, should it ever be discovered. One of these was Bertoni, whose character my relative long before had thoroughly read; and when he described to me the ambition of that character, the desire to mount in the society at any cost, I treasured up his words.

"He entered the religious house, bearing no other name than Lorguette, and I, in accordance with his last request, published that he had been lost at sea, in order that they would not require his body to give it the customary honors. In my heart, then, ambition took the place of my old desire for revenge, and I worked early and late to rise in my profession. I visited my uncle once, and I found him strangely altered—he who had been so worldly-minded, so irreligious, was remorseful and penitent, and he sought to effect the same change in me; he even begged me to give myself up to justice. I fled from him, trusting however, that the strength of his love would prevent him betraying me, and my trust was not deceived.

"Directly after that, accident enabled me to serve young Delmar, and by him, you remember"—turning his eyes from the grate at which he had been steadily looking, to Hubert—"I was introduced to you. I tried to get away from you, to get away from the topic you would introduce in conversation—Cecil Clare's murder—but you were persistent, and you even forced me to accompany you home.

"From that time an image haunted me—both of you understand whose—a face that *would* thrust itself into my sleeping and waking hours; that came when I repelled it most, and that was ever wearing the frightened expression it wore when it met me so unexpectedly in company with him who imagined himself to be the murderer of Cecil Clare.

"I could not resist the fascination that made me appear to return the strange attachment which you"—looking again from the fire to Hubert—"seemed to have formed for me. You fancied you were shrewd, and that you carefully concealed from me the burning secret you carried, when in reality you were laying bare your poor tortured conscience—it was from your own un conscious admission that I knew 'Roquelare' was pursuing you, and I rejoiced because I felt that I was safe.

"You insisted that I should sue for Miss Calvert's hand; I obeyed only too gladly, stifling the thought of my crime which fain would thrust itself between me and the object of my passionate attachment. I did not think then that *your* affection for Miss Calvert was reciprocated, and I fancied that you did not declare your attachment because of your imaginary crime. But when I found that even as you loved, so were you loved in return—when I knew that I, the truly guilty one stood between you—that it needed but a confession from me to remove the wrong impression from your mind, and leave you free to grasp your happiness, I was content to let the wrong remain, for I could not resign to another her whose image so perpetually dwelt with me.

" When the crisis came, and I witnessed her unselfish efforts in your behalf; when I heard entreaties such as in the by-gone years I had been wont to turn from, but which strangely moved me then, when I knew the full force of the sacrifice she was making, there came into my soul such feelings as had been there never before. I resolved to devote every faculty to save you, Hubert—to do all in my power—save give *myself* up, I could not do that.

" As a first step in my course for the defence, I thought carefully of all that my uncle had told me about Bertoni, and I worked upon it, with what result you are already aware; but I found that Bertoni would still retain the case despite his expulsion from ' Roquelare,' of which expulsion I first learned on the day he met us"—glancing at Margaret for an instant—" when we were returning from the prison, and he lifted his left hand to show the crimson bandage about it. From the knowledge my uncle had imparted to me, I knew that bandage was the mark of expulsion. The stamp of the society with which every member must be branded, had been burned out of Bertoni's wrist; and just so long as he retained any hold upon public life, just so long as he practiced his profession, just so long he would be compelled to wear that crimson bandage, to proclaim his disgrace as it were, to every member of 'Roquelare.' If he refused to wear it, spies would track him everywhere, and only leave him when he had felt the full weight of 'Roquelare's' vengeance. If, on the contrary, he had dropped the case, and sunk into obscure life, Roquelare would have been content to watch that he never again emerged into any public career. That he would adopt the latter course was my hope; but, when he hissed to my teeth that he would continue the prosecution in order to defeat me for the sake of revenge, and when I saw the gestures which accompanied his speech in the court, after his expulsion from ' Roquelare," I knew my chances of saving you, Hubert, unless I gave myself up, were meagre indeed. Every gesture of Bertoni's was significant of the society's own rules; expelled member though he was, the body was bound by its own regulations to assist him to the utmost in the prosecution of a case which had begun under its auspices—to assist, that the extreme rigor of the law might be inflicted on the criminal, for any leniency, after a clear case of circumstantial evidence has been shown, would throw discredit on 'Roquelare.' And every time that Bertoni's bandaged wrist came in sight, I knew it was to show how he still felt his power, and my hope grew fainter and fainter.

"I had heard you sometimes speak to Delmar of Hugh Murburd, and of your correspondence with him, and, after your arrest I learned from Delmar the residence of Murburd. I hastened thence in order to sound the mother and son regarding the evidence they might give if summoned to court; but Bertoni's detectives had been before me, and I was foiled. Mother and son were absent; the domestic could give no further particulars than young Mr. Murburd had gone to New York some time before, and his mother had followed him on the next day.

"I returned to the city to study again every point of the case, and to discover, if possible, some loophole by which I might free my client, and at the same time save myself.

"In what way Cecil Clare had been connected with Hubert so as to provoke from the latter the blow which made him imagine himself a murderer, I knew not; that there had been a connection, even a close acquaintance, I already inferred from the conversation which occurred between Delmar and Hubert on the occasion of my introduction to the latter. On that occasion, Delmar, reviving the circumstances of the first investigation of the murder, desired to know what acquaintance Hubert had with Clare that could warrant the bringing of his and Miss Calvert's name before the public; but Hubert made some evasive reply, and in deference to his apparent reluctance to answer, the question was not repeated.

"I questioned neither of you on the subject,"—looking again at Hubert—"because I felt that whatever were the anterior circumstances they would do little for the benefit of the prisoner, and I, with *my* burning secret, shrank from questioning those who were suffering for my crime.

"I hoped that my efforts at least would avert the worst—that you would not die, that you would be free from prison walls sometime, and I tried to harden myself to a feeling of indifference about it; but the face that ever haunted me, came more persistently then— came with its frightened look as I had seen it first— came with its imploring expression as I saw it afterward —came with the entreaties that I heard it make to you to return to your God and your duty—came with low, sweet tender words like my mother used to speak to me years before—and it well nigh wrung *my* secret from me.

"Once, while I waited at the door of your cell, I

heard you express your determination to forego marriage, even though you should be acquitted, because of the crime which you fancied you had committed, and I heard Miss Calvert express a similar determination. Then I knew that *my* crime would have to be acknowledged, if I would give happiness to her whom I loved. I saw her agony, but I saw also her brave, noble resignation, and I was conquered.

"Yet, I would make one more appeal to herself. I would ask her if your acquittal would not be sufficient, and if her own lips again assured me that the murder of which she too believed you guilty, was always to remain an obstacle to your union, then I would obtain one final victory over myself, and accept the bitter consequences. I had fancied that her trust in me was somewhat diminished and I was inclined to attribute it to a betrayal by Hannah Moore, of the confidence which my mother had given her. But when I remembered the woman's solemn oath, and the tender attachment she had felt for my mother, I attributed the idea to my fancy.

"I saw Miss Calvert—I obtained from her the assurance I dreaded to receive, and then I held the final struggle with myself.

"I went for the second time to the religious house in which my uncle abode, and when he learned that the object of my visit was to request his presence in court in order to prove that *I* was the murderer of Cecil Clare, I knew by the glad eagerness with which he received my proposition that *my* secret had borne as heavily and sickeningly upon him, as yours had done upon Miss Calvert.

"It was his voice which spoke from the crowd to Hannah Moore, commanding her to speak—ventriloquism enabled him to do that and it was his sudden appearance which caused Bertoni, to look so strangely, and to exhibit such motion. My uncle's coming was, as it were, from the dead. 'Roquelare,' had believed him drowned, and Bertoni had coveted the high place made vacant by his supposed death. The strange and simultaneous rising of the judge and some of the jurors was due to the sign which my uncle made—a sign that only he, because of the high degree which he had attained in the society, was permitted to make, and which compelled for him whenever he chose to use it, such deference as was then given. He employed it on that occasion to prove his identity, and to insure for his evidence such consideration as would not have been given to the words of another.

"You know what followed. Of the scenes through which *I* have passed—of the time that has elapsed since last I saw you, I may not speak "— he shuddered slightly—" I can only say that there was a long, and painful, and tortuous examination, and death, disgraceful and public for me, and secret and torturing for my uncle seemed imminent—frightfully imminent, until it was shown in a review of my uncle's life, that from the time he had entered the society his career was marked by sacrifices made alone for the common good, by rejected opportunities of honors and emoluments of himself by which he alone would have been benefited, and repeated refusals of even the last high honor, the final acceptance of which was due alone to stern compulsion. These things, together with the fact that he had told me nothing of the true secrets of the society, that I had helped to vindicate the honor of 'Roquelare' by exposing Bertoni, and that if given our freedom we both intended to shut ourselves forever from the world, obtained pardon, and in some measure even kindness from 'Roquelare.'

"I was obliged to submit to an initiation and afterward to have the mark burned out, as they had already done to my uncle "—he rolled slightly back the sleeve from his left arm and disclosed a crimson bandage like that which had encircled Bertoni's wrist—" And now "— he rose suddenly—" I have only to ask that when thoughts of me come unbidden, and perhaps, unwished for, and you remember my willingness to let an innocent man suffer for my crime—nay, the *desire* to have him suffer, which I had at first, balance it with thoughts of the torture which I endured in after months; when you remember my daring aspirations to a pure hand, remember also that I was maddened by a love all the deeper because I felt that it *ought* to be so hopeless; when you think of me as having been willing to win that hand, in pity think also that I was goaded by very desperation to the attainment of a happiness which I felt *ought* to be beyond my reach. If *your* sufferings were severe"— turning slightly to Hubert—"if *you* loved also and yet permitted that fancied crime to come between you and the object of your love, I reasoned that your attachment could not be the maddening thing that mine was, and I did not then know that your love was returned. When, on one occasion I said that we were both drinking of a bitter cup, it was only to believe that mine contained the most wormwood and gall. A *fancied* crime stood between you and your heart's object; a *real* crime stood before, though it did not bar my presumptuous approach to, *my* heart's object.

"Think of these things when you remember my perfidy, but more than all "—his voice sank to a deep, low tender tone, as if the swell of feelings which had grown with every word, had obtained now complete mastery—"remember it was a woman's holy pleadings with another—her devotion, so like Heaven's own love in its pure disinterestedness; her unswerving loyalty to the teachings of her faith; her complete sacrifice of self, which brought to me at last the strength to do right;—that caused desperate struggles in my soul, that frequently made a confession spring almost to my very lips, and that brought back the memory of my mother, and the religious practices of my childhood as they had been brought back never before.

"In my future of voluntary penance, the thought

that you both have fully pardoned, have even perchance sometimes kind memories of me, will be a nucleus about which to gather the prayers and deeds of the remainder of my life."

He shaded his face with his hand as if to conceal its expression, while his listeners seemed too much surprised, and even awed, to speak.

Hubert was the first to recover himself, to give his visitor unmistakable assurances that much more than he requested was granted, and to press upon him the warmest offers of hospitality. But Clare shook his head.

"I must away to-night; and besides, I am pledged to partake of no man's hospitality until sacred walls in a distant country enclose me."

"What Order?" asked Hubert wonderingly.

"I cannot tell yet; my plans will not be matured until I shall have seen the Superior, possibly of such a house as that of which my uncle has been an inmate, and to which he has returned with the intention of entering the Order."

"Why not join your uncle?" questioned Hubert.

"Because I would sever myself from kindred and friends, and everything that could tend to make my renunciation of self less complete."

Margaret, whose true tender heart was much more pained by the recital of suffering she had heard, than her woman's vanity was gratified by the flattering things which had been said about her, seeing that Clare was determined upon an immediate departure, asked if he would not speak to Hannah Moore before he went.

"Certainly," he answered with glad eagerness; "I was about to make the request, for the good creature deserves my gratitude for the faithfulness with which she kept her painful knowledge of me."

And Hannah Moore was put into a state of the most flurried excitement by the unusual announcement that Miss Calvert wanted to see her in the parlor; and with a very hasty smoothing of her apron she left the kitchen to obey the strange order.

Miss Calvert met her in the hall on which the parlors opened, and ushering her into one of them, said, with a reassuring smile:

"He, about whom we have all been so anxious, is waiting to see you."

Withdrawing, she closed the door softly, and left Hannah Moore and the lawyer together.

The interview lasted but a few minutes, and the cook was crying joyful tears when she came forth, and saying, as well as her emotion would permit her to speak:

"It's your mother that's happy in Heaven this night, and it's yourself that God loves, Mr. Frederick, to make you so good at last."

And then she returned to the kitchen, going slowly, and turning often, as if to take one more look of the young man.

Hubert and Margaret, with Madame Bernot, who had joined them as soon as she learned of the termination of their confidential intercourse with Clare, waited in the adjoining parlor, and thither, when Hannah Moore had at last disappeared in a turn of the stairway, the lawyer hastened.

The extreme limit of the time which he had allotted for his stay had expired, and he extended his hands in farewell—extending them to Margaret first, while he looked down upon her with indescribably sad eyes.

He did not speak—the pressure of his hands and his look constituted his "good-by," and she, too full also to speak, only bowed her head; for an instant they stood thus, then he drew his hands away, murmured an adieu to Madame Bernot, and turned with Hubert who would accompany him to the door. Then Margaret threw herself on Madame's breast, and sobbed out all the pent-up feelings of the past hour.

It was raining fiercely, and the wind drove the storm

in a wild dash against the young men as they stood in the open door-way ; Hubert again besought Clare to remain at least for that one night ; but the lawyer firmly refused, and with one last grasp of hands, and one last very sadly, very tenderly spoken: "Farewell, till we meet in Heaven," Clare darted down the steps, and on in the very teeth of the fierce, wild tempest, until his form was lost to sight, and Hubert turned slowly and sadly inward.

CHAPTER XXIII.

THERE was not even the shadow of an obstruction in the way of the marriage of Hubert and Margaret now, and preparations for that event pressed hastily and happily forward.

Louise Delmar at her brother's solicitation accepted the invitation to be Margaret's bridesmaid, and after a few meetings she grew to encounter Hubert without experiencing that strange, undefinable thrill which the very mention of his name had been wont to arouse.

Mrs. Delmar tried to drown in the vanity and gossip of her own select set, the fact that both son and daughter were beyond the reach of her worldly designs, and she schooled herself to look upon them with a sort of quiet scorn which she imagined to be more effective than a perpetual storm of words, and when Louise informed her of her intention to be Margaret's bridesmaid, she shrugged her shoulders, and laughed contemptuously; but when Eugene told her that he had planned a quiet European tour with his sister, directly after the marriage of their friends, in which tour she would be obliged to join, she raved once more in her olden way. She had just gathered about her the society she wished: she had no desire to accompany a couple of straight-laced, Puritanical hypocrites in a solemn expedition round the world. But neither had Eugene any desire to permit her to remain after them, to indulge without restraint the follies in which she delighted; so he firmly, but respectfully informed her of his intention to withdraw all financial support from her should she refuse to make the tour, and the baffled, disappointed woman sunk down into her usual miserable passion of tears.

Happy Margaret! Never had days passed so swiftly and delightfully, never had love bestowed such meed of joy before.

The wedding was to be quiet and simple; the ceremony to be performed by Father Germain at their own residence, directly after which the young couple were to take a trip to their old Louisiana home. Madame Bernot was so well that they could leave her without anxiety for a few days.

The case of Clare, *alias* Plowden, which no one looked for more eagerly than Miss Lydia Lounes, never appeared on any calendar of the city courts, and that lady considered herself especially disappointed and aggrieved by the bungling and mysterious manner in which the press after a long silence spoke of that interesting gentleman. The truth was, that "Roquelare" had ways of its own for hoodwinking even such a potent body as the Press, and for causing a belief to become current that "Roquelare" itself had dealt summary vengeance on the true murderer of Cecil Clare.

When Miss Lounes heard that report, she recorded it in her jourual, while she dropped a few secret, very secret tears.

"They have killed him at last—that dear, distinguished lawyer who won my tender affections, and in whose grave my poor, weary heart longs to repose."

On one of the happy days of preparation for the wedding, Hugh Murburd and his mother were announced, and a joyful meeting followed.

The poor old lady was much enfeebled as if from long suffering, but she was garrulous with all the privilege of her age. She *would* recount minutely all that she had suffered during the time that she had been kept from her son, how that enforced separation was the cause of the painful, tedious illness which had attacked her directly that she had been permitted to join Hugh, and owing to which illness, neither she nor her son had been able to call sooner on the Bernots as they had desired and intended to do.

Then she would have Hugh repeat to Hubert what he had told herself after he knew that Hubert was not guilty—how, when the young men were traveling together, and sometimes in crowded hotels were obliged to occupy the same bed, Hubert had spoken in his sleep of a crime which stained his soul—how Hugh remembered that, when he saw Bernot's name appear in the first investigation of Cecil Clare's murder, and the suspicion which these two facts aroused, led him to preserve and bring home the papers which his mother had found, and which had caused her such perplexity—how, when the pretended Mr. Conyer came with his strange inquiries, and stranger communications, Hugh fancied he understood it all—that Hubert *was* guilty of some crime, and that Mr. Conyer was a detective on his track. Hugh would not write to Hubert lest his friend should become startled, and if he had committed a crime, betray himself by his very fears, and Hugh had not answered satisfactorily the inquiries his mother used to make, because he deemed it best to keep very secret everything he himself knew, or suspected, lest it might come to the detective's knowledge.

And when everything had been explained to the old lady's satisfaction, even to the fact that the telegram desiring her presence in the city, and supposed to have been sent by Hugh, had been only another of Bertoni's diabolical machinations, and when the young men had warmly grasped hands, and had pledged each other's friendship over brimming glasses of rare old wine, and when Madame Bernot had spoken tearfully her thanks to stanch, true Hugh, and Margaret crying and smiling in the same minute was pressing the old lady's hands, then Mrs. Murburd leaned back in her chair and well nigh sobbed from excess of joyful emotion.

Madame Bernot and her son would have detained the Murburds until the wedding day which was now hardly a week distant, but the old lady was anxious for her home from which she had been absent so long; the utmost that pressing solicitation could effect was the prolongation of their visit until the next day, but Hugh promised to return for the ceremony.

Below stairs there were hearts no less happy than those above; there were preparations for a joyful event no less delightful than those making by Madame Bernot and Margaret.

Annie Corbin as Margaret's maid was to accompany the young lady on her bridal tour, and John McNamee with the anxiety of an ardent Irish lover as he was, fearing the effect of even that short absence on the affections of his sweetheart, importuned that their marriage should take place a day or two before that appointed for Miss Calvert's. His request was warmly seconded by Hannah Moore, and the blushing little maid unable to withstand so many entreaties, put her hand into John's great fist, and faltered " yes," and then ran away to hide her happy, blushing embarrassment.

Madame Bernot on learning that, ordered that everything should be done which could contribute to the festivity of the event, and the help were all in a state of delightful anticipation. Hannah Moore sighed only for twenty pairs of arms, that she might do twenty things at the same time; and "Little Sam" experienced constantly a most unaccountable inclination to cut unheard-of capers on the kitchen floor; but he did not permit the temptation to interfere with his duties, and he performed all the cook's errands in so satisfactory a manner that she invariably addressed him with:

"Sam, you're a jewel!"

On the day preceding the evening on which Annie Corbin was to become Mrs. McNamee, Sam was out on one of his numerous little commissions; and while his little slender legs did their duty in the way of quick, important steps, his head was no less busy. It constantly turned to assure itself that people *were* looking at Samuel Lewis, who was such an important person in the Bernot household, and it held itself very high to assure the eyes that *were* attracted by this little specimen of frail humanity, how fully it was aware of its own importance.

But the little slender legs came to a sudden stop, and the elevated head held itself very stationary, for just in front was a small crowd of street urchins round a man who was playing on a cracked fiddle—a pale, thin, dirty, tattered man, who played some melancholy strain, and smiled—a very ghost of a smile—on the boys who seemed to listen admiringly.

The little under-waiter drew nearer, and the man with the fiddle saw him; he stopped playing suddenly, while a faint color came into his face, and putting his instrument under his tattered coat he was moving off. Then little Sam was sure that the poor fiddler was Magnus Liverspin, and his heart was touched at the apparent poverty and distress of the once traveling comedian. He walked after the tattered man, and touched him lightly on the shoulder, whereupon Liverspin turned, and the faint color in his face became a deep crimson.

"You're Liverspin—ain't you?"—said Sam, very softly and kindly.

The tattered man nodded, and then said, huskily:

"Go away—I don't want to see you.—I never wanted to see you any more after I played that game on you."

"But you're poor," said little Sam, softer and kindlier still, " and perhaps I can help you."

The tattered man turned away his head, and did not speak, and little Sam waited, repeating his last remark when he had waited a minute or more, but repeating it so softly and kindly that Liverspin broke down and wept like a child.

"It's the first word of kindness I've heard in many

a day," he said; "and it's broken me down. I *am* poor. I haven't tasted food to-day yet."

Little Sam grasped the tattered man's arm. "Come home with me and we'll give you a good meal of victuals anyway, and after that we'll see what else we can do," forgetting everything but the present suffering of the object before him.

Liverspin shrank from the proffer.

"I could'nt meet them—your fellow-servants—and they knowing the spy I was."

"Tut, tut, man; they'll forgive you when they know as you're sorry, and when they see your present poverty." And, linking within his own the arm of the tattered man, who made but little more, and that a feeble resistance, the magnanimous under-waiter marched off, followed by a couple of the street urchins, who begged for another of "Them 'ere tunes, Mister."

"Little Sam's" magnanimity extended to the length of not asking a single question calculated to discover how the once jolly Liverspin came to be in his present deplorable condition. "For," argued Sam with himself, "he's weak and hungry, and I'll just let him be until he has one good feed.

That generous resolution however, did not prevent him from detailing in prosy length to his dirty companion all the good and wonderful luck which had befallen the Bernot family, and his own delightful anticipations of the happy time there would be at John McNamee's wedding that evening.

Arrived at the house, he stealthily ushered Liverspin into a waiting-room, while he undertook to acquaint Hannah Moore with all that had happened.

It was a little difficult at first to enlist the good woman's sympathies as readily as "Little Sam" desired to do, for her old indignation at "Divilspin," as she would persist in calling him, roused at the very mention of his name; but when the little under-waiter induced her to take a peep at the poor tattered creature warming his hands over the register, and when, after her introduction to him, he looked on the point of again breaking down as he had done under "Little Sam's" kindness, her compassion was as fully enlisted as that of the little under-waiter. And her kindness was not satisfied until it had imparted itself to her fellow-servants, so that Liverspin after partaking of, as Hannah expressed it, "Just a bit to keep the life in him until I get him a good meal," found himself taken to a bath room, and provided with such garments from the wardrobe of the male help as seemed most suitable, so that when he returned to the kitchen he looked, in the language of Miss Moore:

"At least sweet and clean."

He ate with a verocity which he vainly tried to conceal, the substantial meal Hannah had prepared for him, and when the last bit had disappeared down his eager throat, and he had washed it down with a copious draught of the servants' own table ale, he said, with a grateful air that went to the cook's heart:

"I don't deserve what you've all done for me, but I'm thankful for it, and I'll keep the remembrance of it here till my dying day," laying his hand on his heart with a pathetic motion.

"The one that ought to do it, in consideration of of my services in his behalf, refused, when he found he wouldn't need me any more, and that was Bertoni. When I left the court-room after giving my evidence, some strange man picked a quarrel with me and I was arrested; and after that came the things that left my health as broken down as you see it. I wish I could tell you what I went through while 'Roquelare' had me, but I can't, only it was horrible—" he shuddered, and his pale face seemed to grow still paler—"and they kept me, and made me go through frightful things till they'd be sure I'd never divulge what I witnessed when they were examining Bertoni and me. They didn't make me a member; they didn't put any mark on me and that was the mischief of it; for if they had they'd be bound to help me then. When at last they let me go I was too ill from fright, and what I had undergone, to practice my old profession, and somehow, I failed to get employment at anything. I went to Bertoni, but he wouldn't see me when I sent in my name, and so things went on from bad to worse till it came to the starving trifles I could earn with this," touching the cracked violin that lay on a chair near him.

The most incredulous could not have doubted his story, nor the most callous-hearted fail to have been touched by the pathos in his tones; so one and all hands of the sympathetic help were extended to him, and one and all were sincere in their offers to assist Magnus Liverspin to a future course of honest industry. Their kindness even went so far as to invite him to be present at the festivity of the evening, when he rose to depart, and he accepted the invitation.

That evening—that merry, delightful evening, when true Irish mirth, and genuine Irish wit shone forth in all their simple honesty; its memory could never be effaced from their minds even when the changes of years had found them other and separate homes.

There were ardent congratulations to pretty Mrs. McNamee, and toasts and songs, and songs and toasts, and then more ardent congratulations—there were pleasant tales, and pathetic tales told, the latter however, always with a happy ending, and there were witty anecdotes related, such as would have done credit to the best spirits of a much higher grade of society.

"Little Sam" was toasted for the manner in which he had "bamboozled" the great lawyer, and he was called upon to respond in a speech, and "Little Sam" rose, trying to assume an appearance of pompous dignity, but he was very shaky about the legs, and very watery about the eyes, and after a quavering:

"Ladies and gentlemen, I'm proud this night to have the honor—to have the honor—I say I'm proud this night to have the honor," sank into his seat being quite overcome by his feelings. But that was nothing, for everybody applauded, and the pompous head-waiter declared that Mr. Samuel Lewis was a "trump."

And Miss Moore sang, and then requested the company to drink the health of Mr. Plowden, or rather Mr. Frederick Clare, to show that everybody wished even the lawyer well; and then she told them how he had gone beyond the seas to be a holy monk, and for that reason alone everybody should wish him "God-speed;" and Miss Moore's heart was gladdened by the evident sincerity with which the toast was promptly drank.

And Kreble, whom Madame Bernot still retained, though having no essential need of her services, sang in her own language a ballad of "Faderland" hoping when she had concluded—

"Das was agreeable to de company," upon which every one broke into renewed applause, and the broad, red face grew broader with good-natured smiles, and redder from happy blushes.

Then Liverspin performed on a violin which had been procured for him, and which was *not* cracked, Irish airs that alternately set the feet of his listeners into uncontrolable motion, and made their hearts thrill with the exquisite memories of loved Old Ireland.

But the last, last toast which was drank, almost the last, last words that were spoken ere the happy party separated, was a repetition of the first toast, a repetition of the beloved names which had been the first mentioned that evening, and everybody stood up, and everybody drank with refreshing zest to the

"Long life, happiness, and prosperity of Mr. Bernot and Miss Calvert, soon to be Mrs. Bernot."

CHAPTER XXIV.

THE marriage ceremony had been performed by Father Germain, and happy, blushing Margaret, at last a wife, was trying to reply calmly to the hearty congratulations which poured upon her from the little group of friends present.

Louise Delmar had never looked so handsome, perhaps owing to the simplicity of her dress, chosen in deference to Margaret's simple though exquisite taste, and certainly she had never felt so purely, so innocently happy.

The anticipation of her European tour, together with her constant endeavor to rejoice in Margaret's happiness, had won for her a peace of mind to which she had long been a stranger.

Eugene had been groomsman.

Hugh Murburd, true to his promise, had returned in time to witness the ceremony, and Doctor Durant, regarded now with warm friendship, was also present.

Those were all, but they were enough for the happy hearts who panted only for a union which no earthly change could sever.

Father Germain looking as happy himself as the youthful couple, blessed them frequently, and while he gave the counsels the Church so lovingly imparts to her newly wedded children, he felt the little need of it there was in this case; suffering had so purified the two young hearts before him, that there was little doubt since they had been so true to the teachings of their faith, but that they would always be true to each other.

A few hours later, and the happy couple were driven by John McNamee to the pier at which rested the southward bound steamer, and anyone who witnessed the leave-taking between Mrs. McNamee and her husband would have imagined that the little woman was about to make a prolonged tour of the world.

Four days after, the Delmars—including the vain, fashionable mother, who had at last consented to accompany her children, though that consent was preceded by a half dozen attacks of violent hysterics—sailed for Europe, and Madame Bernot, whom the brother and sister had visited every day since the departure of Hubert and Margaret, felt a strange loneliness after this second leave-taking. But her son and daughter, as she delighted to think of, and to call Margaret, arrived on the very day which had been appointed for their return, and not an hour too soon.

Madame was stricken with the old paralysis, the old disease, in all, and its most severe forms.

She could not return the fond pressure of the dear hands; alas! she could not even turn her head to follow their motions. She was lying on the bed whither Kreble had borne her on the very first symptom of a return of the old illness, but she asked to be placed in the invalid chair. The latter, though folded to its portable size had retained its old conspicuous position in Madame Bernot's room. With heavy hearts they opened it and placed the dear sufferer in her old place. Her eyes immediately fastened on the sacred picture, and both priest and physician, who arrived almost together, saw at one glance that her end was at hand.

It was painless at the very last; and, with such a look of heavenly rapture as compelled those who witnessed it to believe that even her mortal eyes had a vision of immortal happiness, the gentle sufferer passed away.

● ● ● ● ● ●

A year passed; a swift, bright year, shadowed alone by the tender memory of the "dear departed."

The Bernots had removed to a handsome establishment on the outskirts of the city, accompanied by every one of the old domestics, save Kreble, who had returned to "Faderland," directly after Madame's demise.

Hannah Moore still held supremacy in the kitchen, with "Little Sam," as warmly attached to her as ever, and between whom and Rosie the chambermaid, strong kindred affections appeared to have arisen—so strong as to warrant very pleasant anticipations of another "match," in Miss Moore's mind.

John McNamee was still the coachman, and his wife Mrs. Bernot's maid, while the pompous head-waiter was secretly thinking of laying siege to the heart of the buxom laundress.

Hubert, that his lovely wife might occupy the position in society which she was so well fitted to adorn, gathered about him many of the *elite*, and distinguished; his own noble qualities, his intellectual gifts, his rare culture, apart from his wealth, made his acquaintance a coveted envied favor, and honors unsought and unwished were lavished upon him. The latest, and one which his benevolence prompted him to accept, was the presidency of a society formed for the purpose of effecting new and salutary improvements in the treatment of the insane; in connection with this honorary office he was about to visit, accompanied by his wife, a certain private asylum. It was a bright, early spring day, and he waited only the completion of Margaret's simple, but tasteful toilet.

Just as she joined her husband in the parlor, blushing with pleasure at his lover-like compliment to her charming appearance, a servant brought in a letter—a foreign letter evidently, from many and divers stamps upon the envelope. Hubert opened it, and with her hand within his arm, they read it together.

It was from Louise Delmar. Either brother or

sister, and sometimes both, had written regularly since their departure; but their letter contained something which made husband and wife simultaneously exclaim; it was the death of Mrs. Delmar—but such a death!

"She had been eager to attend a ball at the Grand Duke's palace," the writer stated, "and Eugene after much trouble procured tickets of admission. But in the very act of dressing she was seized with sudden faintness; we begged her to stay at home—it was useless, and she rallied sufficiently to finish her toilet, even to insist on some change being effected in her head-dress in order to make the latter more becoming. While being assisted to the carriage she trembled violently, but to our entreaties to return and allow us to send for a physician, she laughed and said it was only a chill. She was very still when we had comfortably seated her, and we asked her how she felt. There was no answer, for she was dead."

Hubert and Margaret looked at each other with grave, sad faces—the same thought was in the minds of both—"as she had lived, so had the fashionable woman died in the midst of her vanities."

And then their thoughts fondly and tenderly reverted to their own sainted dead.

At the close of the letter was a paragraph containing:

"In one of your churches which we visited just before mother's death, I saw a monk bearing a most striking resemblance to Mr. Plowden—which name comes more naturally to me than his proper one of Clare—

"He muffled his face with his cloak when he saw me staring so intently at him, and he hurried out of the church. I would have followed, but I feared to lose mamma from whom I already had become separated. Could it have been fancy on my part, Margaret? but I am convinced it was not, for the resemblance was too striking, too sure."

The private asylum which Hubert and Margaret were about to visit had just secured a new superintendent, one highly recommended for his firm, but kind qualities, and his Spanish-looking face seemed to evince the former, if not the latter traits.

Somehow, his countenance impressed Margaret with a feeling of having seen it before, though she could give it no definite place, and the man, evidently knowing who his visitors were, still seemed to be connecting with them some other interest than that which attached simply to Mr. Bernot and his lady.

In a private room, and pinioned so as to prevent harm to himself, they beheld Bertoni—shrieking, mad Bertoni—who had but one word for all times and persons, and that word, "Roquelare."

The superintendent turned to Mr. and Mrs. Bernot, and with a gravity in his manner amounting to reverence, said:

"To that man's insanity I owe the worship and love which I now give my Creator."

And in a few brief words he told to his astonished listeners the singular remark made to him by Plowden on the occasion of his disputing with a friend about the superiority of mind alone; of the subsequent change in his feelings when he witnessed the sudden blighting of that great mind that he had deemed invincible, and of his last interview with Plowden, or rather Clare, just before the latter disappeared forever from the public gaze. Margaret suddenly remembered the swarthy-looking man who had so hurriedly pursued Plowden on the latter's last exit from the court-room, and she bowed her head in silent reverence to God who works good to souls by such inscrutable ways.

They came out into the gloaming of the soft spring evening, meeting on the walk, to the verge of which the carriage in waiting had driven, three extravagantly dressed ladies. They stepped aside to permit the Bernots to pass, and in so doing they all obtained a full view of Margaret's lovely face.

"Why, Lydia!" was the half-smothered exclamation of one, "that's that Miss Calvert. Don't you remember?"

"Hush!" was the response from Lydia, or rather Miss Lonnes, "don't mention the creature's name, I hate her."

"Yes; but don't you know that she is the leader of a very brilliant, and select set now; that she is quoted as the model of beauty, and elegance, and goodness, and dear knows what—"

"Yes; by fools who forget what she was," answered Miss Lounes, "and who shamefully permit such creatures to usurp our place in society."

Ah! that was poor Miss Lounes' secret heart-cry forcing itself up. If she had only refused to take Mrs. Delmar's advice months ago, and condescended to patronize the despised Margaret Calvert might not she herself be now enjoying the society which surrounded Mrs. Bernot, and before this, might not the symphonious cognomen of Lydia Lounes have been changed for one bearing the much envied prefix of "Mrs."?

Gently and, we confess, with some reluctance, we drop the curtain over the sorrowful and happy scenes we have witnessed, and gently and reluctantly we say farewell to the characters who have borne us company so long. The Bernots, happy in their true, faithful love, the Delmars, brother and sister, possibly to marry in the coming years, but always to retain for each other the affection which has made the lives of both better and brighter; the Murburds to remain a touching example of motherly love and filial affection, until the old lady shall be borne to her rest, and Hugh shall take upon himself husbandly cares; and the Bernot help to serve faithfully their beloved master and mistress until the wonted change of death and marriage shall remove them to other spheres, and even Hannah

Moore shall preside in a kitchen of her own. We leave them all with a kindly, tender farewell, not even forgetting him whose sincere and lifelong penance must have atoned for his ghastly wrong, and but for which wrong this story would never have been written.

www.ingramcontent.com/pod-product-compliance
Lightning Source LLC
Chambersburg PA
CBHW020319240426
43673CB00039B/854